FRONTIER COWBOYS
AND THE
GREAT DIVIDE

KEN MATHER

FRONTIER COWBOYS AND THE GREAT DIVIDE

EARLY RANCHING IN BC AND ALBERTA

VICTORIA · VANCOUVER · CALGARY

Heritage House Publishing Company Ltd.
heritagehouse.ca

Library and Archives Canada Cataloguing in Publication
Mather, Ken, 1947–
Frontier cowboys and the great divide: early ranching in BC and Alberta / Ken Mather.

Includes bibliographical references and index.
Issued also in electronic format.
ISBN 978-1-927527-09-2

1. Ranching—British Columbia—History. 2. Ranching—Alberta—History. 3. Frontier and pioneer life—British Columbia. 4. Frontier and pioneer life—Alberta. I. Title.

SF196.C2M373 2013   971.1'03   C2012-907039-4

Edited by Lesley Cameron
Proofread by Karla Decker
Cover design by Jacqui Thomas

Cover photos: Cowboys in Calgary, Alberta, ca. 1883, Glenwbow Archives PA-3603-2 (front); Round-up crew of Lucas Eastman and Waller Ranch, Porcupine Hills, Alberta, ca. 1886, Glenbow Archives NA-1508-5 (back)

The interior of this book was produced on 100% post-consumer recycled paper, processed chlorine free and printed with vegetable-based inks.

Heritage House acknowledges the financial support for its publishing program from the Government of Canada through the Canada Book Fund (CBF), Canada Council for the Arts and the province of British Columbia through the British Columbia Arts Council and the Book Publishing Tax Credit.

Canadian Heritage   Patrimoine canadien   Canada Council for the Arts   Conseil des Arts du Canada   BRITISH COLUMBIA ARTS COUNCIL

17 16 15 14 13 1 2 3 4 5
Printed in Canada

This book is dedicated to the working cowboys and cowgirls of Western Canada who keep the tradition alive.

CONTENTS

Introduction

Dream back beyond the cramping lanes
To glories that have been
The camp smoke on the sunset plains,
The riders loping in
Loose rein and rowelled heel to spare,
The wind our only guide,
For youth was in the saddle there
With half a world to ride.[1]

They were young. Lured from the factories and farms of the east and Europe, or toddling along with their parents in vast wagon trains, they travelled west. A new land was opening up and they wanted to be a part of it. While the search for gold may have drawn many of these young men into the wilderness, it was not so much fame and fortune that they were after as adventure. Starting in Texas and California, they worked their way northward along either side of the rugged Rocky Mountains. And when the gold did not pan out, as was most often the case, they turned to the ranches springing up in the grassland foothills of the mountains. Riders were needed to drive the cattle north or to tend to the growing herds, so they settled for a time into the cattle trade, watching closely those who had been ranch hands for generations, the Mexican *vaqueros* or English drovers who had brought their tools and practices to the New World. They were the cowboys. Their rugged, thankless life somehow captured the imagination of the world. As they trailed their cattle north on either side of the Rockies, they adapted their techniques and gear to suit the northern climate. Over the few decades that it took to carry the cattle culture as far north as the grass would allow, their distinctive styles developed independently of each other.

Charlie Russell, the legendary cowboy artist, famously described the two "species of cowpunchers," making clear the distinction between the cowboy west of the Rockies and his counterpart east of the "Great Divide":

Texas and California, bein' the startin' places, made two species of cowpunchers: those west of the Rockies rangin' north, usin' centerfire or single-cinch saddles, with high fork an cantle; packed a sixty or sixty-five foot rawhide rope, an swung a big loop. These cow people were generally strong on pretty, usin' plenty of hoss jewelry, silver-mounted spurs, bits and conchas; instead of a quirt, used a romal, or quirt braided to the end of the reins. Their saddles were full-stamped, with from twenty-four to twenty-eight-inch eagle bill tapaderos. Their chaparejos were made of fur or hair, either bear, angora goat, or hair sealskin. These fellows were sure fancy, an' called themselves buckaroos, coming from the Spanish *vaquero*.

The cowpunchers east of the Rockies originated in Texas and ranged north to the Big Bow. He wasn't so much for pretty; his saddle was low horn, rimfire, or double cinch; sometimes "macheer." Their rope was seldom over forty feet, for bein' a good deal in a brush country, they were forced to swing a small loop. These men generally tied, instead of takin' their dallie-welts, or wrapping their rope around the saddle horn. Their chaparejos were made of heavy bullhide, to protect the leg from brush and thorns, with hog-snout tapaderos.[2]

While it is generally acknowledged that the origins of many of the trappings of the cowboy and his horse, as well as the techniques of handling cattle, can be traced to Mexico, there has been much discussion about just how these two distinctive styles evolved and how far north they spread before they merged into one.

To uncover the origins of the cowboy and trace the development of cattle ranching in North America, we must look first to the Old World. Two parts of Europe were major influences on the way ranching was done in North America: southwestern Spain and the British highlands. Each of these distinct cattle cultures contributed to the development of ranching in the Americas.

The traditional cattle-raising regions of southern Spain and Portugal were the home of the first mounted herders, referred to as *vaqueros*, or "cowmen." Although these mounted men used braided ropes that they called *lazos* to pull cattle out of the mud (with the rope attached to the tail of the horse in the absence of a saddle horn), they generally used staffs with sharp points, called *garrochas*, to prod the cattle along in what may be seen as the forerunner of the "cowpuncher." The cattle they tended—longhorns—were mostly allowed to roam wild until needed for market. Clearly, this system of mounted herders working semi-wild cattle is the prototype of the North American cowboy.

Far to the north of the salt marshes of Andalusia, in the highlands of Britain, a different way of handling cattle had evolved. Most of the herders, who were primarily old men and young boys, were on foot and used whips and herder dogs to control the cattle. The bullwhip was used primarily for its ability to crack loudly next to a reluctant animal and thus force it to move in the desired direction, but it could also be applied to the hide of the animal to make a point. By far the most common method of herd control was the faithful dog. Because bulls were the most difficult to handle, the British herders developed the bulldog breeds that could effectively drag down cattle by firmly attaching to their lip or loose neck skin, a practice called "bulldogging" from the earliest times. Since it was common practice to mix cattle from different owners together for grazing, the British herders, like their Spanish counterparts, branded and earmarked their cattle for identification purposes. The brand was a permanent mark that could be seen easily on cattle and remained the primary mark of ownership until recent times. Because they were a legal mark of ownership, brands were registered with the governing authorities. In eighth-century Britain and Germany, large landowners used their family coat of arms as their brands. In Spain, the king granted and kept a record of all livestock brands, and this practice carried over to the New World. The only cultural difference was that the British preferred the large block-letter brands rather than the elaborately curved brands favoured by the Spanish.

Both of these Old World cattle cultures contributed to the North American scene, but the Spanish had the first and most significant impact. Columbus remarked on his voyage of discovery to the New World that there was no evidence of horses or cattle. On his second voyage, he set out to remedy that and offloaded 24 stallions, 10 mares and an undisclosed number of cattle.[3] Hernán Cortés used the offspring of these horses when he landed on the mainland in the early sixteenth century. Not long after he conquered the Native Mexican people, he brought cattle to the Mexican eastern coastal areas, where they thrived. From there they spread across the central mountain range. Over time, the Mexican *vaquero* and his cattle spread north from the Gulf coast plains into coastal Texas and along the Pacific coast into California. The Texas and California versions of the *vaquero* flourished in their new locations. Each of these vanguards of Mexican ranching had acquired special characteristics by the time they reached Texas and California. These two regional differences would have a significant impact on the ranching frontier in North America.

Totally independent of what was going on in Mexico, a separate ranching culture was developing in South Carolina, via the British colony of Jamaica, where it was influenced by the black slaves who had been herders in Africa. This mainly British form of ranching spread from the coastal plain and islands around Charleston southward into the interior of the country. From there it spread southward into Florida and Louisiana and northward across the Appalachian Mountains into the Ohio River Valley. This system of ranching used herder dogs, cow whips and block-letter brands, and practised calf capture and castration, free ranging, milking, range burning and stock salting, all of which were common practices in Britain.

Inevitably, as the cattle culture of old Mexico spread across Texas, it encountered the system of handling cattle that was brought west by the English-speaking settlers of the Carolinas. The two distinctive cultures merged into a new way of ranching. The unique Texas blend of handling cattle took aspects of each culture and adapted them to the Texas environment. The Mexican practice of mounting herders on agile, intelligent horses from which cattle were roped with hemp or maguey ropes was the most significant contribution, but the English-speaking Texans made adjustments to the horse equipment that was used. They used a Mexican stock saddle, but the bulky single-cinched saddle with a thick tree-branch horn and closed stirrups was modified to a much lighter design with a slender horn and open stirrups. Because of the danger of losing roped cattle in the brush, instead of wrapping the rope around the horn, they tied it there. For this to be successful, the saddle had to be more secure and a thick-horned saddle that was double-rigged with cinches in the front and back was therefore developed.[4]

Other equipment common to the Texas herders included spurs with small rowels and whips, mostly short quirts. Beyond these contributions, readily accepted from the Mexican *vaqueros,* a majority of the ranching practices came from Carolina and had British origins. Certainly the most enduring contribution to the ranching industry was the Carolina word "cowboy" to designate the men on horses who formed the labour force of the ranching industry. The term was to remain a distinct part of the Texas ranching system for years before popular culture took it over and applied it to all mounted herders in North America. Other significant contributions from Carolina included the British practice of calf castration, British block-letter brands and an emphasis on raising cattle for beef as opposed to hides and tallow. The vocabulary of the Texans included the Carolina loan words "dogie" (motherless calf), "cowpen" (ranch) and "cowhunt" (round-up).

By the time Texas joined the American Union in 1845, stock-raising methods were well established. Texans were influenced by the Mexican ranching practices, which had been successful in southern Texas, and adopted an open-range approach to raising cattle. This involved turning cattle loose on unfenced open pastures and allowing them to run wild and fend for themselves until mounted cowboys rounded them up. This method of raising cattle, and the men who practised it, are described in a first-hand account written in 1860, in which the writer described how English-speaking "cow boys" rounded up wild cattle that had previously belonged to the now-departed Mexican residents. He goes on to describe how "the cattle are permitted to range indiscriminately over a large surface of country, thirty, forty, and even fifty miles in extent from north to south and east to west." It was "no easy task to hunt up and mark and brand the calves of a large stock, still it is done and with tolerable accuracy." This cattle hunting took place in the spring and fall and was accomplished by cowboys organized into "crowds" of 10, 12 or 15 men. Each herder had a "lasso at saddle-bow" as well as a pistol and bowie knife. The calves were driven into a pen, where they were marked, branded and castrated. The account goes on to conclude:

> The young men that follow this 'Cow-Boy' life, notwithstanding its hardships and exposures, generally become attached to it . . . Many of them are not inferior to the best Mexican vaqueros in the management of their fiery steeds . . . they 'rope' or throw the lasso with great dexterity and precision.[5]

At the end of the Civil War there were hundreds of thousands of wild cattle in Texas and a growing hunger for fresh beef in the cities of the eastern United States. These cities could only be reached from the various railheads of railways being constructed across the Great Plains. Cattle drives from Texas to northern and western markets, and later to railroad-loading facilities, started in earnest in 1866, when an estimated 260,000 head of cattle crossed the Red River. The drives were conducted for only about 20 years, eventually becoming unnecessary with the advent of the railroads and refrigeration in the 1880s. But, during that relatively short time, some 5 million head of cattle had gone up the trail from Texas. And with them went the Texas cowboy and his way of handling cattle.

While all this was going on in Texas, another distinctive ranching culture was developing in California. Unlike in Texas, in California the practices and equipment were initially a direct extension of those of the Mexican *vaqueros* who patterned themselves after the *charros* of central Mexico. The first cattle-raising ventures in California were attached to the various missions, where the outlying cattle operations were referred to as *ranchos*. Cattle thrived in the rich coastal valleys, and by 1830 there were over 200,000 head of cattle in California. By the middle of the 1830s the mission system had declined, but private citizens continued the ranching expansion. Because of the remoteness of the area, the primary products of the cattle trade were hides and tallow, which could be shipped without spoilage.[6]

The California *vaqueros*, often referred to as *californianos,* were mainly from the indigenous Native population with a mixture of Spanish, Indian and perhaps African blood. These herdsmen used stock saddles, which had been modified by the addition of a saddle horn. The previously favoured *garrocha* was being replaced by the braided rawhide *reata*, which was wrapped around the saddle horn so that it could slip on impact, a technique called *dar la vuelta* (to take a wrap). *Californianos* developed a style of their own that was utilitarian but also showy. They wore the Spanish large-rowel spur with four or five long, sharp points over a soft boot. Their dress was patterned after the *charro*, with a short jacket, medium-length pants with a red sash at the waist and a low-crowned flat-brimmed hat held in place with a neck string. To protect themselves from brush and to prevent chafing by the rawhide *reata* during roping, they wore deerskin *armitas* over their legs, held in place with drawstrings. The *vaqueros* worked under a *mayordomo*, or ranch foreman, and regularly performed round-ups, referred to as *rodeos*, to supply beef for the missions. By the 1840s, the missions system was disappearing and private owners took over the ranches. On the *ranchos* there was generally only one *rodeo* each fall. The *vaqueros* moved the cattle to higher elevations in the summer heat and then brought them down to the low country for the rainy winter season.

After the Mexican people became independent from Spain in 1821, the government established a system of awarding land grants to immigrants in California. Up until the 1840s, one fifth of all land grants went to people with Anglophone surnames. These new immigrants were the descendants of the early British settlers in South Carolina who had crossed the mountains into the Ohio and Missouri River valleys. The new immigrants mostly settled in the Sacramento Valley, where they encountered the Hispanic cattle and ranching system of the *californianos*. But the newcomer Anglophones also brought with them distinctly British methods of raising cattle. Their influence became even greater after gold was discovered in California in the late 1840s. Over the next 15 years, thousands of head of cattle, referred to as the "mongrel breeds of the western states,"[7] were driven from the Missouri frontier along the California and Oregon Trails to the mining markets near Sacramento. These incredible overland drives were much more difficult in terms of distance covered and difficulties encountered than the later drives north from Texas. In 1852 alone, some 90,000 head of cattle were driven west to California; the following year, another 60,000 head travelled west along the trails. Most of the cattle driven into California were steers destined for the mining camps, but some were breeding stock for the California herds, which had been depleted by the demands of the mining population. Before long, the bloodlines of the cattle began to change, resulting in a "western" type of cattle, mostly Durham shorthorn with a few Spanish traces.[8]

This encounter between the two major Old World ranching systems resulted in an interesting mixture of the two. The practices of managing cattle became more British than Mexican. Whereas the *californianos* had raised cattle mostly for their hides and beef tallow, the huge influx of miners to the goldfields meant that the demand for beef grew exponentially. The largely British tradition of cutting hay to feed the livestock during the summer dry season became regular practice in California. A key aspect of the earlier California system of ranching that persisted with the coming of the Anglophone ranchers was the custom of moving cattle seasonally between pastures. When left to their own devices, cattle have a basic instinct to drift upslope in the summer where cooler temperatures and better forage can be found. The seasonal shifting of cattle was not a new concept to the newcomers from the midwestern states. As a traditional aspect of the British system of raising cattle, the practice had been brought to the Carolinas from the New World. In the mountainous country of California, this procedure was widespread.

What is interesting is that, even though the ranching practices changed significantly, the actual techniques and dress of the ranch workers remained mostly *californianos*. The English-speaking herdsmen did not hesitate to borrow the methods and vocabulary of the *vaqueros*. The most notable borrowing was their name, which was anglicised to "buckaroo" and came to mean "a cowboy of the Spanish California type" for decades afterward. The Anglophone cowhand, coming from a cattle-herding background that required minimal riding skills, also enthusiastically took to working on horseback. In fact, the English speakers' vocabulary of horsemanship was almost entirely Spanish in origin. The buckaroo rode a horse with a hackamore (from the Spanish *jaquima*), decorated his gear with silver *conchos* (Spanish "shell"), led his horse with a macardy (from the Spanish *mecate* for a fibre rope), covered his stirrups with taps (or *tapaderos*), wore chaps (from the Spanish *chaparreras*) and, of course, swung a braided rawhide reata (Spanish *la riata*) to capture cattle. The buckaroo rode a light, single-cinched saddle with a tall, slender horn around which he dallied (from *dar la vuelta*) his reata. His bridle reins were woven together to form a romal. The vocabulary of the buckaroo also covered other aspects of ranch work. He worked for a *mayordomo*, or foreman, participated in *rodeos* (cattle round-ups) and referred to a Native Indian village as a *rancherie*.

The *californiano* method of breaking horses was also adopted by the buckaroos. They used hackamores rather than bits, unlike the Texans. The hackamore consists of a braided leather noseband, or bosal, held in place by a light leather headstall and a woven cotton cord (called a "Theodore," from the Spanish *fiador*). This technique ensured that the horse, to which the bit was introduced late in the training program, possessed what was called a "soft mouth," making it much more responsive to the reins and to the distinctive California "high port" or "spade" bit. Horses to be broken were usually confined in a corral (another California loan word). In the middle of the pen was a "snubbing post" to which the horse was tied for the initial stages of breaking: getting the horse used to the touch of a human and the weight of a saddle. These snubbing posts in the round corral, where an animal could be tied for more effective breaking, doctoring or slaughter, were found wherever the buckaroo went.

The trappings and techniques of the buckaroo spread north with the largely British breeds of cattle. The cattle ranges of Oregon, Nevada and parts of Idaho and Washington were all strongly influenced by the California system of cattle ranching. But they were continually being modified by the influx of settlers from the Midwest, who followed the traditional British practices brought over from the Old World. As mentioned earlier, the British custom of cutting hay to feed cattle during times of shortage of grass had been accepted in California, where the hot dry summers parched the grasslands. This custom was modified in the more northern territories, where hay was required for winter feed. Other aspects of the British cattle-raising system were incorporated in Oregon and Washington, where the majority of ranchers were from the Midwest. Stock dogs could be found on most ranches and, where the young men were mostly from the Midwest and unfamiliar with roping, the use of stock whips was common even though it existed alongside the practice of roping with a braided rawhide reata.

By the time the California system of handling cattle had spread north to Oregon and Washington, it was an interesting blend of Spanish and British practices. The cowboys still called themselves "buckaroos," rode California saddles with largely Spanish tack and adopted much of the vocabulary of the californiano. They accepted the California methods of breaking horses, and they wore chaps and large rowelled spurs. But while the buckaroo looked a lot like the *vaquero* in dress and horsemanship, he handled cattle much the way his distant ancestors in Britain had. He cut hay for winter feed, he moved the cattle from the high country in summer to the lowlands in winter, and the cattle he handled were largely shorthorn British breeds that had been upgraded through selective breeding.

Thus, the two major systems of handling cattle spread northward, one on either side of the Rocky Mountains: the Texan and the buckaroo. Did the two different styles of handling cattle both find their way across the 49th Parallel, one into British Columbia and the other into the Canadian prairies? Can we examine the cattle frontier of British Columbia and find evidence of the buckaroo that far north, and can we see the Texas influence in Alberta? If so, how long did it take before the two cultures merged into one generic "cowboy culture"? In this book we will look at the lives of the cowboys of the British Columbian and Albertan ranching frontiers, the working class of the ranching industry. We will attempt to find out where they came from, how they did their daily work and where they learned to handle cattle. In the process, we will learn much about how they lived, the hardships they endured and the individual joys and challenges that each one of them faced. This book is not a scholarly examination of ranching origins; it is an account of the men and women who were the first of their kind in the ranching frontiers of British Columbia and Alberta and who contributed in many ways to the development of these provinces.

Chapter One

DROVERS

The California gold rush transformed the entire west coast of North America, first drawing in newcomers by the thousands and then, as the original mining strikes ran out, inspiring a search for fresh goldfields. Throughout the 1850s, miners moved relentlessly north from California, from one discovery to the next in hopes of "striking it rich." James Watt, a veteran prospector and packer, later commented:

> Folks now-a-days haven't much conception of the richness and extent of those early placer mines. Why, the whole country from the Blue Mountains [in Oregon State] to the eastern slope of the Rocky Mountains, and from southern Idaho far north into British Columbia, was just one big goldfield. There was rarely a stream that wouldn't "pan at least a color" and practically every square mile of that vast territory was some time or other traveled over and prospected by some of those prospecting parties in the latter 50s and early 60s.[1]

By 1858, miners were moving into British territory north of the 49th Parallel and, when word leaked out of gold being discovered on the Fraser and Thompson Rivers, another rush was on and thousands of hopeful miners rushed to the Lower Fraser River. Understandably nervous, having ceded all the territory north of California as far as the 49th Parallel to the United States in 1846, the British government established the Crown Colony of British Columbia (with an emphasis on the "British") on November 19, 1858, at Fort Langley on the Lower Fraser River.

While the proclamation was being read at Fort Langley, miners were scrambling through the steep cliffs of the Fraser River Canyon and proceeding up the Thompson and Fraser Rivers from that point. Beyond the Fraser Canyon, they began to find coarse gold in an area they called the Cariboo. The Cariboo's riches began to attract the attention of young men around the world, resulting in a gold rush of tens of thousands of would-be miners.

The stockmen of western Oregon and Washington State were watching developments in British Columbia with great interest. American settlers from the midwest states had begun to arrive in the Willamette Valley in the early 1840s, and many of them brought their cattle, mostly shorthorn breeds of British origin. In 1843 an estimated 700 to 1,000 immigrants headed out on the trail in what was called The Great Migration, bringing with them some 1,300 head of cattle. It was soon discovered that Durham cattle survived the rigours of the trail better than the other shorthorn breeds and, from that point on, Durhams were the most common cattle on the trail. This influx continued through the 1840s, and by the time of the 1850 census, there were 20,000 beef cattle in the Willamette Valley.

The cattle brought over the Oregon Trail interbred with the "California" cattle, some of which were the small Spanish "black" (but not necessarily longhorns). This interbreeding resulted in fine beef cattle, described by one breeder as "the thick-loined, deep-quartered, dark red half breed Shorthorn Oregonians, descended from some of the best Missouri and Illinois streams, trailed by immigrants across the plains in the early 50s."[2] The process of breeding up the quality of cattle in the Willamette Valley continued through the 1850s, but the dwindling of the market in California meant that the cattle population of the valley grew faster than the process of upgrading. As late as May 1859, a writer in the *Oregon Farmer* periodical lamented the state of livestock in the state:

> [The] time is now fully come when the raising of cayuse horses and Spanish cattle do[es] not pay in the Willamette Valley. Could this portion of the State be purged of the superabundance of this stock, which has now become a burden, rather than profit to our citizens, room could be given for better breeds, which are already fast being introduced, and the good work of improvement soon be fairly under way.[3]

Fortunately, even as the above passage was being written, a new market was appearing in the goldfields to the north in the new colony of British Columbia. Initially, when activity was concentrated on the Lower Fraser River, cattle could be driven from the ranching areas in the Rogue River Valley, the Umpqua Valley, and the Willamette Valley as far as the Columbia River, where they travelled by boat to Monticello (now Kalama). From there they were driven overland along the Cowlitz Road to the head of Puget

Sound and then by boat to markets in Victoria and the Lower Fraser. This transportation, although costly, was fine as long as the gold areas were along the Lower Fraser. But once the miners penetrated beyond the Fraser Canyon, things got much more expensive. An alternate route was developed between Harrison Lake and Lillooet, but it alternated between land and lake transportation, making it expensive and hard on cattle. But there was another alternate route, this one totally by land, that brought cattle through the "back door" of British Columbia.

This route saw the cattle going east along the Columbia River, either by boat or overland trail as far as The Dalles, and then northward by one of two routes to the mouth of the Okanogan River. From there cattle could be driven northward through the Okanagan Valley to Fort Kamloops and onward to the mining areas. This was the preferred route once the rich Cariboo goldfields were discovered and, in the 10-year period from 1858 to 1868, about 22,000 head of cattle crossed the border into British territory at Osoyoos Lake. This was the beginning of a cattle industry in British Columbia—20 years before one was established in Alberta.

Cattle on these overland drives did not only come from the valleys of western Oregon. The vast Sacramento Valley of central California supplied great numbers of cattle, which, by the time they reached Barkerville in the heart of the Cariboo gold region, had travelled 1,500 miles! With the demand for beef coming not only from the Cariboo but also from the mining regions of Idaho and Montana, there was a major move across the Cascades from western Oregon into the Columbia Basin, closer to the mining markets. Walla Walla and The Dalles, established by American Protestant missionaries, had long been cattle centres where cattle suffering from exhaustion from the Oregon Trail could be exchanged for fresh cattle for the final push into western Oregon. These "pilgrim" cattle had flourished and supplied the missions with ready income. As part of the mission work, the Native people of the area were trained in cattle herding and proved to be naturals when it came to work on horseback. In fact, many of them went on to establish ranches themselves. As other cattlemen began to take up land in the Columbia Basin east of the Cascades, they bucked current trends by hiring Native herdsmen to look after their cattle. This openness to using Native labour on the ranches, not found in any other area in the West, became a notable aspect of these ranches and would carry through to British Columbia. The practice was necessitated by the shortage of white male labourers, most of whom were more interested in taking their chances in the mining regions, and facilitated by the fact that the Chinook trade language made communication between the races an easy matter. In addition to being skilled riders, Native herdsmen soon

Cattle in the main street of Barkerville ca. 1870. Notice that the horse on the left has *tapaderos* covering the stirrups and a braided rawhide rein. BC ARCHIVES A-3771

became adept at using ropes, making them the natural choice for driving and handling cattle.

The equipment of the Oregon cattlemen on both sides of the Cascades was strongly influenced by the *vaqueros* of California. While most of the labourers were not directly of California origin, they saw the advantages of the *vaquero*'s equipment and techniques, and followed the "buckaroo way." This influence carried over to the British side of the 49th Parallel. The "Mexican saddle" could be seen everywhere. Photographs taken in the street (there was really only one) of Barkerville in the 1860s show typical California saddles with short, rounded skirts, solid saddle horns, low cantles, braided romal reins and stirrups covered with *tapaderos*, all characteristics of the saddles found in California at the time.

Three main regions fed cattle into British Columbia during the gold rush days of 1858 to 1868: the Sacramento Valley of California, the Willamette Valley of Oregon and the Yakima Valley in the Columbia Basin. While the methods of herding cattle in these three areas were largely the same, there were subtle differences. The Californians who came north with the cattle were very much buckaroos; California practices took less hold in the Willamette Valley and its appendage, the Columbia Basin. In this chapter we will look at three drovers, each one representing one of the three major areas.

Ken-e-ho

It was a summer day in August of 1861. A hot dry wind blew down the Yakima River valley from the Cascades, rippling the bunchgrass and lifting small clouds of dust. The camp of Klickitat Natives on Satus Creek was still in the heat of the afternoon. Dogs slept in the dust, and the horses, with their bellies full of bunchgrass, dozed contentedly. The camp consisted of about 40 tipis, similar in design to those of their cousins east of the Rockies but covered in woven tule mats, or elk or deer hides rather than buffalo hides. The worn grass around the camp indicated that it had been occupied for some time, the Klickitats only leaving as an entire band to harvest camas roots in June and July or to join with other bands and tribes to fish for salmon in the Columbia River.

The midday tranquillity was abruptly disturbed as two horsemen approached the camp. Dogs roused themselves from sleep and barked savagely at the intruders. Men jumped to their feet and looked to their weapons, for the riders were white and it was uncertain whether they were the vanguard of a much larger group. It had only been two years since open warfare had existed between the white intruders and the tribes of the Interior. The Klickitats had joined their neighbours, the Yakima, in bitterly resisting the intrusion of the Whites and the enforced acceptance of reserves carved out of their traditional territory. Many lives on both sides had been lost, and the scars of fierce enmity had not yet healed.

As the two men came closer and the Klickitats could see who they were, the tension eased. Major John Thorp was well known. He was a tall, powerful man who had crossed the plains in 1844 and been among the first settlers in Oregon. Now in his late sixties, his strength was undiminished and his eye as keen as that of a young man. His son, Fielding Mortimer Thorp, had settled across the Yakima River in the Moxee valley that February. Fielding Thorp had proven to be a man of character who kept his word, and his father was equally well regarded. Major Thorp had arrived in May with 150 head of cattle that he had purchased to graze on the rich bunchgrass of the valley. Since Fielding Thorp's homestead was across the river from the reserve, and both Thorps were known to be decent neighbours, their presence was acceptable. Accompanying Thorp was a blond-haired youth of 16, also well known to the Klickitats. Jack Splawn had come to the area with his brother,

Charles, in 1860 and befriended the Klickitats, quickly learning Chinook, the trade language of the fur traders and Natives of the Pacific Northwest, so that he could converse with the Natives.

The two men rode up to a tipi in the centre of the camp. A tall, handsome woman emerged and stared at them expressionlessly. She was dressed in the clothes typical of her people: a long deer-hide dress extending to her ankles, moccasins, and a buffalo-skin cape over her shoulders. All of her clothing except the cape was elaborately beaded. Thorp addressed her respectfully in Chinook. "Is Ken-e-ho here? We would like to talk to him." The woman turned and said something in Klickitat toward the interior of the tent. From within could be heard a man's voice and, within seconds, a tall Native with a commanding appearance stepped from the tent. He was dressed in a similar fashion to the woman, with a long deer-skin shirt

Tipi typical of the Klickitats and neighbouring tribes. Unlike their counterparts on the Plains that used buffalo hides, the Natives of the Washington interior used woven tule (bull rush) mats to cover their tipi frames. WASHINGTON STATE ARCHIVES AR-28001001-PH001081

extending to his mid-thighs and leggings reaching up to meet the shirt. His dark piercing eyes studied the men as he spoke. "What is it you want with Ken-e-ho, son of Squim-kin?" His manner was one of calm assurance and was not unfriendly.

Ken-e-ho was the leader of this small band of Klickitats. Like many of his people and other Natives in the Yakima Valley, he was experienced in handling cattle. Back in 1847, the Catholic Oblate missionaries had established a mission in the Yakima Valley. Like other missionaries in the Columbia Basin, they had acquired "pilgrim" cattle that had been driven over the Oregon Trail and had taught the Native people under their charge how to handle the cattle. The Natives often drove small herds of cattle to The Dalles for resale. Ken-e-ho had been on several of these drives until the Yakima War of 1856–58 drove the Oblates, who were accused of arming the Natives, north of the 49th Parallel. Some of these Oblates, including Father Pandosy, established Okanagan Mission on the site of present-day Kelowna.

Thorp dismounted and explained that he wanted to drive his cattle northward through the lands of the Yakima, the Okanagan and beyond to the new goldfields in British territory and needed help. Ken-e-ho knew very well that there were no white men in the vicinity who would be prepared to undertake such a journey. He also knew that the tribes whose territory they would cross were not well disposed to white intruders. The Yakima people had killed several small groups of miners in the early years of the gold rush to British territory. Three years earlier, a group of Okanagans had ambushed a party of about 150 miners under the leadership of David McLaughlin and killed 6 of them. And, although things had been relatively peaceful for the past two years, the miners were deeply mistrusted by the Natives of the Interior. It was obvious that Thorp was thinking of a twofold advantage to having some Klickitats as part of his party: the added manpower was valuable but, even more to the point, having Natives on the cattle drive would make the party much more acceptable to the Natives whose territory would have to be crossed.

Thorp offered to pay an honest wage—one dollar a day, the same that he paid white drovers—and suggested that travelling north into the British territory might add a little excitement to Ken-e-ho's life.

A flicker of a smile crossed Ken-e-ho's lips. Thorp was right on both accounts. The Klickitats had lived a miserable existence since being placed on reserves, and extra money would be welcome to buy much-needed goods from the traders. And he had to admit that the thought of travel into territory that he had never visited before had some attraction. Life had been quite boring without the excitement and danger of constant warfare. He agreed to come, but stipulated that he would have to take his wife, Eliza, along, suggesting that she might make a good cook.

Thorp frowned. The last thing he needed was a woman on the trip. But he knew that Klickitat women were as strong as the men and had an exceptional ability to harvest food that no Whites would recognize from the surrounding country. The added cost of another person was more than he had bargained for but, if the profit on cattle in the goldfields was as good as he had heard, there would be more than enough to offset the extra expense. He nodded in agreement.

Thorp added, "Young Jack Splawn will be coming with us as well and I'm also hiring Joe Evans and Paul, the son of the white trader, and his Yakima wife. I'm looking for one more drover if you know of anyone." Ken-e-ho smiled broadly. "Good. I will bring along Cultus John, who is dependable and our best horseman." Thorpe agreed and extended his hand to Ken-e-ho. The two men shook hands, looking into each other's eyes as equals.

Two days later, the cattle drive started out. The party, consisting of Thorp, his partner Joe Evans, Jack Splawn, Ken-e-ho, Eliza, Cultus John and a mixed-blood, Paul, strung out the cattle with Thorp in the lead. Aside from the cattle, there were half a dozen pack horses with the supplies and bedding, and extra horses for each of the drovers. This arrangement, with an equal mix of Native, white and mixed-blood drovers, was typical of the cattle drives from Oregon and Washington into British Columbia at the time. As the above encounter indicates, the Natives were excellent horsemen and drovers; they also brought knowledge of the countryside and a certain credibility to the party as it passed through the territories of other Native tribes. Although open hostilities had ceased a few years earlier, the occasional "excitement" would threaten to erupt into full-out war. That spring, most of the white families in the Klickitat Valley had fled to The Dalles when the Klickitat Natives had risen in support of armed encounters between the tribes to the north and miners travelling to the British Columbia goldfields. The presence of Native drovers was to prove advantageous to Thorp when his drove encountered hostile Natives along the way through Washington Territory.

Most Native drovers dressed like their white counterparts. Lieutenant Mayne of the Royal Engineers, who travelled through the Interior in 1858 and 1859, described the typical dress of the Native drovers:

> The majority of Indian parties have now adapted the dress of Europeans and turn out for the journey in trowsers [sic] and shirt, usually carrying an old coat of some sort, which they are careful to put on when nearing a town . . . Shoes are the one article of European attire which they do not take

kindly to wearing, although they always ask for a pair at starting, which, too, they carry in the pack upon their backs. They either travel barefoot or in moccasins, which are not the pretty things embroidered with beads which one sees in pictures, but a plain piece of deer-skin, laced round the foot with a strip of the same material.

Mayne also mentioned that the Indians always slept around a fire in all types of weather and "no matter how cold the night, the Indian invariably strips to sleep and lies with his blanket about him, feet toward the fire."[4]

The Native men rode on buckskin pads fitted closely to the horse's back, similar to a saddle. Their stirrups were triangular and covered with elk skin, and cinches were made of hair and wide straps of rawhide. Native women on the drives, like Eliza, rode on a saddle made of wood and covered with buckskin with front and back horns. To the front horn could be attached, on either side, large baskets with tight-fitting lids to carry food supplies. The rear horn was much larger and was ornamented with bright beaded cloth.

The drove travelled up the Yakima River valley for a few miles before turning north and heading up the Umtanum Ridge and out of the valley. Thorp planned to stay on the west side of the Columbia River, taking a route that was much more rugged but that avoided having the cattle swim across the Columbia twice. The first day out was especially difficult, with cattle wanting to turn around and head back at any chance. Lunch was eaten on the go as each person chewed on some dried salmon or beef, washed down with water. After proceeding about 12 miles, an average day's journey, the cattle were bedded down on a nice bunchgrass range next to a small creek, where they settled down after the long day.

As long as the trail was well defined, Thorp and Evans could take the less-dusty lead position, but where the trail forked or became less distinct, Ken-e-ho was called up for advice. He had travelled this route many times, most recently in 1855 after defeating the soldiers on the Yakima.[5] He and the other Natives had travelled fast at that time, constantly looking back over their shoulders in fear that the soldiers and their death-dealing howitzers were near.

The trail descended into the beautiful Kittitas Valley, where a glimpse of the magnificent Cascades could be had to the west. This valley provided excellent forage for the cattle, but Thorp did not let them graze for long, the trail north being a long one. The next morning they were off, again ascending out of the valley into the mountainous country to the north. The trail climbed steadily, reaching the summit of Colockum Pass, more than a mile above sea level. This was hard work for the cattle as, at times, the trail was little more than a narrow path on the side of a steep ridge. There was no room for a horseman to pass the cattle, as the animals could only travel single-file. It was with some relief that the drovers saw the trail descend even more steeply than it had climbed, revealing the mighty Columbia River far below. Once they reached the river, it was possible to spread out a little and proceed along the riverbank to the mouth of the Wenatchee River.

The drovers headed the cattle north from Wenatchee along the Columbia River, once again passing along a narrow trail leading around a perpendicular cliff, and proceeded to Entiat through rugged country. Four days later, they reached the Okanogan River and joined the main trail that headed north and was used by miners and drovers.

Jack Splawn, who was 16 years old at the time, left an account of the journey in his book, *Ka-mi-akin—The Last Hero of the Yakimas*, written in 1898.[6] He mentions the continuing presence of Native marauders who attempted to steal cattle as they were driven along the Okanogan River. One night Splawn, showing the impetuosity and strong-headedness of youth, decided he would protect the cattle from potential theft. He "followed the cattle. When they lay down, I did likewise; when they traveled, I traveled." Just before dawn a group of six Natives approached stealthily from a nearby canyon and cut three steers out of the group. As they headed the cattle

Jack Splawn in later years, from his book, *Ka-mi-akin—The Last Hero of the Yakimas*.

off on the run, Splawn fired at them and hit one of the Natives, who later died from the wound. This brave but foolhardy act meant that the entire tribe would be out for retribution. Major Thorp therefore decided they should push the cattle as fast as they could to the British Columbia border. When they were within a few miles of the Customs House, a band of Native warriors under the leadership of the famous Chief Tonasket approached them and warned them that many of their young men were out for revenge. Tonasket agreed to send some of his warriors with the party to keep them from being attacked until they safely crossed the border into British territory.

What is interesting in this account is the fact that, up until that time, no one had felt the need to ride herd during the night. Cattle were simply left to graze and, in the morning, rounded up to be driven forward that day. This frequently meant spending—wasting—time looking for strayed cattle and eventually

Richard Clement Moody.
BC ARCHIVES A-01723

resulted in the stationing of night herders to keep the cattle contained during the night.

Several days later the drive reached the border that marked the beginning of British territory. William George Cox, one of many from the Anglo-Irish ruling class who came to British Columbia in the early gold rush days, was the customs collector at the Osoyoos border crossing. He was also magistrate, commissioner of lands, Indian agent, and coroner in the area. He was indeed "Her Majesty's representative." Cox was a good-natured individual but already had a reputation as a fierce defender of his adopted colony's rights. Originally he had operated out of Fort Kamloops but, when he found out that many of the drovers were taking an alternate route along the Similkameen River and circumventing Fort Kamloops, he set up his customs house where he could keep an eye on the border. He also, without asking permission or drawing attention to his methods, stationed constables south of the border to capture smugglers. His methods were, to say the least, somewhat unorthodox. He once defeated an American drover in a fist fight when his authority was challenged and, in his capacity as magistrate, settled a claim dispute by having the two claimants run a race from the courthouse to the claim, winner take all.

As the cattle were being driven along the Okanagan Lake, the party caught up with a single rider wearing the impressive red uniform of the Royal Engineers. Ken-e-ho had never seen a man ride an English saddle, which resembled a loaf of bannock in some ways: flat with nothing in front or behind. The rider's way of riding also seemed strange, rising on his stirrups at every bounce of the horse, but he seemed to keep his balance quite well.

The man was Captain Robert Mann Parsons of the Royal Engineers, and he was accompanying Lieutenant Richard Clement Moody, Commander of the BC detachment of the Royal Engineers and Lieutenant Governor of the colony. The following day, the drove overtook Moody, who was involved in surveying the trail along Okanagan Lake. They had a brief conversation with Moody and pushed the cattle past his party.

When evening was falling, they were approached by one of Moody's men carrying a small sack. "The Colonel would like to give you these beans to supplement your rations," he said and dropped the sack beside the fire. Then, without any further word, he turned his horse and rode off. The entire party was delighted with this change from the rations that they had been depending upon for so long. If fact, they decided to take the next day off so they could boil up the beans for supper. First thing in the morning, Eliza rekindled the fire and put the beans in a pot to simmer all day. The drovers, filled with anticipation, spent the day in repairing damaged equipment, fishing in the nearby creek or just relaxing. But, by suppertime, Eliza announced that the beans were still quite hard and would need more boiling. The disappointed drovers settled for their usual fare of beef jerky and bannock, supplemented with a few fresh trout grilled over the fire.

By nighttime, the beans seemed just as flinty as they had that morning. Ken-e-ho, desperate for some delicious beans, offered to stay up all night to keep the fire going so that the beans would be ready for morning. So, after his usual night shift, he stayed by the fire, dozing and then waking to throw wood onto the fire. Alas, when morning came, the beans were still in their natural state of hardness. Ken-e-ho, tired and not a little frustrated, asked, "Tell me, do you think British beans are different from American?" Everyone laughed and, after some discussion, decided to bury the beans under a pile of rocks as a monument to Colonel Moody's good will and generosity. There is no questioning Moody's good intentions, but perhaps his cook was guilty of choosing to part with beans that were somewhat past their "best before" date.

The cattle drive continued along the Okanagan Lake and then over the height of land to Fort Kamloops. From there, Thorp combined his herd with that of Henry Cock, and the two men drove their cattle along the south side of Kamloops Lake, crossing the Thompson River at Savona's ferry, operated by a former Hudson's Bay Company employee named François Saveneau, pronounced "Savona" by English-speaking drovers. When the drovers reached the Bonaparte River, near Cache Creek, they found that they were too late in the season to make a ready sale for their cattle. Most miners from the Cariboo country were heading south for the winter. Unsure about what to do, Thorp sought the advice of John McLean, who had been in the country for 40 years. McLean advised him to winter the cattle at Hat Creek, 20 miles farther on, where the bunchgrass was abundant. Seeing no other alternative, Thorp agreed and left Jack Splawn and Henry Cock to spend the winter with the cattle, while the rest of the party returned south.

The rest of the drovers, including Ken-e-ho, headed back to the Yakima and Klickitat Valleys, only to face one of the harshest winters on record. Surprisingly, the cattle left to winter with Jack Splawn and Henry Cock coped very well in the Bonaparte Valley and were sold in the spring for $150 a head. Ken-e-ho and Eliza returned to their home on Satus Creek, where they lived out the rest of their days. Two years after their trip into British Columbia, Jack Splawn returned to the area and spent a night with them. Splawn remembered the visit later:

> Ken-e-ho took me to his lodge, the largest in the village, where Eliza . . . met me. How well I remember her noble character. Though her skin was red, her heart was spotless white. Kind and good, she was a peer of many of her pale-faced sisters. She arranged a place where I could roll up in my blankets, and placed food before me.

Many years later, in 1881, Splawn returned to the area and learned with sadness that his friends Ken-e-ho and Eliza had passed away.

Dan Drumheller

The same winter that Jack Splawn was wintering in the Bonaparte Valley, Dan Drumheller glanced at the thermometer one day as he went out to feed the last of his hay to his starving cattle. It was 40 degrees below zero as 1861 turned into 1862, with no sign of relief. He was bundled up against the cold, but he could still feel the frigid air penetrate his clothing. Hay was now selling at $100 a ton, and Drumheller and his partner, Louis McMorris, had spent all their money on purchasing the 300 head of fine mixed-blood shorthorn cattle at $16 a head. All they could do was cut willow from down by the river to give their cattle some nourishment, and wait for spring.

The 1,000 inhabitants of the frontier town of Walla Walla lay in the grip of winter for 90 days, cut off from the outside world. The rest of Washington Territory and Oregon fared no better. When spring finally came, Drumheller and McMorris had eight head each, calves that had lived on their mother's milk until the mothers succumbed to the cold. In Walla Walla County, Washington Territory and Umatilla County, Oregon, there had been 10,000 head of cattle in the fall; by May 1, 1862, there were fewer than 1,000 left.

Dan Drumheller had come from good pioneer stock. He was born in Tennessee and travelled across the plains by wagon train to California in 1854. He was a rider for the Pony Express in the late 1850s and later became a miner and packer in the goldfields. He had been told by his brother George, who had been in Walla Walla since 1854, that there would be no severe winters in that region and promptly decided to go into the cattle business. Despite his disastrous winter, in the spring of 1862 he partnered with his brother Jesse and Samuel Johnson, who owned a stock ranch 10 miles southwest of Walla Walla in Umatilla County, and bought 240 head of cattle from the ragged remnant of the vast herds of the previous fall. Drumheller was careful to record that these cattle were not scrub longhorns from the Spanish breeds brought to California:

In the early '50s a great number of well-bred cattle of the beef strains had reached California. By 1860, there were but few of the full blood, long horn, Mexican cattle to be seen in California. Governor Gains, one of the early governors of Oregon territory, brought with him to Oregon some splendid Durham cattle. A few years later Sol King of Benton County, Oregon, made several importations of choice shorthorn cattle. Besides, there were many other early settlers of Oregon who owned full-blooded cattle of beef strains.[7]

By 1862 there was a steady stream of cattle heading out from Walla Walla to the goldfields of British Columbia, and Dan Drumheller decided to follow suit. He hired a couple of drovers and headed the cattle north. From Walla Walla, the trail led across the Snake River and north via the Grande Coulee to the Columbia River, which Drumheller and his cattle crossed at the mouth of the Okanogan River. Drumheller lost some cattle in swimming them across the Snake and Columbia Rivers, both of which were at their highest levels in recorded memory. From Fort Okanogan, Drumheller drove his cattle along the old Hudson's Bay Company brigade trail on the east side of the Okanogan River. He crossed the border at Osoyoos Lake and then followed the brigade trail along the west side of Okanagan Lake and over the height of land to Fort Kamloops. Staying south of Kamloops Lake, he crossed the Thompson River at Savona's ferry. Drumheller would have swum his cattle and horses across the river and used the ferry to get his meagre supplies and camp gear across.

Drumheller followed the Thompson River to the mouth of the Bonaparte River, near where the Cornwall brothers, Clement and Henry, had just established a ranch near what is Ashcroft today. He left the cattle there with

Dan Drumheller, January 1864, from his book, *"Uncle Dan" Drumheller Tells Thrills of Western Trails in 1854.*

one of his drovers and rode north to the Cariboo to see what the market was like. Unfortunately, Drumheller was not alone in his desire to cash in on the lucrative Cariboo market. That summer 4,343 head of cattle had crossed the border at Osoyoos, most of them from the Willamette Valley, which had escaped the severe winter. Drumheller found that there was a glut of cattle available for the Cariboo market but was able to sell some to Charles Oppenheimer, who had received the contract to construct a wagon road from Lytton to Cook's Ferry, later renamed Spences Bridge. As there was no market for his remaining cattle, he decided that his best hope was to winter them and try to sell them in the spring. He returned to the Ashcroft area, sent his drovers home and prepared for winter. He partnered with William Gates, a young man from The Dalles, Oregon, who had a herd of cattle on the same range. The two men had time to build a small pine-log cabin, roofed with poplar poles covered with rye grass and then dirt. They even constructed a fireplace in one end for cooking and heating purposes. There were no windows in the cabin. Drumheller and Gates spent the winter in relative comfort, living on their own beef, along with the frontier staples of bacon, beans, dried fruit, sugar and coffee purchased in Lillooet and potatoes traded from Shuswap Natives. Drumheller took a couple of trips to Lillooet for supplies but, other than that, the only work to be done was chopping the watering places open for the cattle and gathering firewood.

The following March, Drumheller drove the cattle to the Fraser River and sold them at an excellent price to Aschel Sumner Bates, an American from

Boston, Massachusetts, who had been one of the first to reach the Fraser River above the canyon and who had switched from mining to cattle ranching. Then Drumheller headed to Lillooet, where he intended to take the Harrison Lillooet Trail back to the coast. While in Lillooet, he noticed a man whom he knew by sight as a well-known villain who, along with several other desperados, had already earned a reputation in British Columbia for murder and robbery. The man, Brockey Jack, was with the notorious Boone Helm and George Lowery and learned that Drumheller was carrying a large amount of gold from his cattle sales. As March was early for miners to be travelling south on the trail and few people would be around, Brockey Jack left a couple of days ahead of Drumheller, no doubt to find a place to lie in wait and rob him.

The Harrison Trail involved crossing three lakes and, between them, taking four portages. Drumheller travelled safely over two of the lakes and found himself in a rough hotel. But he was uncomfortable in the hotel because he knew Brockey Jack was somewhere nearby watching for him, so he decided to spend the night in the woods. In the morning, he hired a man to row him across the third lake. The wind was against them, and it looked like Drumheller would miss the stagecoach that left from the other side, leaving him alone on the shore and at the mercy of Brockey Jack. He got the man to land him on the shore and scrambled through the bush, barely making the stage. That evening, Brockey Jack showed up disgusted at Drumheller's hotel, clearly indicating that he had been stalking Drumheller the whole way. Drumheller later learned that Brockey Jack had been hanged near Wallula, Washington, Boone Helme at Virginia City and George Lowrey at Lewiston, Idaho.

Dan Drumheller returned to Walla Walla, where he was once again lured by the promise of getting rich in the goldfields of the Pacific Northwest. After several unsuccessful attempts at gold mining, he returned to Walla Walla in 1867, determined to make his living in cattle, not gold. He reconnected with Samuel Johnson, who had helped to bankroll his trip to the Cariboo a few years earlier. Johnson had recently purchased 400 head of four-year-old steers in southern Oregon for his ranch 10 miles southwest of Walla Walla. After driving them to his ranch, he was having trouble keeping the steers on his range and asked Drumheller if he would herd them for the winter. Drumheller agreed and, with one man for help, looked after the cattle through the winter. In the spring, Johnson offered him half ownership of the cattle, payable upon their sale. Drumheller purchased 16 saddle horses and 4 pack horses in preparation for driving the cattle north to the Cariboo. He hired three drovers and a Native from California to cook and to drive the saddle and pack horses. On April 15, 1868, they started north with 400 head of fine steers.

On the way north through Moses Coulee, the drove met up with a Chinese man by the name of Chee Saw, who owned a store on the Columbia River near the mouth of the Okanogan. He agreed to travel with the drove and help in any way he could. Drumheller was impressed; the man was "a daring horseman, and could handle a rope like a Mexican."[8] For five days they travelled north and, with Chee Saw's help, got the cattle safely across the Columbia, except for one steer that kept turning back and was finally given to Chee Saw. He returned to his store with a fine steer and stayed for the rest of his life, giving his name to the town of Chesaw.

Drumheller and his drovers successfully drove the steers through to the Fraser River and rested them on a bunchgrass range 20 miles southeast of Lillooet. By then the market for cattle in the Cariboo was very limited, mostly being supplied by the many drovers who had settled on ranches. The depressing situation was brightened somewhat when the well-known cattle entrepreneur, Jerome Harper, rode into Drumheller's camp. Harper explained that he owned more cattle than he could easily dispose of in his various markets. In fact, he suggested that it would only be a matter of time before British Columbia cattle were being driven to outside markets to relieve the overstocked ranges. Nonetheless, Harper agreed to have a look at Drumheller's cattle and rode through the herd, examining the exceptionally fine steers. Drumheller hoped that Harper might offer as much as fifty-five or sixty dollars a head but was not optimistic. Harper agreed that the steers were the best he had seen in a long time and, after dining on freshly killed venison and pan-fried bannock, decided to stay the night. Drumheller described him as "a frail, nervous fellow [who] seldom slept more than four hours." In the morning, he offered to purchase the entire herd if Drumheller would promise not to drive cattle into British Columbia again. When Drumheller agreed to that stipulation, Harper offered him seventy-five dollars a head. Not yet satisfied, Drumheller asked Harper if he would buy the extra 10 saddle horses at what they had cost him in Washington. He only needed five horses for him and his men to ride back on and one pack horse. Harper looked at them and was particularly impressed with Drumheller's best saddle horse, but Drumheller insisted that it was not for sale. When they finally agreed on a price and shook hands on the deal, Drumheller led his best saddle horse into camp and put Harper's saddle on it. He had decided to travel home via the coast and only needed four saddle horses and a pack horse anyway. Harper was delighted with the gift, and Drumheller was grateful for the top dollar he received for the cattle and horses.

Harper departed to Clinton and sent his foreman, Newman Squires, to pick up the cattle and horses. After releasing the cattle and sending his men home on horseback, Drumheller went to Clinton and settled up with Harper, receiving payment partially in gold bars and the balance by cheque on the Bank of British North America in Victoria, payable in US gold coin. Harper held the cattle for winter butchering at his slaughterhouse in Barkerville, where the steers dressed out at 900 pounds on average. He charged fifteen cents a pound for them in mid-December, realizing a profit of about fifty dollars a head. Drumheller later wrote that "This was the best band of 400 steers I have ever handled and for cattle that had been raised and fattened entirely on grass I do not believe their equal has ever been surpassed on this continent."[9]

Drumheller took the BC Express Stage Line to Fort Yale on the newly completed Cariboo Wagon Road and then sailed on a paddlewheel steamboat to Victoria, where he cashed his cheque. Then he boarded an ocean-going steamboat to Olympia, Washington. Then, once again, he travelled by stagecoach to Kalama on the banks of the Columbia River, where he took a steamboat to Portland and on to Walla Walla. His partner, Samuel Johnson, was delighted with the return on his investment and the two men agreed to remain partners in the years to come. Drumheller did the buying as far away as California and sold cattle in the mining camps of Idaho, Nevada and Montana, and Johnson provided the capital and a holding area at his ranch.

In later years, pioneer cowboy and cattleman Jack Splawn was to write about the year 1868:

> After this year there were no more drives to the Cariboo. The country round about was now raising all the cattle the miners could use. Many fortunes were made in the cattle business in the palmy days of this favourite route, but the tramping hooves of the great herds along the trail were heard no more. The stockman's right arm was gone when he lost the Cariboo trade.[10]

Myron Brown

Myron Brown was miserable. The trail through the bush was rough and the cattle uncooperative; when it wasn't raining, the mosquitos were like clouds; and when it was clear and warm, the dust was choking. The rain was pouring down, soaking his wool overcoat, and the cattle kept wanting to double-back home. With every step his horse took, it almost stumbled as the mud sucked up inside its hooves. And worst of all, it was Sunday! Brown was a Methodist from generations back. His ancestors on his mother's side had built a chapel in England in which John Wesley, the founder of Methodism, had preached.

His grandfather had been a church leader in Ohio and later in Oregon. Yet here he was in the wilds of British Columbia working on the Lord's Day. He was surrounded by godless men and could only share his pain in his little trail diary, given to him by his loving mother. As he huddled under his canvas bedroll that evening he wrote, "This is the first Sunday I ever spent without the means of grace. I miss the meetings very much. God grant that it may not last long."[11] But this was only the first of many Sundays on which Brown was forced to drive cattle into the wilderness.

Myron Brown was born in Toledo, Ohio, in 1846, the son of Joseph and Ann Brown. His parents' families had arrived at Plymouth Rock shortly after the Pilgrims. But his parents, with a restlessness that was common in the United States of the day, had moved from Massachusetts to Vermont and then to western New York in search of opportunity. From there they were swept along with the tide of immigrants into Ohio. Joseph Brown, who was a cooper, decided to seek his fortune in Oregon Territory. He packed up his small family, including Myron and his sister, Mary Ann, and headed west to Independence, Missouri, the start of the trail. In the spring of 1852 the family joined a wagon train heading west. That year more than 10,000 people travelled the Oregon Trail and some immigrants reported seeing wagons before and behind them "as far as the eye could see." This put incredible stress on the trail and made it difficult to find water, camping spots and feed for the thousands of head of cattle that were driven along the trail. Because of this, most wagon trains were kept small so that only small campsites and limited grazing were needed. Travellers often changed trains due to a number of causes. As Joseph Brown was a staunch Methodist, for example, he would have refused to travel on the Sabbath, meaning that the family would have been left behind by less committed Christians. Illness and death were common on the trail, with cholera being the main cause of death. A disease known as "hollow horn," possibly anthrax, was common among the cattle. After months of hardship and privation, the family reached Portland, Oregon. Joseph Brown, sick and exhausted from the stress and rigours of the journey, died shortly after they arrived.

Ann Brown, with six-year-old Myron and four-year-old Mary Ann, could hardly turn back, so she travelled south to Oregon City and located a homestead on Clear Creek, which runs into the Clackamas River in the Willamette River Valley. Without a father and husband to work and provide for the family, the Browns were desperately poor and had to depend on neighbours for assistance. That winter, the family subsisted on potatoes and wild game supplied by neighbours. Before long the little community of Clear Creek had its own Methodist meeting house and, as Myron grew to manhood, he felt a call to work in the ministry. However, to help support his family, he worked for neighbouring ranchers in caring for the growing cattle herds that could be found in the Willamette Valley.

When Myron was 21, he was introduced to William Connell of Rockport (now Dallesport), across the Columbia River from The Dalles. Connell had travelled over the Oregon Trail in 1846 and had originally settled in Wasco, just south of The Dalles, and moved north across the Columbia into Washington Territory in the late 1850s. Along with Ben Snipes—who had ranched in California before coming to Oregon—the Thorp family and the Splawn family, he had been impressed by the abundant bunchgrass in the Yakima Valley and established a ranch. When he met Brown, he was in the Oregon City area purchasing cattle to drive to the Cariboo region in British Columbia. In 1864, Connell, along with his partner, Moore, had wintered 400 head of cattle in an area north of Rockport called Parker Bottom and, the next year, had driven them north into British Columbia.[12] The fact that Connell could pasture his cattle on land that he did not own was based upon a common understanding that could be traced as far back as ancient Britain where unowned property, referred to as the "king's land," remained in the public domain and could be used to pasture livestock. This concept of public domain, freely open to cattle and other livestock of all settlers, was central to the open range system of cattle raising. This meant that a rancher could own a relatively small plot of land and pasture his or her cattle on the surrounding public lands. In the United States, the concept of Crown land was repudiated after the Revolutionary War (1775–83), and all such lands were held by the federal government as part of the public domain. In British possessions all over the world, the concept of Crown land remained. In both cases, it meant that ranchers had access to extensive grazing lands that were either leased from the government or occupied until the government saw fit to use them otherwise.

The booming Cariboo mining area was the most lucrative market for cattle from the Willamette, Rogue and Umpqua River Valleys. Robert Lundin-Brown wrote in 1863 that cattle could be purchased in Oregon and then driven:

[b]y the Dalles, Columbia River, Okanagan River, Osoyoos Lake, western shore of Okanagan Lake, Thompson River, Buonaparte [sic] River and thence to the Cariboo country. The profit obtained by persons employed in this business is very large, as may be seen at once from the fact that beasts purchased in Oregon at $10 a head are sold three or four months afterwards in the north at $50 per head and cost literally nothing for food by the way.[13]

In the fall of 1865, Connell was back in the Willamette Valley. This time he purchased 600 head to winter in Parker Bottom, where he built a rough cabin in which to spend the winter. Having successfully driven and sold these cattle in the Cariboo market, he returned and purchased another 1,000 head with the intention of driving them north to the mining areas of British Columbia. While in the Oregon City area, he met Myron Brown, who was herding cattle for a rancher in the area, and offered him a job the next spring driving cattle to British Columbia. Brown reluctantly agreed, knowing that his chances of advancement as a herder in the Oregon City area were limited and that, according to reports from those who had driven cattle north, there were huge profits to be made as a drover. Fortunately, Brown faithfully kept a small "pocket diary," each page measuring 2.5 by 4 inches (6 by 10 cm) in which he, sometimes cryptically, recorded each day's events. The 1867 diary starts on February 22, for which he writes, "This morning rec'd the letter long looked for, the one that calls me from *home*. Mother gave me the picture herself & my baby brother which I shall prise [sic] very highly. Snow and rain falls alternately." A few days later, on March 1, he "said goodbye to the family circle. Oh, how hard to part from friends. I am now alone."[14]

Brown travelled to The Dalles, where he took the ferry across the river and met up with William Connell. The next month was spent rounding up cattle and branding them with "trail brands" for identification purposes. These brands, also called "hair brands," were singed into the cattle's hair, not burned into the hide like regular brands, as a temporary mark of ownership. No doubt Connell had purchased cattle from several cattlemen in the Willamette Valley and had to trail-brand all his cattle before heading out.

Myron Brown's trail diaries provide a day-by-day record of the progress of this 1867 cattle drive as well as two more drives the following year. During this first drive, under the leadership of William Connell, Brown's diary reflects the newness of the experience and the excitement of being on the trail. During the preparations for the trip into British Columbia, he was expected to work on his own if necessary and to cook for himself. In March he was left on his own to herd the cattle:

March 11—I am alone with the dog at camp & lonesome enough with the prospect of staying so all night. I sent a letter to mother today.

March 12—Stayed alone last night for the first time in my life. Have been alone all day and very lonesome.

March 13—I am still alone. This is a hard life to lead alone in camp with nothing to do. I sometimes wish I was at home but cannot be for a long time.

March 15—Spent another night and day alone. I hope it may soon end. It is a dull life to lead for one used to company & the enjoyments of life. Still cold and freezing.

Finally, on April 1, the drove of approximately 500 head of cattle left the Klickitat Valley for the Cariboo. The drive proceeded over the Satus Pass and into the Yakima Valley. The first major challenge of the drive was to swim the cattle across the Yakima River, a task that would prove difficult for the cattle and the newest drover, who wrote, "April 9—Spent the day crossing the [Yakima] river. Only got a part of the cattle over. Fell into the river off the bank and had a narrow escape."

Connell decided to follow the most frequently used route, which involved swimming the cattle across the Columbia at Priest Rapids and driving them through the Grand Coulee before swimming them across the Columbia again at the mouth of the Okanogan River. From there, the drovers pushed the cattle along the old Hudson's Bay Company brigade trail to Fort Kamloops.

Brown's diary records his youthful exuberance at being far from home and experiencing new things:

April 21—Still traveling on the [Columbia] river. The weather is pleasant. I found some round pricklipairs [*sic*].

April 25—Traveled all day in the [Grand] coulee. Went duck shooting in the evening.

May 1—Saw some blue jays this morning & some fir trees. Scenery very beautiful & varied. Passed through McLaughlin's canyon. Made a long drive

May 4—Passed the custom house. I am now on British soil, the first I ever traveled.

May 7—A fine view of the [Okanagan] lake all day. Drove about 8 miles. I like the trip first rate. Went back after a cow.

May 9—In the morning went back after a cow. Shot a pheasant. Traveled about 10 miles through timber & brush web foot fashion.

May 20—Traveled a short distance. I went to Camloops [Kamloops] in the evening. It is a very bad place.

May 23—Crossed the Thompson [at Savona's ferry]. Mailed a letter home. Had a hard day's ride. Rode a horse down. Saw the first white woman from [since] The Dalles. Heavy shower.

Brown's ongoing frustration involved working on Sunday, a fact that he makes frequent reference to:

April 14—Hunted cattle nearly all day. Sent a letter home. I hope I shall not have to work every Sunday.

April 21—Spent the day herding. No religious service. How strange it seems to be without the means of grace.

May 12—Again we were on the road on this holy day. Oh! How I should like to be at Clear Creek to meeting today [*sic*]. I want to hear from home so bad.

The drove of cattle arrived at 100 Mile House in the Cariboo on May 30 and was met by Aschel Sumner Bates. Bates purchased the entire drove of cattle and had them driven to Williams Lake, where the cattle were kept before being driven to the various gold camps in the Cariboo as needed. Brown and his companions turned around and headed for home, arriving in the Yakima Valley on June 24. Brown continued to work for William Connell, cutting hay and herding cattle until winter, when he returned to his beloved mother.

Cattle arriving at Barkerville sometime in the 1870s. BC ARCHIVES C-08743

The following March, Brown was back in the Yakima Valley, where Connell had wintered his cattle on the bunchgrass ranges that lay unused and unclaimed by settlers. After the usual rounding up of cattle, the men pointed the cattle north and began the long trip to the Cariboo. The drove must have been particularly large, as the crew consisted of "five white men and five Indians and withal a rather agreeable crowd all things considered." The drive followed the same trail that Brown had taken the previous year, crossing the Columbia at Priest Rapids and the Okanogan.

It is interesting to note that the cattle were allowed to move and graze on their own through the night, often moving significantly farther down the trail, just as they did with the Thorp party of 1861. This often worked out to the drovers' advantage. Brown notes that, after crossing at Priest Rapids, "Early in the morning moved camp about 10 miles. However we did not have to drive but a few of the cattle as they drove themselves during the night." The downside of this practice was the time lost in rounding up the cattle that had strayed from the herd during the night. Nonetheless, the drovers, probably willing to do some rounding up in exchange for a good night's sleep, did not see a need for night herding.

Brown's trail diary charts his growing self-assurance and maturity as a drover. Early on, as the party travelled up the Okanogan River, he noted:

I saddled up & went ahead, caught the lead cattle about 6 miles from camp on a big hill. With one Indian, I put 300 head of cattle up the hill & counted them, went back and drove up the rest.

A few days later he wrote:

After a good deal of trouble and hard work climbing mountains, we gathered & counted and found 11 missing. Wm. & I then went back. About two o'clock Wm. started to camp with 6 which we had found. I then set out again & late in the evening found the rest & with difficulty drove to camp. Met the boys coming back. Traveled about 10 miles and camped in a bottom.

William Connell appears to have left Brown in charge for much of the drive as he went ahead to make arrangements for purchase, showing a decided trust in the 22-year-old to look after things. On May 21 they arrived at the 150 Mile House, where they were met by Jerome Harper who, along with his partners in the butchering business, Benjamin Van Volkenburgh and Edward Tormey, had purchased the 150 Mile Ranch in 1864 as a staging area for his lucrative business in the Barkerville area.[15] Harper bought all their cattle and, after helping Harper to brand them, the entire crew headed back once again. The return trip, as usual, took very little time. By June 13, Brown and the rest of the crew were back in the Yakima Valley. Brown recorded:

> This morning I felt quite well. With the wind blowing hard and the rain falling fast, we saddled up and started for Yakima where we arrived at 3 o'clock, cold, wet & hungry, the rain having never ceased. Of course we did not stop for noon, the distance is 50 miles. Everything is all right on the Yakima so far as I am concerned. I should like to keep on just four more days longer which would set me at home but here I must stop for a while. Rec'd a letter from my ranch. Today closes me out with the Co. For the present I have due from the Co. $120.

It would appear that Brown had used his proceeds from droving to buy a small ranch in the Willamette Valley near his home. Having settled his affairs, he was able to go home for a visit, only to return to Connell's place in Rockport on August 12. Connell had an offer to make him on his arrival. "In the evening after some talk, Mr. Connell and I entered into a partnership for the purpose of carrying on the cattle trade."

After the usual preparations of purchasing cattle from the small ranchers and trail-branding them, a drove of 205 head of cattle, under the charge of Myron Brown, headed north from the Yakima Valley. This time, Brown decided to stay on the west side of the Columbia River and drive the cattle over a much more rugged trail that crossed the mouth of the Wenatchee River and the outlet of Lake Chelan. He arrived at the Okanogan River 15 days after leaving Yakima. Interestingly enough, when the drove passed the customs house at Osoyoos, Brown paid duty on 223 head of stock, so most probably some calves were born on the drive. Some of the cattle were already worn out from the drive, and Brown sold three head to William Lowe, the customs collector, for $175. When they got to the Bonaparte River, Brown was joined by William Connell, and the cattle were sold, some a butcher shop in Clinton. On the return trip down Okanagan Lake in early November, they encountered a blinding snowstorm and realized they could not proceed. Heartbroken that his trip home was delayed, Brown decided to turn back. The crew sold their horses and walked or paid passing wagons to carry them. They finally arrived at Yale on the Lower Fraser, footsore and exhausted, but the steamer on the Lower Fraser did not arrive. The 10 men, by this time desperate to get home, rented a canoe and went looking for the steamer. Some 20 miles downriver, they found the steamboat firmly lodged on a gravel bar and assisted with extricating it, finally arriving in Victoria on November 21. Brown recorded that "for the first time in my life [I] beheld salt water." From there they caught a boat for Portland, where Brown experienced another first: seasickness. Finally, on November 23, they reached Portland, where the crew split up, some heading upriver to The Dalles or Yakima Valley, and Brown to his home in the Willamette Valley.

It is interesting that some of the practices Brown talks about indicate the growing acceptance of traditional British methods of handling cattle into the California practices. The original techniques, clothing and gear of the Mexican *vaqueros*, already modified in California by cattlemen from the eastern United States, were further influenced by the men who had trailed cattle over the Oregon Trail in the 1840s and 1850s. Brown makes frequent mention of braiding or repairing whips, indicating that this was an accepted method for driving cattle. He also mentions using a cattle dog, suggesting that, at least for herding cattle, dogs were used. Brown also records several adaptations that were designed to contain the cattle for easier handling, such as building a storm fence to keep cattle within a certain area in the Klickitat Valley and the construction of a "branding stall" to facilitate the branding of 150 head of cattle. These go directly against the Texan practices. The Texan method of branding was always on the open range, where cattle were roped and brought to a branding fire. Men who were not as competent with a rope, the inexperienced drovers, like those associated with Brown, found it easier to drive cattle into an enclosure and then a branding chute.

Brown also mentions the usual practice of making hay, recording that he was "raking hay with a horse rake" in the Klickitat Valley. This practice, already accepted in California, was not considered necessary in the open-range system. Clearly, northern ranchers were beginning to realize the need to stockpile winter feed—not surprising, considering the fact that fully 80 percent of the cattle in that region were killed off in the fierce winter of 1861–62. That winter had been so severe all over the North-West that well-known stockman John Jeffries estimated that nine-tenths of all the cattle east of the Cascades had perished.[16]

Myron Brown went on to work as a farmer and a carpenter until he found his true calling as a Methodist preacher. He married Olive Rowley in 1870, and the couple had four daughters and a son. In his capacity as a minister, Brown travelled all over the North-West. His obituary in 1921 read in part:

> As a pioneer preacher, a race now fast disappearing, he served large circuits and initiated the work in many places which have developed into prominent charges . . . He was pastor at Wallace, Idaho during the miners' riot, which

brought in the "bull pen" and martial law. Because of his fearlessness he was often drafted by the sheriff to assist in arresting the most desperate characters. He preached to audiences of miners, that without exaggeration numbered thousands and held them to his message. He was always able to secure their confidence and esteem and contributed much toward the restoration of law and order.[17]

William Connell quit the cattle business after 1868 and invested his money in city property in Portland, making a significant fortune. Unfortunately, he was unable to enjoy it for long, as he died a few years later.

Chapter Two

FRONTIERSMEN

The *Shorter Oxford Dictionary* defines "frontiersman" as "a man living on a frontier, or on or beyond the borders of civilization." During the mid- to late 19th century, the frontiers of civilization in North America pushed westward from the Great Lakes and the Mississippi River and eastward from the Pacific coast. Generally, and especially in the case of the United States, the frontier was a place of lawlessness and lack of government. In Canada, where the Hudson's Bay Company (HBC) controlled most of what is now Western Canada, the frontier remained a place where crime, as we know it, would go unpunished by any higher authority and where individuals moved at their own risk and without any more protection than what they could provide for themselves. In fact, the entire area of the Great Plains and much of the rugged Pacific Northwest remained beyond the reach of civilization to a great extent. The boundary between Canada and the United States, especially on the prairies, did not exist in any real sense. The frontier was the realm of the Native people, who had occupied and fought for their territories for centuries. They were in the majority and, even though treaties had been made and most often broken, one travelled through their traditional lands at their pleasure.

As the mining frontier pushed north and east from California, thousands of men and a small number of women travelled through the wilderness in search of gold. Many of the men who emerged as leaders of the first generation of cattlemen in British Columbia and Alberta had experienced the last untamed and free days of the fur trade. These men were frontiersmen, and the ranching business in British Columbia and Alberta owed much to their efforts.

Jim Christie

The 1870s were a time of stagnation for the ranchers of the new province of British Columbia as the gold-rush activity dwindled and the promised railway connection with the rest of Canada stalled. Various attempts were made to alleviate the overcrowding in cattle and horse ranges, but none were more enterprising than the scheme hatched by Adam Ferguson and James Christie. Ferguson, 32 years old, was originally from Scotland, and Christie, 20 years old, from Ireland. The two decided that there ought to be a market for horses in the Red River area, over 1,200 miles (some 2,000 kilometres) to the east. They knew that there was a trail up the North Thompson River and through the Yellowhead Pass that avoided the prairies, where the Blackfoot still ruled supreme. The two men rounded up 107 head of wild horses in the hills around Kamloops and, on July 7, 1874, headed up the North Thompson.

At that time there was a smattering of settlers in the Heffley Creek area north of Fort Kamloops and, farther on, James Knouff had established a ranch close to the lake that now bears his name. Even farther north, near the old Hudson's Bay Company post at Little Fort, Charles Fortier, a retired HBC man, had settled at the mouth of the Clearwater River. There was a passable trail up to Fortier's cabin but, beyond that, there had been little traffic since the HBC had stopped using the Yellowhead Pass.

During the gold-rush days, some 10 years previously, Viscount Milton and W.B. Cheadle had travelled from Fort Edmonton through the pass

Adam Ferguson BC ARCHIVES A-01291

and described the horrible condition of the trail at the north end of the Thompson River valley:

> The fallen trees lay piled around, forming barriers often six or eight feet high on every side; trunks of huge cedars, moss grown and decayed, lay half-buried in the ground on which others as mighty had recently fallen, trees still green and living, recently blown down, blocking the view with the walls of earth held in their matted roots; living trunks, dead trunks, rotten trunks, dry barkless trunks, and trunks moist and green with moss; bare trunks and trunks with branches—prostrate, reclining. Horizontal, propped up at different angles, timber of every size, in every stage of growth and decay, in every possible position, entangled in every possible combination.[1]

In 1871, two parties from the Geological Survey of Canada under the leadership of Alfred Selwyn ignored Milton and Cheadle's warnings and left Kamloops in August to explore the Yellowhead Pass as a possible route for the Canadian Pacific Railway. The advance party, led by Roderick McLennan, consisted of 135 horses and mules for packing supplies and riding, 26 men in four pack trains, and 40 head of cattle for beef. Their purpose was solely to cut trail for Selwyn's party of 8 men and 15 horses, which left Kamloops on August 19. By the end of August, Selwyn's party had only managed to reach Raft River over a well-cut trail and had caught up with McLennan's party. From then on, "obstructions and difficulties of all kinds increased rapidly."[2] At Murchison Rapids, they were confronted by an impassable river and a seemingly impenetrable forest. By then, any semblance of a trail had disappeared and there was no feed for the horses. They were forced to cut their way through thick timber and swamp. By October 15, the party had reached Canoe River and was dangerously low on provisions. Selwyn decided to push through to Cow Dung (Yellowhead) Lake with Benjamin Baltzly, the photographer, but was unable to make it. On October 28, they turned back to Kamloops, leaving most of the two parties' horses to fend for themselves. The exhausted party arrived in Kamloops with only 26 horses. The ones that had been left to fend for themselves likely all perished that winter.[3]

The following year, survey parties did cut their way through to the Yellowhead Pass, once again finding the area between the North Thompson and Tête Jaune Cache on the Fraser River to be incredibly difficult to travel through. The endless deadfall and difficult travel prompted one of the seasoned leaders of the survey party to complain:

Fallen timber on the North Thompson River as photographed by Benjamin Baltzly in 1871.
McCORD MUSEUM I-69987

These past two days are the hardest I have had on the surveys and we were in constant danger. Once my mule fell with me from the ledge of a cliff into deep water, from which I narrowly escaped drowning; again while climbing a steep mountain side a mass of loose rock and earth began to move carrying me down to within 50 feet of the brink of a precipice 600 feet high—the whole staff were often exposed to such dangers.[4]

These were the conditions that faced Ferguson and Christie and their herd of horses once they had proceeded as far as Little Fort on a passable trail. Beyond there, they were able to follow the trail that had been cut by the Selwyn party three years earlier, but they still had to swim the horses across the Thompson River regularly to obtain better going on the other side. They soon learned that driving horses was a great deal more difficult than driving cattle. Horses are faster and can be spooked by just the scent of a bear or cougar, and they also tend to wander during the night if not corralled. The two men began to lose the occasional horse in the bush. The trail had become quite overgrown in the previous two years and they spent much of their time cutting deadfall. Once they had left the North Thompson River, the trail disappeared entirely. Ferguson and Christie had to cut their way through the bush as far as Canoe River and onward to Tête Jaune Cache. There they turned east and entered the Yellowhead Pass, variously called Leather Lake, Cow Dung Lake or Jasper Pass by the fur traders. The pass itself was open and relatively easy going until they reached the Hudson's Bay Company post, Jasper House.

The trail from Jasper House east was every bit as difficult as the one they had already traversed. It passed through more than 200 miles (350 kilometres) of spruce forest and swamp. In some places, the men had to go ahead with axes to cut a way through the deadfall. Horses sank up to their chests in the mud and swamp and had to be pulled out with ropes or pried out with poles. They were also confronted by several major river crossings. The Pembina River, some 150 yards (160 metres) wide, was one of the toughest. They watched with despair as horses lost their footing and disappeared into the rapid current, some never to be seen again. But the only option was to push forward.

By September 26, they had reached Lac Ste. Anne, a Metis outpost and mission some 50 miles (80 kilometres) from Fort Edmonton. Of the original 107 horses, there remained 72, most in terrible condition. At Lac Ste. Anne, they encountered a party heading west along the same trail they had travelled and sent a letter back to Kamloops to report on their progress. Their remarkable journey was considered newsworthy and was reported on in the *Cariboo Sentinel* newspaper:

A letter was received by us from Mr. AB Ferguson, who with Mr. James Christie left Kamloops July 7 for Red River with 107 horses. The letter was dated Lake St. Ann on September 26, a point 50 miles west of Edmonton. They lost 35 head of horses at time of writing and some of those left were in very poor condition for market. The trail over which they passed was very bad. Eight of the horses lost were returned to Kamloops.[5]

After giving their horses a few days to rest and graze, the two men drove them through to Fort Edmonton. In all likelihood they sold the horses there. Unfortunately, the Fort Edmonton journals and account books for that time are no longer available, so it is impossible to know for sure whether the horses were purchased by Chief Factor Richard Hardisty. But, considering the fact that the horses were larger than those available on the prairies at the time, it is likely that they were eagerly purchased by the fur traders. Once the men had completed their incredible overland journey, Adam Ferguson returned to British Columbia, where he acted as express agent at Clinton and later had a subcontract for carrying mail between Clinton and Lillooet. He eventually settled in Savona.

Jim Christie decided to remain in the North-West but drifted south, where he saw the potential market for more horses in the prairies, which were now being policed by the North West Mounted Police and where a few adventurous types had begun to settle. In 1876, Christie travelled to Montana and bought a herd of horses with the meagre proceeds from his earlier sale and drove them north to Fort Macleod. These horses were considered the first to arrive in southern Alberta for trade or sale.[6] He had no trouble disposing of them among the few white settlers in the area, the North West Mounted Police and the Native Blackfoot. The Mounted Police paid an average of $100 a head. The next year, Christie was back in Montana looking for more horses— and this time he had a sizeable bankroll to back him up. He purchased an even larger herd and easily sold them to the growing population of settlers. Although his prices were relatively low this time, ranging from $40 to $60 a head and never reaching the top price of $100 paid the previous year, he was very successful.

The following year, Christie was approached by Inspector Albert Shurtliff to help establish a Mounted Police Remount Station at Pincher Creek, where horses could be bred to supply the police with remounts and where they could grow winter feed for the Mounted Police's horses. Christie agreed, and for the next three years he was employed in purchasing horses and setting up the Remount Station. In Fort Macleod and Pincher Creek, Christie worked with John Herron, who took his discharge in 1878 and travelled back to eastern Canada full of enthusiasm for the ranching potential of the West. Among those who expressed an interest in becoming involved in a ranching venture was Captain John Stewart, a member of a prominent Ottawa family that had made its fortune in lumber. At the request of Prime Minister John A. Macdonald, in 1878 Stewart had set up the Princess Louise Dragoon Guards to escort visiting royalty and to serve at the opening of Parliament. Stewart had chosen John Herron as his sergeant major in the Guards. Herron returned to the North-West in 1881 to prepare for the visit of Governor General Sir John Douglas Campbell, the Marquis of Lorne, and, at the instigation of Stewart, negotiated the takeover of the Pincher Creek Remount Station for a ranching site.[7]

By then Christie had acquired a considerable amount of money and was looking for a way to invest it. When Herron approached him to manage the new ranch, Christie agreed and offered to invest in it as well. So, in 1881, the Stewart Ranch was established with John Stewart, his brother Macleod, John Herron and James Christie as partners. The partners applied for and received a lease of 23,000 acres in the Pincher Creek area that included the former Remount Station.[8] The ranch, under Herron and Christie's guidance, soon acquired horses and cattle to stock the range. The ranch was obliged to stock cattle to fulfill the obligations of the lease, but the emphasis was most definitely on horses. The partners constructed extensive buildings and stables to house the horses and gained a reputation for breeding fine horses. The Mounted Police purchased many satisfactory remounts from the Stewart Ranch. By 1885, there were 2,400 head of cattle and 400 horses on the range.[9]

In 1888, the major shareholder, John Stewart, decided to sell off his interests in the ranch. Both Herron and Christie retained land in the area, and Christie continued ranching with his wife, Janet. In the spring of 1892, the couple sold their ranch and settled in the Nose Creek area north of Calgary. They brought with them 100 head of cattle and 100 horses, indicating that Christie was still involved in raising fine mounts. Unfortunately, only two years later it was reported that James Christie, "the pioneer horseman of Alberta," was killed a short distance north of Calgary when he was thrown from his wagon.

John Shaw

In British Columbia, after the initial strike on the Lower Fraser River, the quest for gold proceeded up the Fraser Canyon into the Cariboo, where thousands of lucky miners extracted a fortune in gold out of the creeks. The hunt continued through the rugged mountains of the Crown Colony of British Columbia and led Joseph Ashley to Stud Horse Creek, later named Wild Horse Creek, in the extreme southeast corner of the colony in an area called Kootenais after the Native people who lived there. In the fall of 1863, Ashley found gold in paying quantities in the creek. When winter set in, he went to the Hudson's Bay post on Tobacco Plains to buy supplies for the next spring's mining and paid with $150 in gold dust. It was a well-known fact at the time that placer gold varies in colour and consistency from location to location, so it was difficult to keep a new gold find secret for long. Mr. Linklighter of the Hudson's Bay Company was no stranger to the gold-mining scene and immediately noticed that the dust Ashley was paying with was unlike any other from that area. So, when Joseph Ashley returned to Wild Horse Creek the following spring, he was followed by a group of fellow miners eager to share in his new-found wealth.[10]

Among that ragged bunch of miners was a man by the name of John Shaw, who had been born in Upper Canada and had left home as a young man, lured by the promise of fortune in the goldfields of the Pacific Northwest. Shaw had drifted through the mining areas of Oregon and Idaho, eventually ending up in the Pend Orielle area of Idaho, where he heard of Ashley's discovery. Shaw was on Wild Horse Creek in the spring of 1864 and was successful enough in his mining endeavours to stay on the creek for the next four years. Fellow miner Dave Griffiths described the mining camp:

> There were about fifty buildings in the camp, including saloons, gambling houses and others. Everything had to be packed on horses four hundred miles, from Walla Walla. You can bet we had to pay good prices for what we got. Seventy-five cents was the flat price for everything—coffee, beans, flour—everything. I have seen flour selling in the spring of 1865 for $1.25 a pound; tobacco at $15 and they would soak it in the creek all night so it would weigh more.[11]

The mining in 1864 was so successful that there were about 5,000 miners on the creek in 1865. It was a banner year for the Wild Horse Creek gold rush, with millions of dollars of gold taken out. Some men made $40,000 to $60,000 that year. Shaw was extremely successful, averaging about $1,000 a week during the mining season. Most men, like Shaw, acted as if the gold was unending and spent a majority of their hard-earned income in town every Saturday night. The next year, the gold was pretty much cleaned out and no one made much more than wages. Shaw still had a small amount saved and, as the supply of placer gold dwindled, decided to take up land in the beautiful valley. At the end of the 1868 mining season, on December 4, he pre-empted land on a small stream running into St. Mary's River, four and a half miles from the ferry over the Kootenay River run by James William Galbraith.

During the Wild Horse Creek excitement, thousands of head of cattle were driven into the mines from Walla Walla, Washington Territory, and Lewiston, Idaho Territory. There were even herds of cattle driven in from as far away as Salt Lake City to Wild Horse Creek. In 1867, when the gold rush was waning, cattle were still being driven into the area: it was reported that cattle were being driven in from Walla Walla and that cattle that had crossed the Cascade Mountains from the Rogue River Valley in western Oregon were resting on the Klamath Plain before being sent on to eastern British Columbia.[12] As late as 1872, a man named Joseph Freeman was reported to have left Walla Walla with 250 head of cattle for the Kootenays but only sold half of them. He mentioned that "large numbers of Texas cattle" were being driven to the Kootenay mines, where they "sell very low."[13]

John Shaw no doubt took advantage of the low prices for cattle and probably purchased Oregon cattle at a reasonable rate for his ranch in the Kootenay Valley. The cattle fattened up on the rich grasses of his bottomland pastures. Unfortunately, the only market was south of the mining areas in the northern United States and the competition from American drovers was so fierce that little profit could be made. For a few years he was able to drive cattle to the Big Bend of the Columbia, where the newest gold excitement was unfolding, but, by 1874, he was left with a substantial herd and nowhere to sell it. That year he was approached by Father Fouquet of the Catholic Church, asking if he would be willing to sell his property. Shaw agreed on condition that his cattle would be allowed to winter there while he looked for a place to dispose of them the following spring. The deal was made, and the Mission of St. Eugene was established on Shaw's former ranch.

Shaw heard that the North West Mounted Police had arrived on the prairies in the middle of Blackfoot territory that spring, and that there might be a chance of getting a drove of cattle through to Fort Edmonton. During the winter of 1874–75, he looked into driving his cattle through the mountains to the prairies and then northward to Fort Edmonton. It is possible that he talked to Jim Christie, who had successfully driven horses through the Yellowhead Pass and sold them at Fort Edmonton. Christie may have returned to British Columbia via the North Kootenay Pass and encountered Shaw in the Kootenay Lakes region. At any rate, Shaw determined that he would take his cattle to Fort Edmonton the next spring.

The next challenge was to find men to help drive his cattle. He was fortunate in securing Frank O'Keefe and Charles Ashton, both experienced cattlemen, to assist on the drive. It is impossible to tell how he got these two men. Frank O'Keefe was the brother of Cornelius O'Keefe, who had established a ranch at the head of Okanagan Lake in 1867, and Charles Ashton had taken up land in the North Okanagan in 1866. Perhaps Shaw travelled to the North Okanagan and, while there, proposed that O'Keefe and Ashton come with him; or, more likely, the two men were in the Kootenays prospecting when they ran into Shaw. However the meeting came about, in the spring of 1875 the men headed out with a herd of 389 head of cattle, consisting of 200 cows—one, two or three years old—and 187 steers. He also had enough horses that the men could switch mounts if they so desired.

The immediate challenge was to pick a way through the barrier of the Rocky Mountains. It has been suggested that Shaw took the Crowsnest Pass, but at that time it was overgrown and impassible. When Thomas Blakiston of the Palliser Expedition had passed through the area in 1858 searching for a pass through the mountains suitable for a railway, he noted that "by report of the natives it is a very hard road, and seldom used." Shaw and his drove would probably have chosen the North Kootenay Pass, which had been used for centuries by the Kootenay Natives to pass through the mountains to the prairies.

They proceeded south along the Kootenay River to Tobacco Plains and then turned east to the opening of the North Kootenay Pass. From there it was a steep ascent to the top of Flathead Ridge and then an equally steep descent to the headwaters of the Flathead River. They went south along the Flathead River, cutting their way through deadfall and crossing several swollen creeks until they reached the trail that headed upward toward the pass. At the start of the trail there was good water and pasture, so the cattle were allowed time to graze and prepare themselves for the push over the pass. From there the trail ascended gradually but steadily until it reached the top of the Great Divide. The trail was well marked, as the Kootenay Natives had used it that spring to travel to the prairies. At the top of the pass, the trail passed through alpine vegetation growing low to the ground and there was still snow on the ground. The trail then started to descend and, a couple of miles past the summit, they passed what Blakiston had named Hero's Cliff. Before long, they were on relatively level ground as they travelled along a small creek that ran into what is now called the Castle River. Blakiston called it the Railway River because of

its flat, easy going grade. They followed this river and then branched off on the trail that crossed the Crowsnest River and headed out onto the prairies.

The drive was slow going through the mountains, and made slower because many of the cows were calving. Shaw did not want to lose marketable cattle and kept the calves with their mothers, even though it slowed things down. Now that they were on the edge of the prairies, the grasslands were extensive and the cattle were allowed to graze their way along, averaging 12 to 15 miles a day. Charles Ashton later told his daughter Minnie the story of the variable weather they encountered on the way:

> Although my father was not given to reminiscences, I have heard him tell how on that trip on the prairies as they rode herd, they were on one night nearly eaten alive with mosquitoes and on the next they had struck a blizzard that almost froze them in their saddles.[14]

They travelled along the foothills and avoided going onto the open prairies as they were concerned that the Blackfoot might attack. But the North West Mounted Police had been in the country for about eight months and had already succeeded in suppressing the whisky trade and imposing a relative calm over the area. John McDougall, whose father, George, had been a Methodist missionary on the prairies since 1863, commented on the change in the Native warrior:

> who now found it hard to adjust his life at once to these new conditions. Nevertheless here in mid-summer of 1875 the fact remained that the major sense of all men in this big West was to respect the Police and obey the law. Thus without any bloodshed an immense area in the centre of a great continent and hitherto an altogether lawless region was being justly and peaceably administered, and though but a few months had elapsed we were in some measure feeling safe and some of the time could be off guard. This vast country with its latent wealth was just now waiting for the beginning of settlement and the introduction of organized government.[15]

Pack train passing through the North Kootenay Pass.
GLENBOW ARCHIVES NA-700-7

The Methodist Mission at Morley in 1875. The building in the background is probably the Hudson's Bay Company post. GLENBOW ARCHIVES NA-51-2

The cattle drive was allowed to proceed without incident and reached the little settlement of Morley on about August 10. George McDougall and his extended family had just arrived in the Bow River Valley. Shortly after they arrived, the Hudson's Bay Company had established a post at the same location under the supervision of John Bunn, whose father of the same name was a highly respected physician at the Red River Settlement. When the McDougalls first arrived, they lived in tents and began construction of a mission building and residences. The nearest place for supplies was Fort Benton, many miles to the south in Montana Territory.

When Shaw arrived with his weary cattle and men, Morley was a construction zone, with lumber being hand-sawed and planed for the mission buildings and the Hudson's Bay Company post. Shaw intended to stay at Morley for a few days before heading on his way to Fort Edmonton. However, John McDougall informed him that there was likely little to no market for cattle at the Fort and suggested he winter his cattle at Morley.

Shaw then approached Bunn to see if he was interested in purchasing the cattle or if his superiors at Fort Edmonton would consider it. Bunn doubted that there was a demand for cattle at Fort Edmonton but agreed to write to his superior, Chief Factor Richard Hardisty. In a letter dated August 14 he wrote:

Mr. John Shaw from Kootenai arrived here the other day with a band of 450 head of cattle, his intention was to have gone on to Edmonton to sell them but he was told that there was not sale for more than 30 or 40 head at most & therefore he has decided to winter them here—he has some good looking 3 & 4 year old steers included and I asked him what his price was for such. He said $60 & $70! That shut me up.[16]

After further discussion with Shaw, Bunn added a postscript to the letter.

After closing my letter to you, Mr. Shaw called on me to say that he will sell out his whole stock including 9 horses for $38.00 a head, not including 60 spring calves which he will throw in. His stock is as follows:

200 Cows including 1-2-3 year olds
187 steers
9 stout horses
Total 396
<u>60</u> spring Calves, not included in the charging
[total] 456
396 head @ $38.00 = $15048.00

I told him that I did not think there was the smallest chance of your buying them, however as he wished me to write to you about it I do so. No doubt the speck might be a good one but the same difficulty would meet us that meets him, viz—want of a market—he will wait to hear from you by the return of the year.[17]

John McDougall encouraged him to leave the cattle and go to Fort Edmonton to find out for himself. On this advice, Shaw left his cowboys in charge of the cattle, which were feeding happily on the abundant prairie grasses, and headed north. McDougall recalled Shaw's arrival in his book, *Opening the Great West*:

During the autumn . . . the first large bunch of cattle for stock-raising purposes came into the country. These were brought over the mountains from the Columbia Lakes by one John Shaw . . . his intention was to drive them right on to Edmonton. However, on my advice he left his cattle on the Bow and rode on first to see the Edmonton country for himself. Having done this he very gratefully came back and wintered beside us at Morley. These cattle . . . laid the foundation of the stock-raising business since grown to such splendid proportions in southern Alberta.[18]

Shaw and his cowboys settled in for the winter, constructing themselves a cabin where they could keep an eye on the cattle and see what opportunities would present themselves in the spring.

The fall of 1875 saw a flurry of activity down the Bow River from Morley, at its junction with the Elbow River. Inspector Ephrem Brisbois had been instructed to go to that location and establish a fort for the Mounted Police. D.W. Davis, the Canadian representative of I.G. Baker and Company, was given the contract to construct the fort. He hired a crew of Metis and Americans from Fort Macleod to do the work and, by winter, a fort measuring 150 feet square had been hastily completed, with quarters for the men on the west side, shops and storerooms on the east side, officers' quarters and a guardhouse on the south and stables on the north. That fall, John Bunn relocated the Hudson's Bay Company post next to the fort. I.G. Baker and Company also built a trading post, and T.C. Power & Brother constructed a store next to the fort. The little settlement was further enhanced with a billiard hall operated by Harry "Kamoose" Taylor and a group of Metis cabins.[19]

I.G. Baker and Company had also been contracted to supply the fort with provisions but was reluctant to drive cattle all the way from Montana. When D.W. Davis learned that Shaw was holding almost 400 head of cattle

just down the river at Morley, he subcontracted Shaw to provide beef cattle to the Mounted Police. And so, in the spring of 1876, the first beef cattle were driven into the little settlement of Calgary, as it was named by Colonel Macleod of the Mounted Police. Little did the inhabitants know that the dusty little community would someday become the centre of Canada's ranching industry.

Shaw and his cowboys were kept busy through the summer driving beef, a few at a time, to Fort Calgary and, in the process, Shaw's fortune increased. Knowing of the vast herds of cattle and limited markets in British Columbia, he saw the potential for great profit in the North-West. But, to meet the demands that were sure to come, he needed someone to look after business on the east side of the Rockies. The Reverend George McDougall had perished during the previous winter, and the future of the mission at Morley was in doubt, so in the fall, Shaw approached John McDougall, who later recounted:

> Mr. Shaw made me a most surprising offer. When we were riding down the valley together he said, "Now, John, that your father is gone you surely will not remain in missionary work any longer. I want you to join with me. I see a great opportunity in this country for us, you to work on this side of the mountains and I on the other in the stock business. We can handle cattle and horses as I see it to a great profit and I will gladly give you half of all I own at once and thus we may start as equal partners. You have given some of the best years of your life in working for others; come now and do something for your family and yourself. If you continue as you have you, like your father will be found one of these days killed, or frozen or drowned." All I could do was thank him and to say I would consider the matter and answer him later.[20]

A painting of Fort Calgary in the winter of 1876 by William Winder. In the foreground is the I.G. Baker and Company Store and at the right is the Hudson's Bay Company post.
GLENBOW ARCHIVES NA-98-7

The next morning, John McDougall was confronted by his brother, David, concerning the proposition. John McDougall answered, "I have decided to thank Mr. Shaw and decline his offer."

With the possibility of future cattle drives through the mountains gone, Shaw sent his cowboys home to British Columbia with a healthy payout and decided he would head north to Fort Edmonton to see what opportunities might present themselves. He bid farewell to his friend John McDougall and rode north in the company of one of McDougall's brothers-in-law, a man named Gillis.[21]

Charles Ashton and Frank O'Keefe rode south, recrossing the North Kootenay Pass and making their way back to the North Okanagan. When Ashton arrived back in Priest Valley, as Vernon was then called, he met and soon married Philomene Jangrau, who had just arrived from Fort Colville. With the money he had made from the drive to the prairies, he purchased a ranch on Swan Lake just north of Priest Valley. He eventually moved up the valley to the Shuswap River, where he remained for the rest of his life. The community of Ashton Creek is named after him. Francis "Frank" O'Keefe became an excellent rider, teamster and all-round cowhand. He worked for J.B. Greaves in 1881 and, when Greaves set up the Douglas Lake Ranch a few years later, Frank moved with him and spent many years breaking horses for the Douglas Lake Ranch.

George Emerson

The sentry on the palisades of Fort Edmonton shouted down, "Group of men approaching! Looks like another bunch of miners." Chief Trader William Joseph Christie sighed. He hated miners. It was the late summer of 1869, and they had been coming for several years now, settling along the North Saskatchewan River on either side of his fort. Usually, after mining the gravel bars for a few months when the river water was low, they moved on. But, in the meantime, they were trouble. When the water was low and they were diligent and perhaps lucky, they could make anywhere from ten to twenty dollars a day using primitive sluice boxes. This income was attractive enough to lure many of Christie's men away from working for the Company of Adventurers Trading into Hudson's Bay. What's more, the miners demanded, and were able to pay for, supplies, leaving less for the Indian trade. He climbed up the palisade and watched as the bedraggled group swam their horses across the river and rode up the hill to the fort.

Fort Edmonton at the time was the major outpost of the Hudson's Bay Company, perched on the edge of the vast prairies. To the south, the

Blackfoot ruled supreme and only the bravest—or most foolhardy—would venture into their territory. The Company had gathered its employees from various locations and one was as likely to hear Cree, French or Gaelic as English spoken at the fort. Edmonton, with its floating population of about 150, was the largest community west of Fort Garry. Aside from the fort with its bastions and palisades, there were a few shacks housing the Metis freemen and a smattering of miners' hovels housing about 50 souls. Most of these lived on Miner's Bar, upriver from the fort, but a few had located on Tom Clover's Bar downstream, and here and there along the 70 miles of river to the settlement of Victoria, miners' shacks sent their wood smoke curling up along the heavily wooded river valley. The Catholic missions of St. Albert, Lac Ste. Anne, Lac la Biche and Victoria, where the Cree and Metis lived, and the Methodist missions of Whitefish Lake, Victoria and Pigeon Lake completed the population of the region. A further outpost had been established at Rocky Mountain House but, aside from that, the prairies remained unchanged and unsettled, the home of millions of buffalo, as they had been for thousands of years.

The miners approached the fort. They were the usual assortment of rugged frontiersmen, armed and totally ready for whatever came their way, be it Blackfoot or Cree, grizzly or wolf. Among them, one man stood out. He was young, perhaps 20 years old, and solidly built, not unusual among the motley crew of miners. His eyes made him stand out: alert and always taking in what was going on around him in a calculating way. Christie thought to himself, "This one's a survivor. He will still be around when the others are gone." "What's your name, boy?" asked Christie. The man looked him in the eye as if to assess what the question had actually meant. "George Emerson," he replied.

George Washington Emerson was born in the United States, probably Vermont, in 1846 and grew up in Danville, Quebec, about 70 miles north of the US border. After the Civil War, Emerson headed south to Iowa, where he took out a homestead at Council Bluffs. Hearing of the discovery of gold in the newly formed Montana Territory, he headed to Virginia City to try his hand at gold mining. But, as was usual in the many mining communities of the northwest United States, the first comers got rich and those who came later made wages and little more. So, not surprisingly, Emerson joined a group of miners who had heard that the gravel bars of the North Saskatchewan were offering good returns for diligent miners. The journey via Fort Benton and then across the 49th Parallel into British territory had been without serious incident. Emerson had been struck by the hundreds of thousands of buffalo that grazed on the prairie grasses. There had been encounters with the Blackfoot, for no one crossed their territory without them knowing it, but the Blackfoot, although resentful of the miners, were placated by a few gifts of tobacco and other trade goods and allowed the miners to pass in peace.

As had been foretold, the mining was good and the group amassed a fair amount of fine gold over the course of the late summer and fall. But, by the end of October, the weather had turned decidedly cold and most of the miners began to pack up and prepare to head back to Montana. Emerson had a different idea. He noted that many of the HBC employees were deserting and that Christie was having trouble getting the work of the fort accomplished. Emerson approached Christie and asked for work. Christie was no fool. He knew that Emerson was restless by nature and would not remain in his employ for long. But, in the meantime, he would do.

Christie hired Emerson on to drive a dog team delivering supplies to the outlying posts during the winter. He had never driven a team before but, with the help of the Cree and Metis Hudson's Bay men, he caught on quickly. At first he had to set track for the dogs by travelling in front on snowshoes. It required an incredible amount of stamina to keep the pace up for two hours at a time before being relieved. Before long he had graduated to driver and knew the routes to all the surrounding outposts. Once he was accepted by the other sleigh drivers, who spoke only Cree and French, he had to learn their languages, a task that his natural curiosity and intelligence made easy. The wages of two to ten pounds a month—the Hudson's Bay Company operated on British currency—provided Emerson with enough to purchase clothes and other necessities so, when spring came and miners began to appear on the gravel bars of the North Saskatchewan, he decided to stay in the Company's employ.

That spring, he set out with a large collection of Red River carts laden with furs to make the long overland journey along the Carleton Trail to Fort Garry. These carts were made entirely of non-metallic material and were held together with buffalo rawhide, known as *shaganappi*. The ready availability of these materials meant that the carts were well adapted to prairie conditions and could be easily repaired. They were buoyant and could be floated across rivers and streams while carrying loads of up to 1,000 pounds (450 kilograms). The deeply dished wheels were two feet (60 cm) high and could navigate mud and marshes with relative ease. The only problem with wooden wheels turning on wooden axles without grease was the ear-splitting squeal that could be heard for many miles, but this was a small price to pay. The brigades from Fort Edmonton to Fort Garry and back often included over 300 carts. George Emerson was among the hundreds of Metis, Cree and Whites who converged on Fort Garry every summer. For six weeks the crews drank, gambled and fought before loading up with trade goods and heading back.

Emerson settled into his life as a freighter on the prairies. But things were changing in the Canadian West. The Hudson's Bay Company saw that the coming of the North West Mounted Police to the prairies had pacified the warlike Blackfoot and established a post along the Bow River in 1874. The post, little more than a log hut, was constructed near the little missionary settlement that had been established by George McDougall in 1875. This meant that Emerson was frequently sent from Fort Edmonton to deliver trade goods and to pick up furs from the new Bow River Post. By now he was working as a free trader, purchasing goods from the Hudson's Bay Company and trading them directly with the Native people. He was a regular visitor to the various Blackfoot camps on the prairies and, with his facility for language, soon became fluent in Blackfoot. Often he spent the entire summer out on the plains. In fact, when he first left the Company, he was totally on his own and would later comment that he spent the entire summer living on buffalo tongues, wild berries and duck eggs. The Native people soon recognized him as a man who could be trusted and respected, a rare distinction indeed among the Blackfoot, who respected very few of the white newcomers. In later years Dan Riley, an early settler, remarked that Emerson "had possessed in a rare degree something that few of his contemporaries had, and that was the esteem and confidence of the older Indians who had known him in earlier years." The Natives also regarded Emerson with some awe for his ability to swim through water, something the Blackfoot did not excel at.[22]

When the North West Mounted Police decided to construct a post at the junction of the Bow and Elbow Rivers in 1875, Emerson headed up to Fort Edmonton and purchased construction materials and supplies that he freighted to the new post. The commanding office, Inspector Ephrem Brisebois, decided to call the rough log enclosure Fort Brisebois but because of his general unpopularity, it was soon renamed Fort Calgary (after Calgary House on the Isle of Mull, Scotland) by Colonel Macleod.

Seeing the pacification of the warlike Blackfoot and the gradual disappearance of the buffalo, Emerson surmised that it would only be a matter of time before settlers arrived and established ranches on the abundant grasses of the prairies. In the spring of 1876, he headed south to Montana, where he invested in a small herd of dairy cattle, which he drove north, selling a few along the way. He settled next to the new fort and established a small dairy, selling his milk and butter to the Mounted Police.[23] When the Mounted Police decided to expand their land, they found Emerson squatting on the best acreage. In return for his giving up his land, cabin and dairy cows, the

Mounted Police traded him a horse, tent and camp outfit. Emerson would maintain in later years that he had got the best of the deal, trading a worthless piece of land (now downtown Calgary) for these essentials.

When Emerson was in Montana purchasing cattle, he ran into a man whom he had met previously on the North Saskatchewan River. Tom Lynch was an experienced cattle drover who had helped trail cattle from the ranges of Washington and Oregon into Idaho, Wyoming and Montana during the 1860s. Emerson convinced Lynch that there was going to be a growing market for beef cattle in the North-West now that things had settled down with the Blackfoot. In the summer of 1877, when the Blackfoot were preparing to sign Treaty Number Seven, Emerson and Lynch formed a partnership to trail cattle and horses into the new ranching areas. That summer the partners went to Sun River, Montana, purchased about 200 head of cattle and drove them north across the line. They found a ready market among the scattering of settlers in the Fort Macleod area. The following year, the partners were contracted by Cecil Denny, Ephrem Brisebois's successor, to supply 100 head of yearling heifers to the fort.[24] They also supplied 50 head of yearling heifers to Captains Shurtliff and Winder of the Mounted Police at Fort Macleod and A.P. Patrick, a government surveyor, for eleven dollars a head. All these heifers were intended as breeding stock, and those purchased by the Mounted Police would be used to provide the Blackfoot people with their own breeding herds now that the buffalo had virtually disappeared from the northern prairies. When Colonel Macleod saw that the Blackfoot were starving and that they had not yet broken their centuries-old habit of wandering the prairies, he recommended that the stock be fed through the winter by white herders so that they would not all be gone by spring.

From then on, Emerson and Lynch were kept busy supplying cattle to the growing number of settlers in the Fort Macleod area. But their ambition was to own their own land and, with this in mind, they decided that the area north of the Highwood River was best suited for raising cattle. There the old grass was so thick that it was preventing the new grass from growing. So, before heading south to purchase cattle, they set fire to the range on the south side of the river. The fire, fanned by the prairie wind, chased them all the way to the Oldman River. Having established their range, in the spring of 1879 the two men travelled to Montana and purchased 1,000 head of cattle, which they drove back to their ranch. They branded these cattle with a "10" on the left ribs.

In 1880, Emerson and Lynch brought in another 1,000 head from Montana and disposed of them readily.

For the next three years, the partners continued to bring in cattle and horses, selling the majority but also keeping some for their growing herds.

In 1882, Tom Lynch was hired by the newly established North-West Cattle Company to purchase their foundation herd of 3,000 head of cattle and drive them back to their holdings along the Highwood River. In 1883 the partners sold their holdings to Fred Stimson of the Bar U and moved their headquarters west to the middle branch of the Highwood, called Pekisko Creek. But Tom's popularity as a drover meant that he spent little time on their ranch, and Emerson was left to handle the daily operations. In 1884, after they brought in a trail herd of 2,000 head, which they sold to the Quorn Ranch and the Military Colonization Company, the two decided to dissolve their partnership. Rather than spending time and energy on establishing values of cattle and buildings, the partners hit upon the simple solution of having Emerson take the cattle and Lynch take the horses, an arrangement that suited them both. Lynch moved his headquarters down the Highwood to High River Crossing, where he could sell his horses more easily, and Emerson stayed on the property they had claimed the previous year.

Emerson settled down on his ranch, located several miles upstream from the Bar U, where he often found work to supplement his ranching income. For years he had admired the Rocking P Ranch in Montana and decided to give his own ranch the same name. Compared with his neighbour, the Bar U, Emerson's ranch was a small operation. This allowed Emerson to look after the daily activities, which suited him just fine, and he was soon recognized as the dean of Alberta cattlemen. When the High River round-up—which consisted of two complete round-up outfits, the Bar U and the Mosquito Creek pools—convened every June, the representatives from the various ranches involved chose George Emerson to guide the wagons from camp to camp. A.E. Cross, one of the premier cattlemen of the era, described Emerson in a 1919 account of the 1887 round-up:

> A description of the Bar U outfit would not be complete without including a very noted old-timer who is still on deck, he is George Emerson, the pilot who always rode in front of the wagons and horses on a fine strong gentle horse, showing them where to camp and get water. George was the expert calf marker, cutting the under bit from one ear and the under half crop from the other to perfection. Emerson was one of the oldest timers in the West.[25]

Another vivid description of Emerson focused on his physique:

> Emerson was built like an oak tree; his shirts called for an 18½ inch neck and 64 inch chest—from neck to tail 3½ feet. With these dimensions George's

whoops and hollers could be heard for miles . . . Like a lot of frontiersmen he was a silent man; however, his keen eye missed nothing, and he knew by some uncanny sense what everyone around the place was doing and thinking.[26]

In the severe winter of 1886–87, Emerson, like most of the ranchers in southern Alberta, lost 40 percent of his cattle. Undeterred, he began to rebuild his herd and, by 1890, had 700 head. Emerson ran his cattle on the open, unfenced range, where they could feed on free grass, but to control access to water and pasture on his own holdings, he spent $500 on building barbed wire fences. This was typical of the gradual move from open range to a more controlled management of cattle. By 1900, Emerson had built his herd up to 1,000 head.[27]

George Emerson ca. 1900.
GLENBOW ARCHIVES NA-1714-1

In 1905, Emerson sold out to the Bar U and moved east to the short-grass prairie country east of Calgary and south of Brooks, where he and George Lane leased Canadian Pacific Railway land. He leased the land for free because the CPR would have had to pay land taxes if it received any rental income from the land. The CPR preferred to make money off shipping cattle and holding on to land until it could be sold to farmers. The two Georges leased the same land but ran separate operations. To further stock the range Emerson and Lane travelled to Mexico and had a month's visit with Lord Beresford, who had a ranch there, and brought back 1,000 head of Mexican cattle.

That year, Emerson bought 2,000 head of Manitoba steers and turned them loose on the lease. Another 1,500 dogies (as the newly weaned steers were called at the time) were added in 1906. In the spring of 1907, after a particularly hard winter, 90 percent of these cattle lay dead on the range. Undeterred, Emerson formed a partnership with Rod Macleay in 1909 and moved his operation to The Sand Hills, north of the Red Deer River. Having learned their lesson from the vicious winter of 1906–07, the partners moved their cattle west into the foothills every fall. Once again Emerson saw his herd increase and the profits roll in. But in 1914 he sold his cattle to Macleay and spent his time between his beloved High River and his ranch in The

Sand Hills. With his profits from ranching, he invested in a dealership selling a combination oil stove and heater. However, the taciturn Emerson was no salesman and never sold a stove; he lost his entire investment. After a short illness, he died in High River in 1920.[28]

Emerson's life reflected the story of Western Canada. From fur trader to prospector, to cowboy, to rancher, to modern businessman, he saw the opening and growth of the West like no other man.

The Influence of the Frontiersmen

None of the frontiersmen described in this chapter had been raised on a ranch or had spent any time in California or Texas, where they would have learned the practices and techniques of those areas. They turned to the ranching way of life simply because it was a way to earn a living in the difficult land they inhabited. Despite their lack of experience, they each learned enough to have an impact on the fledgling ranching industry. What they all had in common was tenacity and an ability to get the job done. They were unafraid of hard work and, despite the claim that "cowboys hate any kind of work they can't do on horses," these men would pitch hay, build fences or chop their way through a mountain pass if it was required.

These men learned the techniques of handling cattle through bitter experience and from watching the experienced drovers who had learned their trade on the long cattle drives from Texas or Oregon. Even in the frontier period, the cattle ranges of Montana and the North-West were already showing the growing influence of the California way of handling cattle that had spread to Oregon, Washington and eventually British Columbia. During the mining boom around Virginia City, Montana, in the late 1860s, there had been an influx of shorthorn cattle from Oregon, Washington and Idaho. Along with the cattle came some of the practices and equipment from west of the Rockies. Originally these cattle had been driven over the Monida Pass or along the Mullan Road and held for sale to the mining camps. In 1867 cattle from the Yakima Valley in Washington Territory were driven to Montana's Bitterroot Valley. Over the next 10 years, it is estimated that a quarter-million Oregon cattle were driven to Montana. Many of the drovers on these early cattle drives took up land and established ranches in the foothills of Montana, bringing with them the practices of careful herding, winter feeding and seasonal movement of cattle that were characteristic of the California system of cattle ranching.

At the same time, the open plains of Montana were being settled by ranchers who were a direct offshoot of the Texas cattle drives of the 1860s and 1870s. Cowboys there rode a double-cinched saddle and tied their ropes to the saddle horn. The open range system of cattle ranching, in which cattle were allowed to roam the unfenced prairie grasses and no winter feed was put up for them, was very much a Texas transplant. The system was predominant in the Montana Great Plains and in the northeastern part of the territory. In 1880 alone, some 10,000 head of Texas cattle arrived in Custer County, Montana, around Miles City and along the Yellowstone River.

An examination of the earliest photographs of cattle in the North-West indicates that the Texas longhorns were not being imported into the North-West in any numbers. Most of the cattle show distinct shorthorn breeding, indicating that the majority of cattle were coming from breeds that had crossed the Rocky Mountains from Oregon, Washington and Idaho. The cattle that John Shaw drove over the Rockies from the Kootenays would have been of shorthorn background, and the same would apply to the cattle George Emerson and Tom Lynch purchased in the Fort Benton area. In that area, Conrad Kohrs, who had purchased a ranch in the Deer Lodge Valley of western Montana in 1866, was noted for improving his herd with shorthorn bulls—probably the first constructive cattle breeding in Montana.[29]

Along with the shorthorn cattle from west of the Rocky Mountains came such cowboy tools as the braided rawhide reata and the practice of roping with the rope wrapped around the saddle horn, called a "dally" from the Spanish *dar la vuelta* (to wrap around). But the techniques of the buckaroos from the West were not adopted wholesale. The double-rigged saddle was still the preferred one on the frontier, primarily because roping the large shorthorn cross cattle required a saddle that was firmly secured to the horse.

As cattle were driven onto the open prairie around Fort Macleod, they were allowed to free range like the cattle in eastern Montana. In fact, this was the great attraction of the Canadian prairies, where cattlemen did not have large capital outlays for fencing or putting up hay. In this practice, they were following the Texas way of cattle ranching, where the cattle were left pretty much on their own to fend for themselves. However, this system turned out to be less suited to the colder northern climate of the North-West.

Chapter Three

MOUNTIES

In June 1870, an Imperial Order-in-Council approved the transfer of the vast area known as Rupert's Land and the North-Western Territory from the Hudson's Bay Company to the Dominion of Canada. This new territory was called the North-West Territories. Recognizing the diminished authority of the Hudson's Bay Company, traders from Fort Benton in Montana established a number of trading posts across the 49th Parallel in British territory. These posts were generally referred to as "whisky forts" after their principle commodity of trade. Several of these posts were built along Battle Creek, which runs through the Cypress Hills.

On June 1, 1873, a group of "wolfers" entered the Battle Creek valley, where the trading posts operated by Abel Farwell and Moses Solomon were located, opposite a camp of some 200 to 300 Nakota (Assiniboine) people. They were looking for a large number of horses that had been stolen from them just across the border in Montana Territory and had tracked the horse thieves into Canada but then lost the trail. The wolfers got their name from their practice of poisoning the carcasses of buffalo left behind by robe traders, and then harvesting the furs from the dead wolves and coyotes that ate the tainted meat. Indian dogs, and sometimes the people, too, were also killed this way.

The animosity that the wolfers already felt from losing their horses was fuelled by the flow of alcohol from the trading post. After much drinking, a misunderstanding over another missing horse led to a mixed group of wolfers, whisky traders and Metis freighters opening fire on the Nakota camp, resulting in 23 confirmed Nakota deaths and the death of 1 wolfer, Ed LeGrace. Both trading posts were subsequently abandoned and burned.

Although it took several months for the news to filter back to the eastern press, when the story did break, the country became enraged. The slaughter was seen as a clear indication that the Canadian West was in danger of becoming like the wild frontier south of the border. The American involvement in the incident was particularly disturbing. The free movement of Montana traders across the international border was seen both as an infringement of Canadian sovereignty and as a blatant disregard for Canada's desire to have a peaceful frontier under British law.

The massacre convinced Sir John A. Macdonald to push through a bill to establish a force of 300 men "who should be mounted as the government should from time to time direct" to police the North-West Territories. The creation of the North West Mounted Police was intended to establish friendly relations with the Native people of the North-West, to put an end to the whisky trade and to maintain law and order. The force was a combination of military men and police with the authority to try law breakers and mete out punishment as required. This meant that the duties of the "Mounted Police" were quite diverse. They were expected to deliver the mail, provide medical services and relief supplies, record census information, collect customs duties, take meteorological readings, and report on livestock and crop conditions. They also helped to supervise Native affairs and functioned as Justices of the Peace. In short, the Mounted Police were the government representatives in the North-West Territories.

Because of their broad mandate, the Mounted Police were in touch with almost every aspect of frontier life, and they soon became knowledgeable about a wide range of subjects, from the quality of livestock to the various remedies for fever. Their regular reports to Ottawa provided valuable information on the state of affairs in their isolated region.

The first men to be appointed to the Mounted Police in the fall of 1873 were officers, most of whom had previous military experience. In general, these officers came from the elite of eastern Canada and brought with them the values and norms of their class. These ideas influenced their social expectations and even their attitudes toward crime. Since they saw their first duty as maintaining order on the frontier, they had to understand the difference between crimes and frontier exuberance. Their first assignment was to recruit the rank-and-file members of their force from specific regions of the country. Recruiters went to the Maritime provinces, Quebec and Ontario. By late in the year, the Mounted Police consisted of three troops, A, B and C, and comprised 150 men. They were dispatched over the Dawson route from Port Arthur's Landing (today's Thunder Bay) to Stone Fort, Manitoba (now Lower Fort Garry). The following year the Mounted Police added another 150 men and troops D, E and F.

Upon arriving in the North-West, the Mounted Police set to work, and in short order the whisky trade was eliminated, the Native peoples' confidence won, and law and order more or less established. The Mounted Police, at first unresponsive to the demands of the fledgling ranching community, soon developed a strong connection with the ranchers. Most often, the two groups shared a common background and interacted socially. The Mounted Police were involved in protecting against cattle theft, illegal branding and related cattle crimes, and ranchers were quick to respond with unwavering support for the police. Close relationships developed between the police and the ranchers, especially as many Mounties became cattle ranchers after discharge.

William Winder

Captain Winder was sound asleep in his room at Fort Macleod when the pounding at the door awoke him. Shaking his head and rubbing the sleep from his eyes, he went to the door. Constable Ed Wilson stood there and announced excitedly, "There's been a theft of horses! John Hughes, Miller and Bastien have had 30 horses stolen by someone who is heading toward the border." Winder thought before responding, "We will go after them at daybreak. Get everything ready." As soon as dawn broke, Winder, Wilson and two other constables headed to the Oldman River, where the ranchers had recently squatted. The Mounted Police had no trouble picking up the trail and, with fresh mounts under them, quickly closed the gap between the horse thief and themselves. They soon spied the culprit swimming the horses across the Belly River. As soon as he spotted the Mounties, the man roped one of the largest horses in the bunch and quickly changed saddles. He rode off at a gallop with the Mounties in hot pursuit. The chase continued for 15 miles before Constable Ed Wilson closed to within 100 yards of the thief, who waved his rifle in an attempt to slow down the Mountie. Wilson fired at him, at first too high, but the second shot passed between his arm and his body. The horse thief threw up his hands in surrender, and the Mounties took him into custody. The horse thief turned out to be James "Slim Jim" Brooks, who had a notorious reputation as a horse thief in Montana.

Although the Native people had been stealing horses from each other for over a century, Slim Jim was one of the first white men to steal from other white men in the area. He was sentenced to five years in jail. The only problem was that the nearest penitentiary was at Stony Mountain, near Winnipeg. Six Mounties had to escort Slim Jim there. The journey took a month, and Jim served as teamster and the cook during the trip.[1]

Captain William Winder had been born in the village of Cookshire, near Lennoxville, in the Eastern Townships of Quebec, where English was the language and agriculture the lifestyle. As a young man, he loved the outdoors

Captain William Winder in full dress officer's uniform. GLENBOW ARCHIVES NA-1385-2

and spent every possible moment on horseback. He became a member of the local militia, with the impressive name of the Cookshire Cavalry, in which he rose to the rank of captain. When the bill was passed to form the North West Mounted Police, Winder was one of the first officers enlisted on September 25, 1873. He was given the task of recruiting among the Eastern Townships and was appointed Captain of C Troop on the March West. Crossing the prairies, he was impressed by the countless thousands of acres of grass and saw the possibilities for raising livestock once the buffalo were gone and the Native people settled on reserves. Winder's wife, Julia, joined him at Fort Macleod in 1876, along with Mrs. Macleod. The couple were signatories of Treaty Number 7 at Blackfoot Crossing in 1877.

The following year, Captain Winder, along with Captain Shurtliff, bought 50 head of cattle from George Emerson and Tom Lynch and turned them loose on the open range near Fort Macleod. These cattle were branded with the Slippery Moon brand, which Winder and Shurtliff chose to keep as theirs. That two Mounted Police had ventured into the ranching business was a fact that did not go unnoticed in the east. In fact, in the House of Commons, Prime Minister John A. Macdonald was recorded as remarking that some "officers especially those of a commercial or speculative turn of mind, have been employing themselves looking after herds of cattle, etc., and have thrown off the soldier too much to indulge in such pursuits."[2] This resulted in an official rebuke from Commissioner Irvine but did not extinguish Winder and Shurtliff's ambition to get into the cattle business.

In September 1879, while still in the Mounted Police, Captains Winder and Shurtliff participated in the first round-up in southern Alberta, only to find that a large number of their cattle had gone missing. Winder pointed out the likely cause in his annual report for 1879. "The Indians are suffering and the Mounted Police supplies are short. Complaints of cattle-killing by Indians came in almost daily from March to October. Yet we could find no clue of guilty parties, though I investigated the cases personally."[3] Unlike some of the other cattlemen, Winder and Shurtliff had little choice but to leave their cattle on the open range and accept their losses as part of doing business.

The issue of Mounted Policemen owning their own cattle continued to be a matter of concern. None other than Crowfoot, the great chief of the Blackfoot, complained to Governor Edgar Dewdney, the newly appointed Indian Commissioner of the North-West Territories, that Captain Winder was branding Native-owned calves with his own brand. Crowfoot's people were so desperate that they were eating dogs and gophers, so this accusation was taken seriously. Dewdney investigated and concluded that Winder actually had no brand of his own. While this took the heat off Winder, one wonders whether he had been saved by a technicality. Winder and Shurtliff had adopted the Slippery Moon brand that had come in with their cattle and may very well have been using it on unbranded calves, even though it was not "officially" recognized as theirs.

After the fall round-up of 1879, Winder was given leave to return to his home near Lennoxville, Quebec. He shared with excitement his experiences in the North-West and his belief in its potential for raising stock, and his words did not fall on deaf ears. He and his wife went to visit her father, Charles Stimson, who was a successful Quebec businessman, and his son, Fred Stimson, who had been managing his father's large farm in Compton County since he was 18 years old. The farm had specialized in cattle breeding, and Fred Stimson had been in regular contact with the Honourable Mathew H. Cochrane, a Member of Parliament and an acknowledged breeder of shorthorn cattle. In 1877, Cochrane had organized a sale of his shorthorn cattle at Bowness on Lake Windermere in Cumberland, England, that had caused a tremendous stir in the British livestock world and resulted in previously unheard-of prices.[4] Cochrane, who had been a Member of the Canadian Senate since 1872, was most interested in what Winder had to say and, in 1880, submitted to Sir John A. Macdonald's cabinet a series of recommendations that were to have a profound influence on the method of granting Crown lands for grazing on the prairies of southern Alberta. In the United States, grazing rights were usually granted once a particular tract was occupied, but Cochrane declared that, on the Canadian prairies, large sums could not be successfully invested without better guarantees from the state. Despite setbacks, he attained his main objectives: in December 1881 a minister's order set aside up to 100,000 acres of pasture land per breeder, for a period of 20 consecutive years at a modest annual rental of ten dollars per thousand acres. It also exempted ranchers from paying duty on cattle imported from the American prairies.

Before Winder left for the North-West, he had convinced the Stimsons and their friend Matthew Cochrane that ranching on the Canadian prairies was going to be not only viable but also extremely lucrative. Within two years the legislation had opened up millions of acres for ranching, and Matthew Cochrane had applied for the first of these leases. Not to be outdone, the Stimsons approached Sir Hugh Allen, owner of the Allen Steamship Line and the wealthiest man in Canada, to invest in the North-West ranching industry. Sir Hugh sent Fred Stimson to the North-West to investigate and subsequently formed the North-West Cattle Company in March 1882, with Fred Stimson as manager. This company, most commonly known as the Bar U, was to play a major role in the western ranching frontier.

Winder was also in the east to raise capital for his own venture. He approached a number of Quebec businessmen and, by the time he left for the West, had tacit approval to invest in a stock-raising venture from a consortium of men, including John L. Gibb, a Quebec City merchant; J.M. Lemoine, a Compton stockman; and George Barry and Charles Stimson, both Montreal merchants. The company also included W.M. Ramsay of Montreal and Charles Sharples of Quebec City. The Winder Ranche Company ("ranche" was a common spelling of the word at the time) was established in 1880 but, before it secured its lease, Winder had to return to Fort Macleod and complete his term of enlistment.[5]

Winder retired from the Mounted Police on April 1, 1881, and began to focus all his energy on the ranching venture. Not having the financial wherewithal of a Hugh Allen or Matthew Cochrane behind him, he considered a lease of 50,000 acres to be sufficient. He decided that an area along Willow Creek at the north end of the Porcupine Hills would be ideal in terms of climate, grass and water. But he was dismayed to discover that a group of businessmen in Halifax, with the support of Sir Charles Tupper, were looking at leasing the same area. He contacted his father-in-law, Charles Stimson, who urged the deputy minister of the interior, A.M. Burgess, to act on the Winder Ranche Company's request. Proving once again that "it's not what you know but who you know," the lease was given to Winder's company in 1883 and the Halifax group was given a lease farther south.

Winder immediately set about stocking the ranch. He purchased 1,200 head of mixed cattle from a man named Mitchell who was ranching on nearby Trout Creek. But, having been in the West long enough to know the value of good horses, he also purchased 75 Oregon mares to form a breeding herd. Winder's brand, the Double Crank, basically a counter-clockwise swastika, was well known in southern Alberta and found on good livestock.

Winder never actually lived on the Winder Ranche. He preferred to live in Fort Macleod with his wife, Julia, where he operated a store. In 1882 he hired Charlie Sharples, the son of one of his shareholders, as ranch foreman. Winder was involved in all management decisions for the ranch and remained active in Fort Macleod activities. In 1885, when the Riel Rebellion sent the entire white population of the North-West into shock, he organized the Macleod Guard and was chosen as captain with frontier lawyer Frederick Haultain, who later became the first premier of the North-West Territories, as his first lieutenant. The Guard held weekly parades, conducted drills and carried out night patrols of the streets. When the Native people of the area refused to join Riel and the rebellion was put down, the Guard was disbanded.

William Winder died from a fall in 1885 and was remembered years later by pioneer journalist Lester V. Kelly:

> The death of Captain Winder, manager and founder of the Winder Ranch occurred during the fall ... As a police officer he had established an enviable record, and as a ranch manager he was proving to be one of the most progressive, his horses especially, bred from good Oregon stock, grading by good breeding into choice remounts.[6]

William Winder was survived by his faithful wife, Julia, and two sons. His elder son, George, became one of the top cowboys in the area.

Edward Maunsell

The thrill of adventure was beginning to wear off for Ed Maunsell. Born and educated in Ireland, he had come to Canada at the age of 18, seeking adventure and fortune. Upon arrival, he immediately joined the newly formed North West Mounted Police and headed out on the March West with about 150 other new recruits from Toronto to Dufferin, Manitoba, via Fargo, North Dakota. They had spent a few weeks organizing their Red River carts and packing them with supplies. By the first week in July they were on their way, 300 men in six troops off to liberate the West from desperados and whisky traders. They started off amid great pomp and ceremony, with large advance and rearguards of mounted men in crisp red uniforms. As ammunition against the whisky "forts," they dragged along two nine-pound cannons and two mortars.[7]

But before the impressive body of men had gone very far, things began to go wrong. The horses purchased in eastern Canada found the prairie grasses unpalatable and soon began to fail. The Mounted Police soon found themselves travelling mostly on foot. Then their provisions began to run out and, true to the axiom "an army marches on its stomach," the pace began to falter. In the morning, Maunsell and the rest of the men were each issued a half-baked lump of dough and a small cube of boiled bacon. This was intended to sustain them for the day until a meagre supper was presented to them. And to make matters worse, the entire column was under attack by fleas. The infestation of these "cooties" was aggravated by the scarcity of water in which to wash.

This was far from what Maunsell had signed up for. As he later recorded:

This was very different from what we had pictured ourselves doing when we joined the Force. We were all young men and inspired with a spirit of adventure. We had imagined ourselves mounted on spirited horses chasing desperados over the prairies. We had also thought that perhaps the Indians might not appreciate the motive of our coming and prove hostile. All of which would have been much more exciting than fighting hunger and cooties.[8]

However, it's a long road that has no turning. Within a few days, buffalo were sighted and the provisions situation was solved. The men were put on a straight ration of buffalo meat and, as young men who had known hunger, their appetite was enormous. The fact that the first buffalo they encountered were old bulls whose meat was tough and stringy did not deter the men one bit. Boiled buffalo meat for breakfast, lunch and dinner was just fine. Each morning the men were allowed to take in their haversack enough meat for the day, and an average of 10 pounds of meat each seemed to be enough to satisfy them, although the nutritional balance was not ideal. Fortunately, as they skirted the Cypress Hills, they found an abundance of chokecherries, which provided a welcome addition to their diet of pure buffalo meat.[9]

Although they had grown accustomed to being more or less always in the company of buffalo, they were unprepared for the sight that greeted them as they approached the Sweet Grass Hills:

The east also presented a sight which no eye will ever witness again. As I stated, we were camped on high ground and as far as the eye could see were vast herds of buffalo moving slowly south, their black bodies a stark contrast against the snow-covered prairies . . . It was impossible to calculate their vast numbers. Who would have predicted then that the buffalo would almost become extinct in a few years![10]

Maunsell observed of the buffalo that "their condition convinced me that the native grasses were most nutritive, I thought the time would come when this vast country would prove one of the greatest meat producers in the world."[11]

The Sweet Grass Hills marked the end of the March West, and Maunsell, as a member of D Troop, turned around and headed back to Swan River in Manitoba, where he remained until reassigned to Fort Macleod in 1876. When he arrived at Fort Macleod, he found that the Mounted Police had quickly put an end to the illicit sale of liquor to the Native people and, at that time, had very little to do. Their main activity was to patrol the border and intercept the occasional whisky trader who attempted to cross into the territory, most often with the intention of supplying it to the police themselves. Around Fort Macleod, a small town had sprung up. Maunsell described it:

> Shortly after Fort Macleod was built, a small frontier town sprung up close to it. It contained three stores, the principle one belonging to I. G. Baker & Co., who had the contract to supply the police. T. C. Power & Bro. was the next largest and next came Tony La Chappelle. These stores expected to get all the trade that formerly was given by the Indians to the whisky traders. They would no doubt have done a large business had not the buffalo become exterminated. These stores also catered to the police and a considerable portion of the trade consisted in selling substitutes for whisky.[12]

After attempting to bring in "brandy peaches" (essentially brandy with a few token peaches), which the authorities soon put an end to, the traders brought in patent medicines that contained a high percentage of alcohol and were extremely hard on the body. The preferred method was to smuggle in actual whisky (or what passed for it in those days), making for a grand game of hide-and-seek between the Mounted Police and the traders. Maunsell looked upon this game between the Mounted Police and otherwise law-abiding citizens as hypocritical, as the Mounted Police were just as fond of a drink as their fellow community members. He was far from convinced that the grand purposes of the Mounted Police were being accomplished and took his discharge when his three years were up in 1877. He had other plans:

> In 1876 I saw in some Old Country newspapers that live beef had been shipped from the U.S. to England. This decided my future life. I reasoned that when the Mounted Police had established law and order, it would not be many years before settlers flocked in and we would have railway communication. It appeared to me judging from the condition of the buffalo both in the fall and spring that domestic cattle could be raised here at a minimum cost.[13]

After his discharge, Maunsell returned to Ireland, where the cattle producers were in turmoil over the fact that live cattle were being shipped from the US and cutting into the lucrative market in Britain. Maunsell could say little to discourage their concern. He told them that he had seen millions of acres of grasslands on which the buffalo became fat and saw little reason why domestic cattle wouldn't do the same. This convinced Maunsell and his family that investing in cattle would not be a losing proposition. So, with the encouragement and financial support of his family, he returned to the

North-West. His brother George, who had enlisted in the Mounted Police in 1875, decided to join forces with Edward, and a few years later a third brother, Henry, joined them.

At that time, there were few cattle in the North-West. Aside from the herd brought in by John Shaw that had been quickly disposed of, Joseph McFarland had brought in some milk cows in 1875; Annie Armstrong had brought some milk cows from Montana to her place six miles west of Fort Macleod; and in 1877, Emerson and Lynch brought in their first herd of 200 head and sold them in the Fort Macleod area. So Maunsell travelled back by way of the Missouri River and Fort Benton. He purchased a horse and a Montana saddle and rode from there to Fort Macleod, where his brother George awaited him. The two brothers contracted with Charles E. Conrad of the I.G. Baker Company to purchase 100 head of cattle and 3 bulls, with delivery scheduled for the fall.

The matter of cattle having been dealt with, Edward and George went to look for a likely spot to settle. They purchased an old wagon and some house furniture, consisting of a cookstove, three chairs and a table, and loaded the wagon with provisions from I.G. Baker. On top of it all, they placed a borrowed tipi and headed out to explore. They were not the only ex-Mounted Police who had the idea of settling. Crossing the Oldman River and heading about six miles west, they encountered Thomas Boys and then Dave Allison, both retired Mounties, who informed them that John Hollis had settled in the Porcupine Hills and "Dutch Fred" Wachter had located on the Belly River at Standoff. Farther down the Belly River, ex-Mountie James Bell and Robert Paterson, who was still enlisted, had settled. With no survey or system of registering homesteads in place, all the men simply "squatted" on land that they found unoccupied. Most of these men had taken Native wives in the manner of the West. These wives proved to be faithful and devoted helpmates to the green ex-policemen, who would not have survived without their wives' knowledge and experience.

The Maunsells travelled a short distance down the north side of the Oldman River, past Boys and Allison, and set up their tipi. As they awaited the arrival of their cattle, they decided they needed a permanent house, but neither of them had a clue about how to proceed. They approached Tom Boys and asked if they could borrow a man named Al Rutherford who was working for him to help with the house. Fortunately, Rutherford knew about log construction and told the Maunsells to cut 90 logs. This was not without its challenges. Neither man had worked an axe before and most of the nearby timber was too small for house logs. But, in true pioneer spirit, they persevered and managed to get out the necessary logs. Then, with more enthusiasm than wit, they decided to peel the logs to enhance the appearance of their future home. When Rutherford arrived, he shook his head and said, "You've made a mistake." They proceeded to erect an 18- by 30-foot cabin, and Rutherford showed them how to chink the gaps between the logs. That's when the extent of their mistake emerged. The mud chinking did not adhere to the peeled logs very well. In fact, they had to be careful not to slam the door, or the dry mud would fall out. Nonetheless, the house was completed by fall, despite the fact that the brothers spent much of their time in the fall cutting hay for the Mounted Police winter feed. They purchased two half-windows from I.G. Baker, and a police carpenter made them a door and a frame for the window. A mud floor and pole roof covered with prairie sod completed the cabin and, without help, the brothers built a corral for their horses. Having seen the need for winter feed for the Mounted Police horses, they started cutting swamp hay with a scythe, there being no such things as mowing machines in the area.

Their neighbour Henry Olsen who, in partnership with Joseph McFarland, had been in the country since 1875, advised them to hold off receiving their cattle until spring. This was wise advice, as cattle arriving tired and footsore in the fall would have a difficult time surviving a harsh winter. So for this reason and the fact that their money from home had not yet arrived, the Maunsells asked Charles Conrad to wait until spring to deliver the cattle. They then spent the winter cutting fence rails and living on prairie chicken and deer meat.

In February 1879, the long-awaited money from home arrived. But, to the men's chagrin, it was in the form of a letter of credit on some bankers in Deadwood, South Dakota. The Fort Macleod merchants wouldn't cash it and suggested Edward Maunsell travel to Helena, Montana, where there was a real bank. Maunsell heard that Tony La Chappelle, long-time frontiersman and trader, was making the trip and would be happy to carry the bedding if Maunsell rode on horseback. The party, consisting of La Chappelle, his adopted Native son, Patsy, and two other men, headed out on February 11. After two days' travel they reached Lee's Creek, where Cardston is now, when it began to snow heavily. The others turned back but La Chappelle, who was an experienced plainsman, decided to push on with Patsy and Maunsell. The snow did not let up, and the party was forced to make camp out on the prairie with only buffalo chips for fuel. But the next day dawned bright and clear, and they saw that they were only a short distance from the Milk River and a coulee called Whisky Gap, where the trail to Fort Benton ran. That night, another blizzard made travelling conditions impossible and they set up camp. The horses had been tied to the wagon but, during the night, they were turned loose to keep them from freezing. All the next day the blizzard raged, and the party was obliged to stay in camp.

The next day the weather was clear and cold again—and the horses were nowhere in sight. Maunsell was preparing to go look for them, but La Chappelle insisted that he would go and headed out into the snow. Maunsell busied himself collecting buffalo chips until he had a huge pile. As darkness set in and there was no sign of La Chappelle, Maunsell lit a large fire and melted a fry pan full of grease until it started to burn. He then occasionally threw snow on the grease and it would flare up. La Chappelle was able to use the flares as a guide and stumbled into camp around midnight—without the horses.

The next morning the party started out on foot with Maunsell carrying their meagre supplies and bedding. As night fell, the men were so weak, they had to stop and eat. Maunsell went out to collect firewood and, thirsty and exhausted, tried to chop a hole in the ice of the Milk River, only succeeding in stepping into open water and soaking his feet. Not wanting to tell La Chappelle, he brought back the firewood and the three ate a small supper, then began to walk toward a cabin on the St. Mary's River. Maunsell's feet were frozen and excruciatingly painful, but he continued to plod on. At dawn the sun brought some warmth and they arrived at the cabin, which was occupied by a man known only as "the Jew" (possibly a Jew named Ursinger who sold horses at Treaty Number Seven). There they managed to thaw out and discovered that Maunsell's feet were badly frozen. They wrapped his feet in rags soaked in coal oil and got him to Fort Macleod, where it was believed he would lose both his feet. He stayed in the Mounted Police hospital for a month and, in a measure of his youth and stamina, walked out to resume his ranching endeavours.[14]

Their cattle arrived at Fort Macleod in June 1879 along with other cattle brought in by Lynch and Emerson for Sam Bruard and ex-Mounted Police Bell and Paterson; Mounted Police Winder, Shurtliff, Neale and Steele also bought cattle with the intention of cattle ranching when their time was complete. The cattle in the Fort Macleod area amounted to close to 1,000 head that summer.

Ed and George Maunsell knew nothing about handling half-wild range cattle, as was demonstrated when the cattle were let out of their corral at Fort Macleod. They had been in the corral all night and were thirsty and agitated from being branded, so when they were let out, they headed on the dead run for the nearest water. Fortunately, there was a prairie slough nearby and, after they had drunk their fill, the cattle started grazing. The Maunsells feared that the cattle might start running again during the night and decided to ride night herd around them. But having been fed and watered, the cattle were

Edward Maunsell mounted on the right and Joseph McFarland on the left. The man in the middle is unnamed. GLENBOW ARCHIVES NA-1071-2

quite content to settle down for the night. They were allowed to range on the open prairie and occasionally wandered and mixed with neighbours' cattle, but the Maunsells knew that could be sorted out at round-up time.

What the Maunsells and their neighbours had not factored in was the state of starvation that most of the Native people were experiencing. Although there was a strong case that some of the cattle left on the range had just wandered off toward Montana, the great likelihood was that the Natives were butchering cattle that they found on the open range and hiding the evidence. When the fledgling ranchers of southern Alberta gathered in the fall for the first round-up in the region, Edward Maunsell was among the 16 riders who took part. At the conclusion of the round-up, the Maunsells found that, of their 103 head of cattle purchased a couple of months before, there remained 56. This was extremely disheartening.

The Maunsells and the other ranchers, the majority of them Mounted Police or ex-Mounted Police, appointed four men to approach the authorities to discuss the situation. Ed Maunsell was one of the four, along with Joseph

McFarland, Henry Olsen and Annie Armstrong's foreman, Morgan. The four representatives approached Governor Edgar Dewdney, the federal government's official representative in the North-West Territories, to present their case. They said that they depended on the government and the Mounted Police to maintain order and protect property. They insisted that they wanted to stay in the country and would do so if the Mounted Police would protect their cattle. They knew that Dewdney intended to purchase cattle to supply the Natives and offered to sell theirs at cost and wait until conditions were more favourable. Dewdney, and later Colonel Macleod, refused to make good their losses, refused to purchase their remaining cattle and expressed the feeling that it was too early for ranching in the area.

The Maunsells had little recourse but to take their few remaining head and drive them back to Montana, suffering the further indignity of having to pay duty to bring them across the border. They had no intention of residing in Montana and made arrangements to have the cattle looked after by a rancher named John Miller. The two brothers then returned to hold down their squatters rights and to try their hands at farming. They purchased a breaking plow and broke about 30 acres, into which they planted oats, thinking that the Mounted Police would be ready customers. The conditions that summer turned out to be ideal, and they realized $1,200 from their meagre crop, which they cut with scythes and threshed with flails.

In April 1880, Ed Maunsell had another encounter with the prairie weather. He had been told that three head of his cattle had been seen near the mouth of Lees Creek and set out to retrieve them. He found the cattle all right but encountered a spring snowstorm on the way back. When the snow let up, the sun came out and Maunsell had to squint to see through the glare. Before long he was virtually blind and began to wander west instead of north. He encountered some Blackfoot who guided him and his cattle to Standoff at Dutch Fred's place. Maunsell asked Dutch Fred to look after his cattle and then paid a Blackfoot to lead him back home. He endured several weeks of excruciating pain before he could see again.

As the area began to be settled and the government opened vast areas of the foothills for grazing leases, the Maunsells, now joined by their brother Henry, decided to return for their cattle, which John Miller was holding in the Choteau country up the Teton River from Fort Benton. When they arrived, the three Maunsell brothers joined the round-up that was in progress. Most of the cattlemen in this area had been ranching for many years and had brought their stock to the Teton and Sun River ranges. When the round-up was complete, Miller sorted out 50 head that had the Maunsell brand on them. Oddly enough, there were no yearlings in the herd. Miller's herd, however, had more than the average number of yearlings. Knowing that there was nothing they could do, the Maunsells decided to cut their losses and drive the small herd to their ranch. Bell and Patterson also brought their cattle back from Montana and resumed ranching.

By the time they had returned from Montana, the federal government had leased immense tracts of land to large investors from the east and Britain. When Ed Maunsell made inquiries, he learned that no one in the North-West had the authority to grant leases and that one had to be in Ottawa to get any help, so he had a friend in the east find out where leased land was available. To his consternation, he discovered that all the good land near Fort Macleod had already been leased, much of it by speculators who had no intention of stocking it, so he took a lease of 6,500 acres on poor land west of Fort Macleod.

Ed Maunsell was very critical of the government leasing system that favoured the huge ranch companies. By 1884, some 41 individuals and companies held government leases of 1,762,690 acres.[15] The owners of these huge leases left their cattle to range freely, leaving little room for the small rancher. Maunsell noted that:

The large ranch companies came in, the result of which was that '83 was the last year I saw my cattle together. The nearest large ranch to me was the Oxley Company. They had acquired several hundred thousand acres of lease, part by grant, part by purchase. On this they turned out many thousand cattle, which immediately scattered in all directions, and Grier's [Maunsell's neighbour] and mine became mixed with them. No effort on our part could prevent this. All the large companies endeavored to conduct ranching, same as was pursued in more southern countries. No effort was made to provide feed for their weak stock in the winter and I had to follow suit . . . Instead of this leasing system being an improvement on the U.S. open range system, it was much worse as far as inducing small stockmen to engage in the business.[16]

Maunsell bemoaned the fact that experienced stockmen from Britain were reluctant to invest their capital in a lease that might be cancelled in a few years. "These men would want to have their cattle under control; they would want to provide feed during the winter, and breed a type they preferred. None of this was possible where cattle were running on the open range." [17]

As Maunsell pointed out, he had no option but to let his cattle graze on the open range. But his concerns were borne out by the winter of 1886–87, which ravaged the cattle on the open range and killed off a significant portion of the Maunsell herd. It was estimated after the spring round-up that the average losses amounted from 50 percent to 60 percent in the High River to Oldman River country.[18] This was a huge setback for the Maunsells, and George left the partnership to establish his own ranch. Ed and Harry stayed in partnership, undeterred. They decided that Ed would run the Ivy Ranch, named for his IV brand, and Harry would run the adjacent farm.

Ed decided that the only way to survive was to keep expanding. Over the years he became one of the leading cattlemen in the area. In 1900 he leased the entire Peigan Reserve and, in 1901, added another 700 head to his herd. In partnership with John Cowdry, a private banker in Fort Macleod, he purchased a 200,000-acre grazing lease west of Medicine Hat. When the Cochrane Ranch lands were sold to the Mormon Church in 1905, Maunsell bought its entire herd for $240,000. At its peak, around 1910, the Maunsell ranch had about 15,000 head of cattle.[19]

Edward Maunsell continued to endure the ups and downs of the ranching business and, when he died in 1923, he was acknowledged as one of the great men of Canadian ranching.

The Mounties' Contribution

The original intake of men to fill the ranks of the North West Mounted Police included many young men with farming backgrounds. This is not surprising, considering the largely rural nature of the country at the time. These men were used to a physically demanding way of life that did not have set hours and that made them especially suited for the job. The ability to ride a horse was also a qualification, but that was commonplace at a time when almost everyone used some form of horse transportation. So it is not surprising that a large number of men decided to stay in the North-West upon completion of their service contract. For example, of 39 men discharged in 1881, 25 of them stayed in the region. The prospect of owning their own land in a region that was obviously destined for a large influx of settlers was enticing, even if it was merely for speculative purposes. Many of these men became involved in ranching and stayed in the region for the rest of their lives.

It would appear that few of the ex-Mounties had any significant experience in cattle ranching, although a few would have been involved in farming practices that included the breeding and care of cattle on comparatively small holdings. None of them would have been familiar with the open range practices that predominated in Montana. The techniques and equipment that they came into contact with would have come entirely from the experienced cowboys on the North-West ranges, most of them from the US. One piece of equipment that seems to have been immediately accepted by the Mounted Police was the western stock saddle. In 1879, Colonel Sam Steele wrote of his duties at Fort Macleod:

> We were almost self-supporting, herded and slaughtered our own beef, cut and hauled our own hay and fuel, repaired our transport, made our sleds for winter travel, etc. "B" division at that time was the only one using the California stock saddle; the rest had the universal cavalry pattern, which kept the saddlers busy repairing them. Having had experience with both, I recommended the stock saddle as best for our purpose, being the most durable, the easiest on horseflesh and the most comfortable, especially for winter. I had ridden mine 6,800 miles in the year 1879-80 in all weathers. It had been used since 1875 and was still in perfect condition, never once having been repaired.[20]

It is interesting that Steele calls his saddle a California stock saddle. It has been documented that the earliest cattle drivers into Montana in the 1870s rode what was called a Plains saddle. It featured a large Mexican horn, straight fork, half-covered seat, rolled (Cheyenne) cantle, large skirts and double rigging. On the northern plains of Montana, the riders felt less need for a double-rigged saddle and many simply threw away the rear cinch, while others adapted the front and rear rigging straps to make a single cinch. These riders met Oregon drovers who were mounted on the California/Oregon-type saddles, which had straight bound cantles; fully covered seats; tall, slender horns; small, round skirts; and single (centre fire) cinches. It is generally agreed that the influence of the buckaroos from west of the Rockies was slight until about the mid-1880s and that most saddles were double-rigged and half-covered. Nonetheless, the influence of the Oregon or British Columbia buckaroos could be seen in the occasional saddles that had slender horns and single-cinches.[21]

As Steele points out, the North West Mounted Police had ordered British Cavalry Universal saddles for the March West, even though they were considered obsolete by the British Army. The men were not happy with the choice. Not only was the saddle heavy, but it also needed constant repair and the steel stirrups rusted, chilled the feet in the winter and were slippery in summer. On their arrival in the North-West, "B" Division of the Mounted Police began to look at the stock saddle as an alternative. In 1876, 30 "California" stock saddles were tested at Fort Walsh. The saddle was more a Plains saddle, being double cinched and having a wide skirt and half-covered seat. But the slender horn and straight-bound cantle were more Californian in style. The deep saddle, with a high cantle and pommel, wooden stirrups and straight-legged seat made for a much more comfortable ride. The double girth kept the saddle in place in rough terrain. As well, it distributed the weight of the rider over a much larger area. Still, some of the officers were not convinced and preferred either the US Army or English saddle. After several months of testing, the "Californian" proved to be a better saddle in every way. It was used until the horse was replaced by the automobile, although the English saddle was still used for ceremonial purposes. The first "Californians" were purchased from American companies for $23.50 (1884) each but, by 1887, a Canadian supplier was found, the Hutchings Company of Winnipeg.[22]

As can be seen by the comments of Edward Maunsell, those Mounties who had a background in raising cattle in eastern Canada questioned both the granting of huge leases that cost a fortune to stock and the open range system that did not put up winter feed. But they had little recourse but to follow the practices of their neighbours. Even William Winder, who had extensive exposure to the more intense "British" practices of raising cattle in the east, should have questioned the practice of free ranging all winter. But the lure of easy profit and the mild winters of the late 1870s provided all the incentive they needed to follow the lead of the American cattlemen who readily adopted the Texas style of cattle herding. They did not foresee the painful consequences of their choices.

Metis scout for the North West Mounted Police showing the regulation California stock saddle.
GLENBOW ARCHIVES NA-635-2

Chapter Four

HORSEMEN

On his second trip to North America in 1494, Christopher Columbus dropped anchor off the north coast of Hispaniola, Haiti, and unloaded 24 stallions and 10 mares. They were the first of their kind in the western hemisphere, and their descendants would dramatically change life in the New World. These horses were descended from the Barb horses of North Africa that the Moors brought with them when they fought Spain in 711. They were unlike the heavy, powerful horses of Northern Europe that had been bred to pull a plow or carry a knight in armour. They were raised primarily for riding in the hot, dry climate of North Africa and Spain and were lean and quick, qualities that were especially favourable both for combat and for chasing the half-wild cattle of Andalusia.

Columbus brought the first horses to the Caribbean on his second voyage in 1493. The Conquistadors brought them to the mainland of Mexico in 1519, where the short grasses and unbounded plains and mountains made them even wirier. Over the next centuries, these small, wiry horses escaped from their owners and wandered northward into territory that would become the United States. In their wild state, they grew as fleet as deer and as strong as oxen. Generation after generation of horses lost size and gained "wind." What they lost in beauty, they gained in utility. They were made for running and making quick turns, and their lungs, expanded from generations of freedom, gave them the ability to run all day.

These superbly conditioned horses moved northward onto the Great Plains and through California into the mountainous and wet climate of the Pacific Northwest. In Oregon and the Great Basin area, they encountered and bred with larger horses that had descended from the Norman and Breton breeds introduced into New France and used by the fur traders who moved into the area in the early 1800s. The result was a stockier, heavier horse that still possessed the speed and stamina of the Spanish breeds. The Hudson's

Bay Company (HBC) in Oregon Country (today's Oregon, Washington and British Columbia) used these horses to carry trade goods into, and furs out of, northern British Columbia. By the 1840s the HBC had established breeding programs at some of its forts in the Pacific Northwest, including Fort Kamloops. As the Company needed large horses that could carry heavy packs, not riders, the horses were bred for size, something that the French Norman and Breton horses were known for. This gave them strength and endurance. As the fur trade employees, mostly French Canadians, left the HBC and took up land in the Pacific Northwest, they brought these horses with them. Their bloodlines were further enhanced by the introduction of new breeds, notably Morgans and thoroughbreds, by settlers arriving from the eastern US on the Oregon Trail. Before long, the horses of the Pacific Northwest were acknowledged as among the finest on the continent.

With the signing of the Oregon Treaty in 1846 between Britain and the US, the territory south of the 49th Parallel was lost to the HBC. The Company's forts south of the border, notably its farm at Cowlitz, were instructed to move their cattle and horses north to Fort Kamloops, where the bunchgrass ranges were plentiful. As a result, the HBC moved a large number of horses, including 200 brood mares, to Kamloops, where they flourished.[1] The Shuswap people proved to be excellent herders and, in the process, obtained horses for themselves. A large number of the horses escaped into the wild and added a genetic boost to the wild horses already in the area.

The HBC horses were used by the fur brigades that travelled through Fort Kamloops all the way to Fort Alexandria on the Fraser River near modern-day Quesnel. These horses were particularly valued during the years of the Cariboo gold rush, which brought thousands of would-be miners to the area. In the years following the gold rush, horses proliferated on the bunchgrass ranges of the British Columbia Interior, and thousands of wild horses roamed the hills through the Okanagan, Nicola, Cariboo and Chilcotin regions.

BC Horses

The ranchers of British Columbia were closely watching the developments across the mountains. When the Canadian government opened vast areas of land for ranching leases in 1881, it was obvious that a ranching industry that would soon eclipse the one in British Columbia would develop. But the good news was that the ranchers there would need good quality cattle and, especially, horses. In both of these categories, British Columbia was second to none. And, even though there was lots of livestock available in Montana, the quality of that stock was generally inferior to British Columbia's, especially the horses. On the open range, each cowboy had eight or more horses for round-up: tough circle horses for rounding up, a sure-footed gentle pony for night riding, a cutting horse for working herds, a roping horse and a good horse for swimming rivers. Most of all, cowboys were looking for horses that could handle large, heavy cattle and preferred the bigger BC stock over the smaller American cow ponies. Drovers like Ferguson, Christie and Shaw had proven that the Rocky Mountains were not a barrier, and better trails through the mountains were being developed, particularly in the Crowsnest Pass, which opened in the east to the primary ranching area. During the 1880s there was a huge influx of BC horses and horsemen to Alberta.

In 1882, Oscar Rush, who worked for Johnny Wilson of the JW Ranch in Grande Prairie (now Westwold), drove 150 horses through the Okanagan Valley. The herd was then crossed into the United States at Osoyoos and given a temporary permit to cross US territory on the way east. Normally a special envoy accompanied the herd through the US at a cost to the drovers of four dollars a day plus expenses to ensure that the horses were not sold in the US without customs duty being charged. Rush and his cowboys drove the herd down the Okanogan River (as it was spelled in the US) to Omak Lake and then across the Colville Indian Reservation. The herd was swum across the Columbia River and then via Spokane Falls to cross back into Canada at Bonners Ferry. From there they travelled through the Crowsnest Pass to Fort Macleod, where they were broken. When Rush heard that the Oxley Ranch was looking for horses, he drove them to the Garnett brothers' ranch near Pincher Creek, where he held them for inspection. John Craig, manager of the Oxley Ranch, was impressed and bought 116 of them. Craig later noted:

> The first purchase of stock for the Oxley Ranch was a band of 116 horses from a Mr. Rush, who had brought them in from British Columbia and was holding them at Garnett's ranch. They were a very good sort, and cost seventy dollars per head.[2]

The ranchers in the area were impressed with the quality of the horses. One wrote, "These 'BC' horses, as they were locally called, were derived from Morgan and thoroughbred crosses on Spanish foundation stock. Exceptionally active, good-looking mounts, they were big and tough as rawhide."[3] This reputation was to make "BC" horses particularly valued in the next few years and would allow the ranchers of British Columbia to sell off a large portion of their excess horses in southern Alberta.

When word got back to the British Columbia Interior that there was a good market for BC horses in the North-West, others were prompted to get involved. In the spring of 1883, William Roper Hull, who had come to British Columbia from Somersetshire, England, in 1873 with his brother John, decided to try driving horses to the North-West. The brothers purchased 1,200 head of horses, a number of them from the BX Ranch in the Okanagan Valley. These horses were descended from a herd of 400 horses that Barnard's Express stagecoach company had purchased in Mexico and California in 1868. The ranch had been established in 1864 by Francis Jones Barnard to raise horses for his growing express business, Barnard's Express. In the early 1870s, Barnard took on partners, and the company was renamed the British Columbia Express, but it maintained its popular nickname, the BX. The horses had mostly Morgan blood and had been chosen for size and speed. The company had stipulated that they would not purchase any horses that had been broken. The horses had been driven to the BX Ranch and then carefully broken to use for pulling stagecoaches. This meant that they had to be able to maintain a brisk trot of about 6 miles an hour on level stretches for an average of 18 miles before they were changed. These stage horses were never really broken for riding but were superb examples of horseflesh and smart enough to be trained as expert cow horses.[4]

The Hull brothers purchased the horses from the BX Ranch and drove them south along Okanagan Lake and through Washington Territory, then back across the Tobacco Plains and through the Crowsnest Pass to the prairies. When they arrived at Fort Macleod, the herd was greeted with the same enthusiasm the Rush herd had enjoyed the year before. One of the cowboys on this drive was Joseph Harrison "7U" Brown, who would figure extensively in the ranching history of southern Alberta. Out of the herd, 300 horses were sold to Fred Stimson of the North-West Cattle Company, which ran the Bar U Ranch southwest of Calgary. Joseph Brown was responsible for getting them to the Bar U and, once there, remained to help break them. He stayed at the Bar U for the next 15 years. Among these horses were Fallback Roan, a particularly handsome horse, and Circle Bar Sorrel, who would achieve fame at the Bar U. Fred Ings, a cowboy and rancher in the area, remarked of the two:

These were the first two horses [George] Lane rode on roundup. They were by no means gentle, in fact, they were only half-broke. It was customary when a new man came to an outfit to give him something tricky in the way of horseflesh . . . John [Ware] and I went to give Lane a hand, but he didn't need any help. He was quite equal to the task.[5]

Later, in 1883, Alex Burnell of Crows Bar, near Lillooet on the Fraser River, drove 500 horses along the same route to the North-West and sold them for $6,000. While the horse drives seemed like a way to earn easy money, they weren't always simple. As straightforward as it may sound, driving horses is far from easy. Usually a large band of horses included mares in foal or with colts, making travel slow. If mares foaled on the trail, they usually wanted to stay where they were and had to be urged along. Occasionally the entire herd would grow homesick and head for home, making night herding essential. Cowboys had to ride around the herd at night and turn back horses if they headed back down the trail. The horses' tendency to want to return to their home territory was accentuated when the herd had to be swum across a river or on a rainy night, making the cowboy's life miserable. Most old-timers agreed that a herd of horses was much more likely than a herd of cattle to stampede. The merest whiff of a cougar or whisper of an unfamiliar sound could send the herd into a mad panic, and woe betide the cowboy who got in their way.

The influx of BC horses continued in 1884. Frank Barnard, owner of the BX Ranch and the BC Express stage lines, eliminated the middleman and sent another 350 horses with Arthur Best of Mission Valley, later Kelowna, who was driving his own herd that way. J.C. Haynes and William Lowe in the south Okanagan drove a herd of their HL Connected–brand horses into the North-West. They were all purchased by the Mont Head Ranch on the Highwood River, which adopted HL as their cattle brand as well. Thaddeus Harper sent Newman Squires along the same route with 200 horses, and William Roper Hull took another band of horses to the North-West. When Squires returned through Kamloops, he remarked that numerous people were travelling the same route, indicating that the Crowsnest Pass was the preferred way into the North-West.[6]

Even after the railway was completed in 1885, there was still a demand for BC horses and cattle in the North-West. In 1886, 8,000 head of cattle and 1,500 horses came into the area by rail from British Columbia. William and John Roper Hull, after driving horses into the North-West for several years, decided that they would set up a butchering and livestock-trading business in Calgary. They went into partnership with Walter Trounce, forming Hull, Trounce and Company. William and Trounce moved to Calgary to run the head office, and John Hull stayed in the Kamloops area to look after the British Columbia end of the business. That spring, the first consignment of stock ever shipped into the North-West by rail from British Columbia arrived in Calgary. By the end of the year, they had brought in from British Columbia 500 horses and 3,000 head of cattle. About two thirds of the livestock were sold, and the remainder were used to stock the 25 Ranch, near Nanton. The partners were the first to integrate cattle raising, meat packing and retailing on a large scale in Alberta.

That same year, Senator Matthew Cochrane travelled to Ashcroft, BC, and met with Thaddeus Harper, who was looking to liquidate his assets to cover a growing debt load. Cochrane was interested in Harper's horses, located on the Gang Ranch, with the intention of selling them to the British cavalry. He ended up purchasing 500 of them and had them shipped to his newly incorporated British American Ranch Company, which had been established on the original Cochrane range and since abandoned for a new lease southwest of Fort Macleod. The Gang Ranch horse herd, referred to as the Harper Band, was considered "one of the finest in the West."[7] The cattle were purchased and driven to Ashcroft, where they were loaded onto stock cars and shipped to Calgary for $130 per car. From Calgary they were driven west to the ranch to augment the growing herd. Unfortunately, it seems that the British cavalry did not purchase the horses: the assets of the British American Ranch were sold to the Bow River Horse Ranch Company in 1887. The Bow River Horse Ranch, with the Harper Band as part of its foundation stock, operated successfully until after the First World War.

Interest in BC horses continued for some time. As late as 1890, the Bar U purchased 152 head of horses from British Columbia. That same year, the Canadian Pacific Railway shipped 66 horses to the British Columbia market, indicating that the tide was beginning to turn. But, for the better part of 10 years, the ranges of the BC Interior had provided horses and horsemen to the fledgling cattle industry in the North-West. In the process, many of the horse-breaking techniques and much of the horse equipment of the west coast had been imported as well.

"Wild Horse" Johnson

One of the cowboys who drove the JW horses with Oscar Rush through the Crowsnest Pass in 1882 was a young man in his early twenties named Edward Johnson. He had been born in Hampshire, England, and left home at the age of 14 to work for the largest horse-breaking and sales stable in the south of England. After a couple of years there, he worked as a deckhand on the full-rigged sailing ship *Selvedere* and arrived in Valparaíso, Chile, where he secured a job breaking horses for the Chilean army. During the 1879–83 war between Chile and Peru, he was put on transport duty, assisting with shipping horses to the front. After that, he took a boat north to Victoria, British Columbia. From there he travelled to the Interior and began breaking horses for a ranch in the Ashcroft area before getting a job with the JW Ranch in Grande Prairie in 1881. Johnson's extensive experience in breaking wild horses inspired someone to give him the nickname Wild Horse.

Johnson returned to BC but decided to move to Alberta permanently in 1887. He went into partnership with Charlie Priddis on a horse ranch at Sheep Creek. At that time, there was still a demand for quality horses, and Wild Horse and his friend Charles Berry contracted with J. Dean of the Herd Ranch on the Elbow River to go back to BC and capture 500 wild horses and ship them to Calgary. The Canadian Pacific Railway made travel and livestock shipping a simple matter compared with the pre-railway days, but catching wild horses was not a job for the faint of heart.

Johnson and Berry travelled to the Big Bar Creek area along the Fraser River, where there was an abundance of wild horses on the open ranges. The two men arrived on the range in the early spring when the wild horses were at their weakest, having scratched through the snow all winter for feed. In the spring, while there was still snow on the ground, a big, healthy, grain-fed horse could outrun the wild horses. Johnson and Berry built a stout corral, up to 10 feet (3 metres) high, out of jack pine logs with log wings 200–300 yards (180–270 metres) long, fanning out from the entrance to the corral. Then they located a band of wild horses and drove them sometimes for miles until they could be funnelled into the corral. It took nerve and a fine horse to drive a bunch of wild horses through the brush and timber, and bruises and scrapes were guaranteed. Once they had the horses headed into the corral, one of them would have to be right at the tail end of the herd of wild horses to close the gate to the corral, as the horses would turn on a dime and head out once they realized they were trapped. The corral would always be round, as a wild horse could make short work of a man trapped in a corner. Then came the job of breaking the horses. A contemporary account describes the process involved in breaking a horse:

A band of what one might truly call wild horses is driven into an enclosure, called a coral [sic]. A lassoer (one expert in throwing the lasso) enters the coral [sic], and awaiting his opportunity, throws a noose of a lasso around the neck of the animal he intends to break. The horse, considerably astonished as well as terrified by his novel necklace, dashes around the coral [sic] in an impetuous manner until he is snubbed by the end of the lasso being twisted around a post and the slack drawn in. As soon as the horse will allow himself to be stroked and handled he is saddled and bridled, his trainer or "breaker" as he is called, having blindfolded the "cayoosh" he proceeds to mount him.

As soon as he is fairly seated in the saddle he removes the bandage from the horse's eyes, and spectators eagerly await further developments. If the animal commences "bucking" then the enthusiasm of the spectators rises in proportion to the height of the jumps or the number of evolutions gone through by the "cayoosh."

In "bucking" the animal arches his back, puts his head between his front legs, stiffens his limbs, springs into the air and comes down on "all fours" and . . . the rider consequently receives a jar which very often sets all the conflicting emotions and feelings of the mind considerably on the jar. The first "buck" very often suffices for some riders who, considering that the firmer but less solid position is on the ground, hurriedly dismount, not in the usual manner, however, but over the horse's head, an undignified, but speedy manner of dismounting. If he is fortunate to escape a broken neck, he may probably obtain a view of the starry heavens, no matter what hour of the day it may be. Now, a horse that is *en fait* at springing into the air and coming down as described above will vary the monotony by wheeling while in the air, so that when he reaches the ground his head will be where his tail was before, and his tail where his head had been. A spring sideways is very effective. But to resume the subject of "breaking," after a horse has been ridden about a week's time by his trainer, he is "broken for the saddle" and is often warranted not to "buck" in the future, but such guarantee is by no means reliable. A man who follows the occupation of "breaking horses for the saddle" is in common parlance term'd a "Buckero" or "Buckeero" (I am doubtful of the orthography.).[8]

Some of the terms used in this article, originally written by Hugh B. Walkem for the *Ottawa Citizen* in 1881, were unique to the regions west of the Rockies and show the continuing influence of the *vaquero*. The term "corral" (spelled "coral" in the article) was another Spanish loan word that had travelled north from California. It denoted an area enclosed by logs or pickets for breaking horses or slaughtering cattle. "Buckaroo" derives, of course, from the Spanish *vaquero* and, as we have seen, was used exclusively west of the Rockies and spread northward from California. All these terms, as well as the technique of "snubbing" a horse (roping it and tying it to a post) before breaking it, were introduced from the south and illustrate the enduring influence of the Spanish *vaquero*. Some 29 years after the gold rush cattle drives, the terminology of California prevailed.

Slowly but surely the wild horses were "green broke" so that they could be trained into tough, hardy saddle horses, but their wild-horse instincts were never fully quashed. They therefore had to be carefully herded into Ashcroft, where they could be loaded into stock cars bound for Calgary. Johnson and

Horsebreaking corral at Hat Creek Ranch, BC. Note the snubbing post in the middle.
HISTORIC HAT CREEK RANCH

Berry returned with the horses and delivered them to Dean at the Herd Ranch. They then headed back to Calgary to spend some of their hard-earned money. It was winter, which meant few jobs for cowboys, so Johnson spent some time as a bartender at the Grand Central Hotel in Calgary. There he met Mandella Midthrone, whose parents had died when she was 11 years old. She had come to Saskatchewan from Oakwood, Ontario, and eventually ended up in Calgary. The two were married in the fall of 1888. That winter, the couple travelled to British Columbia, where Wild Horse drove a BC Express stagecoach on the Cariboo road.

Mandella and Johnson returned to Alberta in the spring of 1888, and Johnson worked for the Oxley Ranch, as he had when had first arrived in 1881. He had worked for the Oxley during fall round-up and continued to do so for a few years. But, like most cowboys, he found the idle time in the winter to be difficult, especially now that he was a married man and had a family to support. So, when he was offered a job by Lesley Hill on the Glenbow Horse Ranch in 1891, he jumped at the chance. While there, he saved enough money to move to the ranch he and Charlie Priddis owned on Sheep Creek. In 1903 he moved to Midnapore, where he built the Dominion Hotel and ran it for a few years.

Edward "Wild Horse" Johnson with his family in 1907. GLENBOW ARCHIVES NA-2583-8

In 1913, Johnson leased a small place west of Okotoks, where he could raise his family and indulge in his favourite activity, raising and breaking horses. He and his two sons, Sam and Bill, who were also cowboys, helped to organize the first rodeo in Black Diamond in 1915. Wild Horse later moved back to Midnapore, where he finished off his days. He died in 1949 at the age of 91, one of the last old-time horse breakers.

"7U" Brown

Joseph Harrison Brown was born in Ashfield, County Cavan, Ireland, in 1856. While Joseph was still a youngster, his father immigrated to America and then sent for his wife and four children. The boat on which they sailed was quarantined in the New York harbour because there was typhoid fever on board. Of the four children, only Joseph and his sister Mary survived. The reunited family settled in Peterborough, Ontario, where three more children were born.

Brown left home in 1882, travelling around the Horn and arriving in British Columbia that same year. He travelled to the BC Interior, where he managed to land a job at a lumber mill. He did not prove adept at the job and one day, while piling lumber in a shed, he dropped a plank on the foreman's head. The irate foreman headed up one side of the scaffolding, and Brown headed down the other, never looking back. And so Joseph Brown ended his career in the lumber industry.

Eventually he got a job at the BX Ranch in the North Okanagan, where the stagecoach horses were raised. Brown proved to be very talented in handling the highly charged BX horses and in training them. But, once again, his career took a turn. In 1883 he was assigned the task of seeing the 1,200 BX horses purchased by the Hull brothers across the mountains to the North-West. Three hundred of these horses were purchased by the North-West Cattle Company for the Bar U Ranch, and Brown was in charge of delivering them. His adeptness with the horses impressed Fred Stimson, the Bar U manager, who hired him on the spot to break and care for the horses. For the next 15 years, he was in charge of the Bar U's horses.

By 1886, Brown had saved enough to buy a small herd of 50 heifers and go into partnership with Bar U neighbour Frank Bedingfeld, who had arrived with his mother, Agnes, in 1884. Mrs. Bedingfeld was quite a remarkable woman. Her husband, Captain George Longueville Bedingfeld, had been a colonel in the Indian Army and had died in India. She decided not to spend

Southern Alberta round-up crew in 1901. Joseph Harrison 7U Brown is seated on a chair in the middle, in front of the Mountie. GLENBOW ARCHIVES NA-1035-5

her time grieving and instead took her only child, Frank, to America with the intention of taking up land. They first visited Morton Farm in Iowa in 1881 but then decided to come to Canada. Frank had been educated at Westward Ho School, Clovelly, England, at the same time as Rudyard Kipling, but Frank took to the western way of life with enthusiasm. While his mother agreed to act as a housekeeper to the Stimsons, Frank, at 16 years of age, came under the tutelage of some of the best cowboys in the country. George Lane and Herb Millar both worked for the Bar U at the time, and legends like George Emerson and John Ware worked for the outfit occasionally.[9]

Frank soon wanted a place of his own and, when he turned 18 in 1886, he and his mother filed homestead claims on adjacent quarter sections a mile up Pekisko Creek from the Bar U. Frank constructed a log house and went into partnership with Brown, who continued to live and work at the Bar U. The partners picked the brand 7U for their cattle. Given the number of Browns on the southern North-West ranges, Joseph soon became known as 7U Brown, a name that was so universally used that most people forgot—or never knew him by any other—his first name. Brown also used the BX brand in memory of his first employer in the ranching business.

Brown's attitude toward ranching was definitely old school. He believed that his cattle, apart from his calves, should be able to rustle for enough to keep themselves alive through the winter. He swore that, if he could get through the winter on whisky, his stock could survive on snow. And there is no question that whisky was one of his main food groups. He always had jugs or even cases hidden in various places on the ranch, in haystacks or in outbuildings. Despite his prodigious consumption, he never missed a day's work in his life and considered the cost of whisky to be a necessary running expense.

Brown stayed at the Bar U in charge of horses until 1898 and then moved onto the ranch with the Bedingfelds. His thrifty attitude toward winter feed, and belief that any cattle that couldn't get themselves through the winter weren't worth keeping, kept their expenses down and profits high. The partners did extremely well and, when Frank married Josephine Maitland in 1910, Brown was able to buy his own place just south of the Bedingfelds' place. There he ranched and kept to himself, happy to have a life that he loved.

Brown's sister Jean came to live with him in 1915 and, the following year, his sister Sara joined them. The sisters provided their bachelor brother with creature comforts that he had not previously known, but that did not change his ways. At the age of 71, he was still actively ranching when he had a serious accident. His horse fell, breaking Brown's leg and tearing his scalp open. Undeterred, Brown had a cowboy cut a willow post and tie it in place

7U Brown ca. 1920. GLENBOW ARCHIVES NA-2467-38

above and below the break and then pulled his hat down on the side of his head to hold the scalp in place. The frontier doctoring complete, he rode back to the ranch for more extensive repairs.

Brown died in 1936 at the age of 80. Considering his full and happy ranching life, he would have been happy to learn that his sisters, who inherited his place, carried on running the ranch according to his practices and policies. After the sisters died, the ranch was operated, at their request, as a refuge for needy and destitute ranchers and cowboys and their families, a fitting legacy for 7U Brown.

Tom Lynch

For Tom Lynch, the decision was easy. For years he and his partner, George Emerson, had been driving cattle and horses up from Montana and beyond into the North-West. In the process they had acquired a large herd, which they held on their land on the middle fork of the Highwood River. By 1884 they had about 1,200 head of cattle and 200 horses. Tom had worked for the Bar U Ranch until that time, while keeping an eye on the livestock he and Emerson had acquired. Now it was time for the partners to go their separate ways so they could pursue their own interests. But the question remained of how to divvy up the livestock. At first they looked at a clean split of cattle and horses, but Tom had expressed an interest in keeping all the horses. Emerson, a man of few words at the best of times, looked him in the eye. "You take the horses and I'll take the cattle." Tom's eyes lit up, but his reply was equally terse. "Deal," he said and the two shook hands. Tom Lynch was now free to pursue his true loves: horses and what came with them, racing and gambling.

Lynch was born in Missouri in 1843 and moved to the Pend Oreille country with his family in the 1850s, when there was a gold rush to the area. As a young man, Tom found work helping drive cattle and horses from Washington, Oregon and Idaho into the mining camps and ranches of Wyoming and Montana. Always willing to take a chance, he travelled north through Blackfoot country in the early 1870s to pan for gold near Fort Edmonton on the North Saskatchewan River. There he met George Emerson, who was working for the Hudson's Bay Company and panning for gold when he had a chance. Tom headed back to Montana where, a few years later, he met Emerson again and joined with him in driving a few head of cattle into the North-West. The two formed a partnership and successfully drove herds of cattle from Montana into the Fort Macleod area, where settlers were beginning to arrive. In 1882, Lynch had been hired to drive 3,000 head of cattle from the Lost River area north of Pocatello, Idaho, into the North-West for the North-West Cattle Company, which was more commonly called the Bar U after its brand, registered in 1881. Following that, Lynch drove thousands of cattle north, delivering the foundation herds of the Military Colonization Company, the Quorn Ranch and many other ranchers in the Fort Macleod and Pincher Creek areas.

Lynch had always had an eye for good horseflesh. On one long cattle drive in 1884, when a herd of 2,000 head of cattle was being driven north for the Quorn and the Military Colonization Company, Lynch had appointed Joe Johnson as trail boss. Lynch was following behind with a herd of unbroken horses. One of the cowboys on the drive, Sam Howe, later said, "God, how we hated to see Lynch show up," for he would inevitably bring a fresh bunch of unbroken horses for the weary cowboys to break out on the trail.[10] No doubt these horses could be sold for a better price if they were broken, and, as usual, Lynch was on the lookout for a fast horse for racing.

Lynch is credited with importing more horses than any other person of his time. He was a major supplier to the Mounted Police. Around 1885, he bought 800 horses from the Nez Perce Natives in Idaho for ten dollars a head and drove them back to Canada. Many of these were branded Rocking P high on the hip, and his former partner, George Emerson, liked the brand so much, he chose it for his cattle. Lynch, with the assistance of John Ware and Mike Herman, drove a large portion of these horses to Blackfoot Crossing, when the Blackfoot were being given their annual treaty money. He was able to sell most of the horses and, as treaty money was paid in one-dollar bills at the time, ended up with a pillowcase full of dollar bills. The Blackfoot encouraged him to stay for the horse racing that inevitably followed treaty day and Lynch, who had been expecting this, pleaded that he only had his buggy horse to race with. The buggy horse was his blue roan, Satan, a general purpose working horse that could run like the wind when there was a race to be had. After some persuasion, Lynch unhitched his horse and accepted the invitation to enter the races. Mike Herman agreed to ride him, as Lynch was a large, heavy man, and Satan won every race going away. Lynch rode home with even more dollar bills stuffed in his pillowcase, and Satan went on to become famous as a quarter-miler in races all over the North-West.

Lynch was one of the most respected cattlemen in the North-West, and his easy-going but no-nonsense manner made him a favourite wagon boss during round-up. He was on his way to financial independence in 1886 when he bought 290 "dogies" or "stockers," cheaply obtained cattle from Ontario, Manitoba or even Mexico that could be fattened up on the range and sold for a profit. Unfortunately, the winter of 1886–87 was brutal, and the dogies, unused to cold weather, were decimated. In the spring, Lynch could only find 80 of them that had survived the winter. Discouraged, and not getting any younger, in 1887 he went back to work building up his herd.

That year, in partnership with Duncan McPherson of the High River Horse Ranch, he travelled to Washington State and bought in a herd of 800 horses. These were fine horses, the offspring of range mares and thoroughbred or Percheron stallions. Lynch kept 100 for himself and sold 700 to the High River Horse Ranch. Out of this herd came the half-thoroughbred Grey Eagle, who went on to fame and fortune as a racehorse. A man named Jim Owens had laid out a racetrack on a flat beside the Elbow River in Calgary, and Grey Eagle, with Ed McAbee riding, was considered the fastest half-mile horse in

Canada. McAbee had come to the area with his three brothers and two sisters from British Columbia to work for BC butcher Benjamin Van Volkenburgh.

After this, Lynch bought a place on Sullivan Creek back in the hills, where he set up his TL Ranch. There, in the seclusion of the foothills, he could indulge in his favourite pastime, breeding and racing fine horses. The secluded location of the ranch had other advantages. Lynch lived to race horses and, on his numerous trips south of the border, invariably returned with a few new horses. His favourite opponents were the Blackfoot, who had some very fast horses, many of which appeared from south of the border, much to the disgruntlement of their owners, who would spend hours looking in vain for them. Lynch was not above using the same tactics. Often, a strange horse of excellent conformation and condition would appear in his corral in the early morning after a trip across the border in the dark of night.

On one occasion, an American named Reynolds came north with four excellent racehorses, hoping to make some money to pay off his debts down south. But his propensity for spending money wasn't matched by the ability of his horses to win it. When his money was gone, he was forced to mortgage his horses and leave them in Calgary. When Tom Lynch, ever sensitive to other horse owners' woes, heard of the situation, he took Reynolds aside and offered to help. Reynolds returned to the States, and the horses mysteriously disappeared from their stalls shortly afterward. The route they followed after that is believed to have been to the Lynch Ranch and then south to Flat Creek and through the foothills and mountain trails to a spot Lynch had fenced at the mouth of Cataract Creek on the Highwood River. It is uncertain how long they remained at Lynch's hideout, but what is for sure is that only three of the horses returned to the US. The fourth, a dark-brown mare that Lynch lovingly named Sangree, remained on the range with the TL brand of Tom Lynch on its side. When the mare had been there long enough to become sufficiently dishevelled that it no longer looked like a finely groomed racehorse, it was brought to Calgary, where it won races against all challengers.

Sangree was bred to the Quorn Ranch's Eagle's Plume and produced two colts, both fillies. After that she raced again and continued to outmatch the competition. Lynch eventually sold her to an American buyer along with one of her fillies, May W, and Sangree returned to the land of her birth. Her continuing success in the south brought her to the attention of the public, and she was discovered to be Reynolds's missing thoroughbred, Froila. Lynch pled innocence and appears to have avoided serious consequences. Froila's daughter proved to be every bit as good as her mother and won many big races in the US.

Tom Lynch died at his ranch in 1891 at the age of 48 years. His wife survived him, but there is no record of her name and no surviving photos of Tom Lynch. What does remain of Tom Lynch is a legacy of courage, determination, kindness and enthusiasm, a legacy of someone who lived life to the fullest and influenced a generation of ranchers and cowboys.

Horse Culture

From the first days of ranching in the North-West, ranchers and cowboys alike recognized and acknowledged the superiority of the horses bred west of the Rockies. Fred Ings, who had worked as a cowboy on the 1883 round-up and later owned the Midway Ranch, wrote in his memoirs, "We needed good horses and big ones; we never rode small horses like the American cowboy. Our cattle were larger and we needed the size and weight."[11] This is not to say that the smaller horses of the southwest did not have a place. In later roping competitions, the reason for the difference between the smaller, agile horses and the larger, stronger ones was remarked upon:

> The range stock of the South-West, of Texas, New Mexico, and Old Mexico, is quick, light, and as speedy as most horses, while the range animals of Alberta and Montana are grade Shorthorns and Herefords, huge, clumsy, well-fed brutes, whose best gait is a lumbering gallop, and whose agility compared with that of the Mexican steer is as a tortoise to a hare. Canadian stock was half as big again as the South-Western range beasts, twice as slow, and not a quarter as agile. A Canadian rope-horse was picked for strength and weight to oppose the weight and strength of the heavy steers; the Arizona and Texas and other American steeds were picked for speed, sure-footedness, and dodging ability.[12]

The "BC horses" brought in from across the Rockies fit the bill for strength and weight and were universally accepted as the best horses on the southern prairies. Included in this category were the same type of horses from Washington and Oregon that were brought in via the Montana foothills. Tom Lynch, the greatest of the early horse drivers, invariably purchased his horses from the Sun River area and points west in the foothills, occasionally going as far as Washington State to find the best horses available.

The importation of horses from British Columbia continued well after the railway had been completed. It simply meant that horses could be purchased and shipped by rail instead of being driven through the mountains. As late as 1900, the Kamloops *Inland Sentinel* recorded that Joseph Christian of Okanagan Mission (Kelowna) had shipped 3,500 horses to Alberta in the past year. In 1903 the Gang Ranch was contracted by a Mr. Hawden to round up 250 wild horses and ship them to Toronto. The round-up took a month, and then the horses were driven down the Cariboo Road to Ashcroft, where they were shipped in 10 carloads to Calgary. There was such a good market for them in southern Alberta that they were all quickly sold, and Fisher Williams of Olds sent the cowboys back to the Alkali Lake Ranch to round up more wild horses and ship them to Calgary.

Not surprisingly, along with the horses came horse-breaking techniques. The use of the hackamore, derived from the Spanish *jaquima*, was widespread in the North-West. Fred Ings wrote about encountering "a bunch of young horses from the hills that had never been handled in any way." After corralling them, he and his friend Dan Riley chose two to break:

> These were two chestnuts, both handsome beasts ... The only way to handle nags like these was to catch them by the front feet with a rope and with a twist throw them and while they were down, put on a hackamore and blindfold them and then let them up. A blindfolded horse will usually stand when held without too much fuss 'til the saddle is on. You ride with a hackamore which is a braided rawhide halter with the headstall fairly close fitting and the nosepiece adjustable so that pulling on the shanks smothers a horse down by cutting off his wind and making him possible to control. The half breed, Henry Miensinger, made very good hackamores.[13]

The method of breaking horses with a hackamore can be traced back to California, as can the practice of "forefooting" them to throw them to the ground.[14] The use of a hackamore was considered by most California *vaqueros* to produce a soft-mouthed horse, responsive to the reins. Once a horse was trained with a hackamore, it was usually replaced with a bit. This technique was unheard of on the Great Plains, where a bit was the standard piece of equipment in horse breaking. So it would seem that the California methods of horse breaking travelled to the North-West via Oregon, Washington State and British Columbia.

The same cannot be said for the single-cinched saddle. Once again, Fred Ings explains:

> The "76" brought in some Texas cow ponies, small, tough and active as cats. They were a revelation to us. How they could carry big men and what they could stand. It was only when they tied onto a big steer or bull that they were not so good. The men from the other side [of the mountains] generally rode centre fire saddles, the cinch in the middle. These proved not as efficient as our double rigged ones in roping and holding large animals.[15]

It is apparent that the more solid double-rigged saddles were prevalent in the North-West.

Another importation from the western side of the Rockies that saw limited success was the braided rawhide rope. Fred Ings talks about using his "rawhide rope" in managing a particularly difficult stallion.[16] Mike Herman, known as The Emerson Kid for his association with George Emerson, was rated "a good hand with stock and one of the best with a rope." He once roped a wolf that proceeded to gnaw at his rope, "a nice rawhide."[17] In another incident, when he and another cowboy were dealing with a neighbour's bull, however, the rawhide rope proved to be his downfall. The cowboys managed to throw the bull and thread Herman's rawhide rope through its nose. The bull got up and headed off on a run, stretching the rope until it snapped and the knot flew back, hitting Herman on the jaw and knocking him out cold. Other cowboys were described as being "good at rawhide work," indicating that, although rawhide ropes were rare, they were not unheard of.[18] As rawhide ropes were usually individually made by rawhide braiders, it is not surprising that they were uncommon in the North-West. The mass-produced manila and maguey ropes were available everywhere, and most ranches purchased spools of rope to supply their cowboys.

In the area of horses and horse equipment, the influence of British Columbia and the Pacific Northwest was pronounced. The large, tough horses of these

regions were just what were needed for the improved breeds of cattle that were larger and slower than the Texas longhorns that had come as far as Montana, with few of them making it into the North-West. Along with the horses came certain aspects of the buckaroo horse culture. Certainly, the methods of breaking horses seem to have been readily accepted in the North-West, and the use of the hackamore was very popular. Other aspects of the horse culture, namely single-cinched saddles and braided rawhide ropes, were less prominent.

Ultimately, the use of equipment came down to a matter of familiarity and preference. There was always a selection of equipment available that could be obtained if the rider wanted it. The excellent southern Alberta history *Leaves from the Medicine Tree* contains a good summary of the situation:

> The early Alberta horsemen, like his [*sic*] mount, was imported. There were men from west of the Rockies that used hackamores and centre-fire (single cinched) saddles, and used the dally or Spanish method of roping. Riders from the south used rim-fire (double cinched) saddles and "tied" their ropes, Texas style. Canadians were divided in their choice of saddle, and used both styles of roping. The well-ribbed Alberta-bred horses could carry a centre-fire saddle without the need of a breast collar.[19]

Alberta cowboys in 1893, showing typical large horses and cattle. In this staged photo, George Emerson is fourth from the left. GLENBOW ARCHIVES NA-5182-1

Chapter Five

Top Hands

In every profession there are those who rise to the top through a combination of natural skill and determination. The cowboy profession is no different. The ranches of Western Canada were populated by young men from every nationality imaginable, most of them fresh-faced youths. Inevitably, the romance that initially attracted them wore off as they found that the life of the cowboy ranged from mindless tedium on the cattle drives to extremes of weather that tested the spirit of even the toughest character. Only those who could withstand the gruelling way of life and enjoy the natural setting in which they found themselves were willing to stay. These "top hands" found that the ranching way of life fit like a glove. They were the men who stayed, often drifting from ranch to ranch but always offering their best and giving full value for their wages. From among these lifetime cowboys, there rose a few who possessed that unique combination of intelligence, physical endurance and love of the cowboy way of life. They were the ones who were chosen by the owners of the large ranches to manage important aspects of the operation.

Considering that ranching in British Columbia and the North-West developed relatively late, after the cattle cultures of California and Texas were well established, it is not surprising that the majority of the men who rose to the top of the frontier cowboy hierarchy were from the United States. They had learned their trade on the cattle ranges of Oregon, Wyoming or Montana and brought what they had learned with them. Joe Payne, the first cow boss of the Douglas Lake Cattle Company, and Ebb Johnson, of the North-West Cattle Company, had learned their trade in Wyoming. George Lane, who was cow boss of the Bar U Ranch, and William Kerfoot, who managed the Cochrane Ranch, had started out ranching in Montana. These men, who landed the best management positions in western Canadian ranching, were but a few of the many American cowboys who contributed to the growth of cattle ranching in BC and Alberta.

The large ranches of Western Canada were generally owned by investors who had little knowledge of the details of raising beef cattle, the notable exception being the Gang Ranch, which was owned by Thaddeus Harper, who had learned from the ground up. Nonetheless, they sought out the best possible men to handle the daily operations of their ranches. These men had to have "cow sense," the ability to read the range and its capability and the sensitivity to know what was best for the cattle. They also had to be leaders of men, who could inspire the average working cowboy to persevere through the coldest winter or the wettest spring and give their best "for the brand."

Long after they had crossed the Great Divide, the names of these men lived on. Those who had worked for them would later boast that they had ridden with Newman Squires, or Sam Howe or Ebb Johnson, and sigh, "Now there was a cowboy!"

Newman Squires, King of the Range

As the sun peeked over the ridge, lighting the distant hills rimming the Caw (as the Kansas River was then known), the travellers on the Oregon Trail awakened and began to prepare for another day on the trail, only to realize that 39 head of cattle had disappeared during the night. A scramble ensued as each man ran to find his horse and saddle up to follow the fortunately obvious footprints leading north. In the forefront of the searchers were the two young Brown brothers and 14-year-old Newman Squires. As the leaders of the wagon train, John "Mac" McAbee and Mr. Brown proceeded cautiously with their weapons ready, but the three boys raced ahead and soon came upon the cattle, who were being held in a narrow riverbed by local Natives, probably Osage. The Natives surrounded the boys, whom they greatly outnumbered, and began to threaten them and relieve them of their valuables, knives, money and rings. Then, to the boys' astonishment, the Natives indicated that they were free to drive the cattle back to their wagons. In this case, their youth had probably saved them. So it was that a chastened trio of young men drove the cattle back to the wagon trail and proceeded on their way to California. Newman Squires's life of adventure had begun.

James Newman Squires was born in Henry County, Missouri, in 1839, the son of George W. Squires and Lucinda Crow. The Crow family had been stock raisers for generations, starting in Kentucky and moving onto the Salt River bottomland bordering the Mississippi River in eastern Missouri. There they employed the British traditional system of raising cattle, using British breeds, herder dogs, block-letter brands and salting. The cattle were not allowed to become too wild and were easily controlled. When news of the discovery of gold in California reached the stockmen of Missouri, they immediately saw the possibilities. The new goldfields were a potential market for their surplus cattle and a source of fine grazing land as well.

Walter J. Crow, a great uncle of Newman Squires, drove 800 head of Durham cattle across the plains from northeastern Missouri to California in 1850 and established the Crow Ranch in the Sacramento Valley. After the death of Walter Crow, his sons returned to Missouri in 1852 and organized another cattle drive to California. The sons were exuberant about the possibilities of raising cattle in California and, in 1853, convinced more than 30 of their Missouri relatives to join them in moving there. In May 1853 the two branches of the Crow family set out across the plains in small clusters of wagons, driving herds of cattle along with them. The last of the family to start out was under the leadership of Squires's grandfather, 63-year-old James Rankin Crow. His party consisted of three wagons. Along with the wagon owned by John "Mac" McAbee came the three Squires boys—James Newman, Robert and John— who had lost both of their parents a few years earlier. As the oldest of the three, Newman was expected to make a contribution and rode herd on the large drove of cattle that accompanied the Crow-McAbee wagons.[1]

The incident with the stolen cattle took place early in the journey. Throughout the long months of the summer, the cattle were slowly driven along the trail west, passing through Salt Lake City in August and continuing on to the Humboldt River and out into the desert. When they reached the Sierra Nevada Mountains, fall was approaching, and the party headed into the seldom travelled Walker River trail. The way was criss-crossed with fallen logs and covered in snow well into late summer. John Ebbetts, a member of a railway survey party sent out to describe the route in 1853, wrote in a San Francisco newspaper that the route was the worst he had ever seen, and he discouraged others from using the trail the following season.[2] Nonetheless, the Crow-McAbee party persisted. In stretches where the wagons passed along steep hillsides, the party had to dig trenches for the upper wheels and blindfold the oxen. Finally, the emigrants arrived in Sonora and joined all their relatives who had preceded them.

The Squires boys stayed with John McAbee and his wife, Susan, who pushed on to Sonoma County, north of San Francisco, where they stayed only a short time. They then moved north to Mendocino County, where they ran a cattle and dairy farm. Mendocino was the site of two Mexican land grants: Rancho Sanel in Hopland, in 1844, and Rancho Yokaya, which forms the majority of the Ukiah Valley, in 1845. There, the Spanish techniques of handling cattle would have influenced the young Newman Squires, who had already gained extensive experience in handling cattle on the trail west.

Newman Squires was strongly influenced by the *vaquero* in the way he handled cattle and horses. Most of the ranches in the central valley that he worked for were owned by Anglophones to the extent that, by the late 1850s, 81 percent of all the large cattle ranches were Anglophone-owned. Large numbers of English-speaking men like Newman Squires had joined the Spanish-speaking *vaqueros* to work on ranches once the diggings in the goldfields became less productive.

The demand for cattle in the California goldfields was dwindling by the late 1850s, and ranchers began to look to other markets for their cattle. Fortunately, the mining frontier was pushing north and there was a growing demand for cattle in Oregon, Idaho and Nevada. British Columbia was the newest source of mining excitement in 1858, and a few years after that, Newman Squires went to work for the Harper brothers, Jerome and Thaddeus, beginning a relationship that would last for the next 25 years.

Beginning in the spring of 1860, Jerome Harper had been buying herds of cattle and driving them north to British Columbia. As very few young men in California were interested in driving cattle instead of mining for gold, Harper was always looking for experienced drovers to drive cattle all the way to the wilderness of British Columbia. He was especially looking for someone dependable to head up the drives, leaving him to look after the British Columbia end of the business. In 1865 he met Newman Squires, who seemed to have all the qualities he was looking for. At 26 years of age, Squires had been looking after cattle all his life and was already an expert with a braided rawhide lariat, having studied under some of the best *vaqueros* in the business. He was hired on as a drover and, before long, put in charge of all the Harper cattle drives from the border at Osoyoos. Squires made sure that customs duties were paid to the colonial officials and then pushed the cattle up the trail through the Okanagan Valley to Fort Kamloops and all the way to the Cariboo. By this time the Harpers had established holding areas where they could keep cattle and feed them into the Cariboo market as required. The first of these was just south of the border at Osoyoos. Cattle would be purchased during the winter months and, weather permitting, moved in large droves to the border area, where they could be kept until spring. Harper did not limit himself to beef cattle; he usually had up to 50 head of dairy cattle, as well as a certain number of good horses. Squires would pick up the drove at the border and move them north, dropping some of them off at the Harper Ranch, east of Fort Kamloops on the north side of the Thompson River.

Squires's years of experience in handling cattle were evident on these drives, and he soon rose to prominence as one of the best. He showed an incredible memory for the cattle under his charge. After a few days on the trail from Osoyoos, he had all the cattle fixed in his mind. The cattle would be kept under night guard and counted every morning. Squires and one of his cowboys would take their places about 30 yards apart, and the cattle would be slowly drifted between them so they could get a good count. If two or three had wandered off during the night, Squires would describe them in detail, such as "the big line-backed steer with one drooping horn" or "a big spotted black and white steer." The cowboys would laugh at him but inevitably, when the missing cattle were found, he would have described them accurately.

Squires's skills as a cowboy were unequalled. Having worked with the buckaroos of California, he was an expert with the braided rawhide reata, able to drop a loop over the head of a specific steer in a herd of milling cattle or to neatly rope the back legs of a calf to drag it to the branding fire. His skills in breaking horses the California way were also renowned. If any cowboy was having trouble staying on a bucking horse, Squires would get on it and ride it to a standstill. He was also a crack shot, be it with a six-shooter or a Winchester rifle. He was known as "a wonder with the Colts revolver," and with him it was "head or no chicken" at 25 paces.[3]

With all his rough-and-ready cowboy expertise, Newman Squires was a man of sterling character. Through all his life, he never drank or used tobacco in any form. He was a man of his word and could be relied upon to follow through on his promises. He was truthful, and what he said could be trusted as the truth as best he was aware of it. Despite all his talents and experience, he was not a boastful man and was always happy to let another man take credit for things that he had done. He was a born leader of men. Those who had worked for him on the numerous cattle drives always spoke with pride that they rode with Newman Squires.

The last Harper cattle crossed the border at Osoyoos in 1870, when a total of only 264 head crossed. By then, the gold rush in the Cariboo was slowing down and the British Columbia ranges were able to supply any cattle that were needed for that market. The Harpers were content to expand their land holdings, and Newman Squires figured in their plans. They put him in charge of their cattle ranges east of Kamloops on what came to be called the Harper Ranch. This suited Squires perfectly. He was being paid good money to do what he loved to do: look after cattle.

By December 1871, Jerome Harper's health had begun to decline and he announced that he wanted to retire from business to Santa Barbara, California, where the family owned a large estate.[4] Three years later, the people of the Cariboo—and indeed all of British Columbia—were shocked to learn that Jerome Harper had died in his bathtub at Santa Barbara; he was only 42 years old. As the *Cariboo Sentinel* put it, his reputation was synonymous with "energy and industry."[5]

With Jerome's departure, the remaining Harper business interests were transferred to the care of Thaddeus, who, although an astute cattleman, did not possess his brother's business sense. While Jerome believed that accumulating land was the best means to acquire wealth, Thaddeus was more of a speculator, and he proceeded to invest ranching profits in a mining venture in the Horsefly area of the Cariboo. Upon the death of his brother, Thaddeus inherited $176,000 and land valued at $300,000.[6] His land included the Harper Ranch east of Kamloops, comprising 3,957 acres, the Perry Ranch near Cache Creek, comprising 906 acres and, in the Cut Off Valley near Clinton, the Kelly Ranch, eventually comprising 14,797 acres.

As markets in the goldfields dwindled, the cattle herds increased and more pressure was put on the precious bunchgrass ranges. The depressed state of the economy and the surplus of cattle in the Interior pushed the price of cattle to record lows. By 1876 prices were as low as twelve dollars a head for cows with calves, seventeen dollars a head for market steers three years and older, twelve dollars for two-year-old steers and six dollars for yearlings.[7] Ranchers were able to market some of their cattle to the growing coastal cities of New Westminster, Victoria and Nanaimo, but they could only handle a portion of the surplus cattle. The railhead at Cheyenne, Wyoming, was across the Rockies and seemingly impossible to reach. But Thaddeus Harper, in a move that would have made his enterprising brother proud, announced in the spring of 1876 his intention to drive a herd of beef cattle to Chicago! The *British Colonist* newspaper in Victoria reported on the venture:

> Beef Exportation:—Mr. T. Harper proposes to take some 800 head of beef cattle from British Columbia to Chicago. He intends to drive via Salt Lake and then take the railroad. At present there are large numbers of cattle in the interior; the market is limited and a band of beef cattle would hardly realize $15 per head. At present, at Chicago, cattle will net over the cost of driving and railroad expense about $40 a head. A few shipments to that point would tend to relieve the market in the interior and consequently give stockowners a better opportunity of disposing of their cattle.[8]

There was only one man whom Harper would trust to undertake such a drive: Newman Squires. Harper had a large number of surplus cattle at his Kelly Ranch near Clinton and knew that the area north and west from there was full of cattle that could be had for a very reasonable price. He and Squires went around the Dog Creek, Canoe Creek and Alkali Lake areas and purchased about 800 head of cattle, aged from three to eight years old. The fact that there were eight-year-old steers, well past the usual marketable age of three to four years, indicates the overstocked nature of the ranges. The cattle were gathered at the Kelly Ranch, and Squires hired cowboys to work with him on the drive. The list includes some of the best cowboys of the time: Antoine Allen, Charlie Connor and his partner, Tom Moore, Johnny Twan and Natives Joe Tenice, Louis Eneas and Jimmy Joseph. Bill Hart, another man on the drive, was listed as a clerk in Barkerville in the 1875 voters' list and may have been involved in the Harper operation there. The drive also included a man named King and a boy named Jimmy Rendell. Each cowboy was responsible for providing his own horses and was paid sixty dollars a month with all food supplied. Most of the cowboys on this drive carried guns, mainly because of the threat from predatory animals and perhaps to pick off a few grouse to supplement their rations on the way. Many of these men spent their lives as cowboys in British Columbia, and their names recur frequently in the stories of ranching in the province.[9]

Squires was an experienced drover and moved the 800 head of cattle at a leisurely pace of 10 to 12 miles a day. This allowed them to graze along the way and so maintain their weight. By May 16, 1876, they were reported to have reached a point "a little above Clinton, bound for Salt Lake City."[10] The report also mentioned that, although a few of the animals looked poor, the majority were good "beeves." The cattle were moved slowly, grazing on the spring grass along the route that ran along the old drover trail of the 1860s. They swam cattle across the Thompson River at Savona's ferry and drove them along the south side of Kamloops Lake, past the budding village of Kamloops and over the height of land from Monte Creek to the North Okanagan. At Cornelius O'Keefe's ranch at the head of Okanagan Lake, Squires decided to rest the cattle for a few days. The north Okanagan ranchers were located far from the coastal markets and were concerned that their grasslands were being slowly overgrazed by the abundance of cattle. Harper purchased an additional 428 head from the ranchers in the area. The drive continued through the Okanagan Valley and crossed the border into Washington State at Osoyoos. From there they followed the Okanogan River to its mouth, where the cattle were swum across the Columbia River. They then travelled along the trail through the Grand Coulee to eventually cross the Snake River near Walla Walla into northern Oregon. By then, they had been on the trail for five months and winter was approaching. After conferring, Squires and Harper decided to winter the cattle and to wait to see market conditions in the spring. Squires decided that he didn't need all the cowboys for winter herding, so some of them, including Jimmy Joseph, who was the last survivor, came only as far as the winter camp, where they were paid off and headed home.

When spring broke and the drive was set to continue, Thaddeus Harper assessed the situation. From the Columbia River to the nearest rail transportation at Kelton, Utah, north of Salt Lake, was a drive of about 600 miles. Shipping from there to Chicago would have cost about $250 for a car of 20 head, and prices in Chicago had plummeted to between $16 and $17 for three-year-old steers, about the same as the stock had cost in British Columbia. There appeared to be no alternative but to bide their time and spend the summer of 1877 in Idaho Territory, where there was an abundance of grass and water. Squires and a couple of his cowboys spent the summer months holding the cattle and allowing them to fatten up until Harper could decide what to do with them. Keeping cattle through the summer in Idaho was not as easy as it may sound. The Salmon River area, which is most likely where they were pastured, was well settled by cattlemen in 1877, and Squires would have had to keep the cattle moving or make an arrangement with a local rancher to use his rangeland. So, as fall arrived and winter approached, Squires was happy to hear Thaddeus Harper announce, "We're moving them to San Francisco." Harper had found out that there were drought conditions in much of California and the market for cattle was strong. Squires nodded acceptance and pointed the cattle southwest across the Great Basin, a region that he knew well from his early drives with the Harpers.

As he drove the cattle into the San Francisco area a few months later, Squires could smile at Thaddeus Harper's ability to land on his feet. With the Harpers' characteristic combination of business acumen and sheer luck, the story ended happily. The *British Colonist* reported the following February:

> British Columbia Feeding California with Cattle.—Some eighteen months ago Mr. Thaddeus Harper drove from British Columbia into Northern Idaho 1200 head of beef cattle. These cattle were summered during 1877 in Idaho, where there was scarcity of neither water nor feed. The drought in California during the same year caused the death of many thousand head of stock, and now Mr. Harper's band is coming into market at San Francisco. The cattle are large and well-grown beeves, rolling in fat, and have been sold at $70 per head.[11]

During the construction of the Canadian Pacific Railway, beginning in May 1880, the railway workers needed to be fed. Thaddeus Harper, along with his partners of the gold rush days, the Van Volkenburghs, secured the contract to supply beef to the construction crews. The arrangement saw

Harper responsible for keeping a steady supply of cattle arriving at stockyards located at Emory City, just south of Yale. As Harper's main cattleman, Newman Squires made cattle drive after cattle drive down the Fraser Canyon or over the Coquihalla Trail to the supply centre. In the spring of 1881, Andrew Onderdonk, the railway construction contractor, brought in 2,000 Chinese labourers, and the demand for beef became even greater. It was estimated that the demand for beef just in the Lytton to Ashcroft section of construction amounted to 10 head a day, each an average weight of 700 pounds—or a staggering 3,600 head of cattle weighing a combined 2.5 million pounds a year.[12] In 1884 the contract to supply beef to the railway construction crews was taken over by J.B. Greaves, who had formed the Douglas Lake Cattle Company, and the Harper/Van Volkenburgh partnership was dissolved.

But Thaddeus Harper was not done. For years he had been eyeing the lush bunchgrass ranges on the west side of the Fraser River across from Dog Creek. Because of their inaccessibility, the vast ranges had not been pre-empted to any extent. Harper had coveted the land across the Fraser for years and now moved to acquire it. Under the Land Act of 1884 passed by the provincial legislature, the pastoral lease system was discontinued but unsurveyed agricultural land could be purchased outright. The standard price for purchasing this land was $2.50 an acre, but the act specified that "mountainous tracts of land, which are unfit for cultivation and valueless for lumbering purposes, may be purchased at the rate of $1 per acre." This was the opportunity that the cattlemen of the Interior had been waiting for, and over 71,000 acres were purchased by Interior ranchers. Foremost among these purchasers was Thaddeus Harper, who purchased 12,146 acres across the Fraser River. Thaddeus Harper, who appointed Newman Squires in charge of the ranching operations at this new ranch, known thereafter as the Gang Ranch.

Thaddeus Harper, ever alert to the potential to make a dollar, observed that there was a growing ranching industry developing in the North-West Territories (later known as Saskatchewan and Alberta) and, with it, a demand for good horses. During the early 1880s several herds of horses had been driven across the mountains into the District of Alberta, now southern Alberta. So, in April 1884, Newman Squires assembled a herd of 200 horses in the Dog Creek area and, accompanied by several Gang Ranch cowboys including Hector McLean, brother of the infamous McLean boys who had terrorized the Interior of British Columbia in 1879, began the long drive to the North-West Territories. On reaching Kamloops, Squires rested his horses for a couple of weeks and had a number of them shod to withstand the hard travelling ahead of them. By early May he and his cowboys were heading through the Okanagan Valley. The herd was then crossed into the United States at Osoyoos and given a temporary permit to cross US territory on the way east. Squires and his cowboys drove the herd down the Okanagan River to Omak Lake and then across the Colville Indian Reservation. The herd was swum across the Columbia River and then via Spokane Falls to cross back into Canada at Bonners Ferry. From there they travelled through the Crowsnest Pass into the prairies. Reaching Fort MacLeod, Squires and his men sold all the horses at a good price and then turned to travel back to British Columbia. The Kamloops *Inland Sentinel* reported that Newman Squires passed through Kamloops in late November on his way back to the Gang Ranch. The account also mentioned that Squires had encountered numerous people travelling over the same route, indicating that it was the main thoroughfare through the mountains at the time.[13]

This long cattle drive may have been the last work that Newman Squires did for Thaddeus Harper. By 1885, Harper was in financial difficulty, and he began to divest himself of many of his holdings in the BC Interior. Sometime during this period Harper sustained a serious injury, which impaired his ability to carry on the rigorous life he had led up to that point. Depending upon the account, Harper was either kicked in the face by a horse on the Gang Ranch[14] or thrown from a horse at Lac la Hache. Either way, he sustained brain trauma from which he never recovered.[15] Harper sold his entire lands and cattle to the Western Canada Ranching Company in 1888. It is said that at this point the Gang Ranch covered 38,472 acres. The sale also included Harper's ranches at Canoe Creek, Clinton and Kamloops, and the Perry Ranch (17,000 acres) at Cache Creek. Broken and ailing, Thaddeus Harper who, along with his brother, was once considered one of the cattle kings of British Columbia, died in Victoria on December 9, 1898.

Squires married a Shuswap Native woman named Sophie. They had two children, Lucinda and Charles, and eventually purchased a ranch at Copper Creek, on the north side of Kamloops Lake, where Squires raised his own cattle and kept a few racehorses. Like most of the men who had been in British Columbia during the gold rush, he dabbled in mining, having an interest in several copper claims near his ranch. His son served in the Boer War with Lord Strathcona's Horse and then returned to North America. A born horseman like his father, he travelled with Buffalo Bill's Wild West Show for several years before settling on a ranch near Calgary.

Newman Squires died from heart trouble in November 1898, at the age of 59. His funeral was widely attended, and he was buried in the Kamloops cemetery. His obituary in the November 29, 1898, Kamloops *Inland Sentinel* was accompanied by a poem that was signed simply "D."

NEWMAN SQUIRES

Hang the saddle up, tie the lariat on, the rider's day is past and o'er;
Turn the old horse loose on the range to feed, thro' day and night for evermore;
The snow lies light on the hill tops white, drapes the pinetrees, drapes the plains;
Nature weeps and supplies a shroud for the old time King of Rope and Range.
Never again shall the untamed steed feel the master's hand and the master know
Never again shall the rope fly swift from the master's hand with his one sure throw;
Never again shall the driven steer hear the master's voice on the overland trail.
Never again shall the wild range see his form 'neath the sun or the moonlight pale.
Oh! Newman Squires, when the canting friars have lost their jobs and God puts men true,
True to the best that exists in man, to corral the sinners, He'll call on you.
Oh! Newman Squires, God speed you well, o'er the narrow trail that all must go;
At peace with God, at peace with men, 'neath the green turf sod in peace lie low.

Sam Howe

Sam Howe was a cowboy's cowboy, a man of humour, warmth and cow sense. He was a hard-living, hard-drinking man who never rose to own a large ranch but, if a rancher wanted his cattle looked after in the best possible way, Howe was his man. During his career, Howe started many young men on the way to becoming real cowboys. A large, handsome man, he was the perfect picture of a cowboy as he sat on horseback on the prairies, and it was said that "one could not have found a more typical specimen of the old-time cowman who helped to drive the first herds of cattle over the buffalo trails of yesterday."[16]

He came from a family that had lived a life of adventure as they headed west to pursue the American dream. His father, Samuel Howe senior, emigrated from England in 1856 and joined an overland trip to Utah as part of a Mormon colonization venture. His party was poorly equipped and set out too late in the year to walk the 1,400 miles (over 2,250 kilometres) to Salt Lake City. Many would-be settlers perished in the snow, but Howe made it and married into a pioneer family in Nephi, Utah. With their family of eight children, the Howes moved by covered wagon to Willow Creek, Montana, about 40 miles (over 60 kilometres) north of Virginia City. Sam was three years old at the time.

His father homesteaded on Willow Creek and had a rowboat that he used to help people across the creek when it was at high water. One day, Sam's father was down by the creek near sundown when a stranger appeared on the other side and pulled his horse to a stop. Mr. Howe, a simple God-fearing man, was a little concerned at the speed with which the man had approached and shouted across, "Are you a man escaping justice?" The stranger quickly drew a Winchester rifle from the saddle scabbard and placed a bullet between Howe and the boat. Howe made record time across the creek, loaded the man and tied his horse to the boat, and made record time back. The man, a big, bearded individual who was armed to the teeth, reached into his pocket and withdrew a five-dollar gold piece that he handed to Howe. When Howe protested that there was no charge for the ride, he smiled and galloped away. Sam, seven years old at the time, witnessed the scene and recounted the story many times.[17]

Sam Howe's first job was herding work oxen for a freight outfit near Virginia City. One morning, while looking for a strayed ox, he came across three dead men hanging from a cottonwood tree. They had been caught robbing sluice boxes and had undergone frontier justice. This gruesome sight, a reminder of the quick and brutal form of retribution common in the mining regions of the United States, stayed with Howe for the rest of his life. When he quit this job, he went to work on ranches in southern Montana, Wyoming, Idaho and Utah, doing everything from chasing wild horses to herding cattle. He became an expert horseman and a good cowboy, rough and tough but always considerate of the animals under his care. He would often remark, "A human can talk, but an animal tells you nothing" as justification for taking the time to understand and care for his horses and cattle.

Howe was almost 18 years old when he was hired by Tom Lynch to help drive a herd of cattle from Lost River, Idaho, into the North-West Territories of Canada. The herd was destined for the Highwood River, where a new ranch was being set up by the North-West Cattle Company. It was 1882, and there were 12 cowboys on that cattle drive, including the trail boss, Abe Cotterell and Cal Morton, who served as cook. Among the cowboys hired for the drive was John Ware, who would become a legend in Canada. They were accompanied by 100 saddle and wagon horses, a chuckwagon, bed wagon and calf wagon (for newborn calves that were born on the trail until they were able to travel with their mothers). The cattle were driven at a leisurely pace to avoid their losing weight and were night herded, with each cowboy taking a two-hour shift. Howe had never learned to read or write, but he could figure out his wages at the end of the month: thirty dollars for 30 days.

The cattle were driven over the Monida Pass into Montana and then northward to the border. It was a long trail, and the long hours began to take their toll on the tired cowboys. But, by the end of August, the herd of 3,014 head of cattle had crossed into Canada and begun to proceed north. The *Macleod Gazette* reported on this, the first large herd to be driven into the area:

The herd of this company passed through here . . . en route to their ranges on High River . . . it consisted of 3000 head of the best grade cattle in Idaho, among which are 70 pedigree cows and 10 thoroughbred bulls. Several of our leading officials and stockmen visited the herd and were surprised at the condition of the cattle after so long a drive. The number of calves was conspicuous to everyone. This is evidently one of the most successful drives ever made in this country and Captain Stimson is to be congratulated on having secured the services of such an experienced stockman as Tom Lynch.[18]

When they finally arrived at the crossing of the High River, the herd was rested so the trail-weary cattle and men could rest. But there was no rest for Howe. He, Tom Lynch and Fred Stimson, manager of the North-West Cattle Company, rode upriver to where the buildings for the new ranch were being constructed. Stimson was obviously impressed with Howe. After 10 days' rest, when the herd was driven to the home range and the crew paid off, Stimson hired Howe to haul logs to the home site. The names of those who spent the winter constructing ranch buildings would live on in ranching history: John Ware, George Emerson, Herb Millar and Jim Meinsinger.

Howe was still with the outfit in 1884 when Montana cowman George Lane took over the job of wagon boss. Somewhere around that time, Sam made a discovery that created much excitement among the cowboys on the Bar U, as the ranch was called. He was riding back to camp in the Calgary district beside the railway track when his horse shied at something in the ditch. Howe investigated and found that it was a 20-gallon keg of whisky. But how would he get it back to camp? He wrapped his lariat around it several times, dallied it to his saddle horn and set off back to camp. Very little rope was left behind the horse, and the keg kept thumping along close to its rear legs, which made the horse jump and plunge away from the bouncing menace. Howe managed to get the keg back to camp, but left a wide swath behind him as he and his skittish horse made their way. Needless to say, the boys had a grand time that night.

In 1888, Howe settled down on his own ranch on Sheep Creek in the present-day Turner Valley, and the following year married Emma McAbee. Her parents, John and Susan McAbee, had taken the orphaned Newman Squires and his brothers to California and raised them in Mendocino County, where they eventually had six children of their own. At the urging of Newman Squires, the McAbee children had come to British Columbia and, in 1887, had travelled to the North-West.

Howe was especially pleased by the fact that his ranch was next to that of his friend, the famous black cowboy John Ware, who had been with him on the cattle drive from Lost River, Idaho. The two men became lifetime friends. Howe built up a herd of cattle and horses and worked in the general round-ups in the Sheep Creek area. Before long, Howe and his wife had a daughter, Beatrice, and it looked like the family was settled down to stay.

However, with a restlessness that marked much of his life, Howe sold out and bought the Atlantic Hotel in Calgary. He and Emma had operated the hotel for less than a year before the South African War broke out and Howe joined the Lord Strathcona's Horse Regiment along with many other cowboys of the North-West. Howe served in South Africa and, when the war was over, he bought a horse and travelled through Southern Rhodesia, the Transvaal, Pretoria, Bechuanaland Protectorate, the Orange Free State and Basutoland. During this time, friends and family began to think that he must have been killed in action but, after getting the travel bug out of his system, Howe returned to Calgary and the Atlantic Hotel. There he was rudely greeted and told that he didn't own the hotel anymore. Emma, thinking he was dead, had sold it and pocketed the money. After trying to settle things through his usual method, his fists, Howe hired his friend, lawyer R.B. Bennett, and was able to recover some of his investment. With that in his pocket and Emma out of his life, he headed out to British Columbia to prospect for gold. A year later, he was back in Alberta, wiser but no richer.[19]

Howe's next venture was to invest in a cattle ranch with John Ware on the Red Deer River north of Brooks. They spent a winter cutting logs for a cabin, and things were looking quite promising. When spring came, the Ware family moved into their comfortable new home and, once again, Howe decided to move on. He spent the next four years working for George Emerson on his lease on the Bow River and then went back to the Bar U, which had been purchased by George Lane in 1902.

The Bar U was grazing tens of thousands of head of cattle on the open ranges of mixed-grass prairie that were unsuitable for farm settlement due to a lack of water. Each spring, a round-up crew would set out from the Bar U to gather three- and four-year-old steers of the different brands owned by the Bar U and drive them to the CPR shipping point at Namaka. This drive would take two months and would consist of two wagons, the chuckwagon and a wagon to haul bedrolls, tents and equipment, with each wagon pulled by a four-horse team. The bed wagon would also carry the rope and posts for a rope corral. The crew would consist of a boss, a cook, eight cowboys and a horse wrangler. Experienced riders would be required to ride out 10 to 15 miles on either side of the wagon and cut out mature steers, which would then be driven to the main herd. This was the type of work that Howe loved.

He stayed on his horse from morning to night, and his trained eye could pick out the steers that were ready for market.

The cowboys worked slowly, allowing the cattle to graze as they were being moved, the objective being to get them to the shipping point as fat as possible. For this reason, the round-up would halt at a point north of Fort Macleod to rest the cattle for a week. Then they would cross the Little Bow River and join up with the Circle Ranch crew, who would help ensure that no Circle cattle were being gathered up in the Bar U herd.

A young green cowboy named Chris Christianson recorded the first time he met Sam Howe:

> I first met Sam when the Circle wagon and the Bar U met at the Driftwood Bend on Bow River, south side, in June 1905. Billy Henry was the Bar U wagon boss, Bally Buck the Circle boss. I being just a kid, was full of questions and remarked to Henry, "Why do these men wear so many clothes?" Billy answered, "Well, these Bar U critters are slow in shedding this year." Henry had a full crew of men that year. I saw Shell Gillespie, "Six Shooter Joe" Reynolds, Mike Herman, Rube Warren, Harry Geroe, Pete Smith, Eddy Marino, Jack Christianson and Sam Howe. The Circle outfit at that time also had a big crew of cowboys. This was the hey-day of the open range work in Alberta. Some of these boys wouldn't have traded their saddle for the best homestead in the country.[20]

Howe worked for the Bar U until 1908, when he and Billy Playfair started up a livery stable and a sort of restaurant in Bassano. Once again, Howe realized that town was not the place for him and sold out to Playfair. He headed south to Montana to see his aging mother and then headed to BC's Cariboo country, where he purchased four fine freight wagons and eight Percheron horses and shipped them to Ashcroft. But when he set out on the Cariboo Road, he was immediately stopped and told that his wagons were too wide for the road. Disgusted, he sold his wagons at a loss and headed back to Alberta.

With his remaining money, Howe bought a saddle and a long rope and went back to cowboying. He worked for George Emerson along the Red Deer River and, when he sold out to his partner, Rod Macleay, Howe became foreman of the Macleay outfit, based at the old John Ware cabin that he had helped to build. Howe stayed there for the next 18 years. His first wife, Emma, had died in 1905 in the southern states, and Howe married the widowed Mrs. Tessie McDonnel in 1921. Macleay raised only steers on his ranch and let Howe build up a herd of his own. By 1928 he had 600 head of cattle

Sam Howe in 1925. GLENBOW ARCHIVES NA-3250-37

showing his DC brand, but he had taken out a mortgage on his herd, and it was called at a time when cattle prices were low, so he had to start out from scratch again. Fortunately, Howe had acquired a small ranch five miles north of Dutchess, so he went back to ranching. While this ranch never amounted to much, it gave the Howes a place to finish off their days. Sam Howe died in 1947, by then one of the best-known cowboys in Alberta and the epitome of the old-time cowboy. Tessie died a couple of months later.

Ebb Johnson

Everett Cyril "Ebb" Johnson was a Virginian by birth and, even though he spent only a few years in that state, he remained "the man from Virginia" throughout his life. When the American novelist Owen Wister was looking to write a novel about the West that went against the popular image of the cowboy as a rough, untamed drifter, he picked Ebb Johnson, whom he had met in Wyoming, as the perfect example of the strong, quiet, wholesome cowboy. His resulting novel, entitled *The Virginian* after its hero, changed the image of the cowboy forever.

Johnson's roots went deep in Virginia. His great-grandfather, William Johnstone, came to Virginia from Scotland in time to fight in the American Revolution. As a reward for his service during the war, he was given a land grant in Powhatan County. His son, Thomas William Johnson, changed his name to match the deed to his land in Goochland County, Virginia. Ebb's father, George, had a plantation called Henry House, near Manassa. At the outbreak of the Civil War in 1860, the year Ebb was born, his father fought for the Confederacy. He was wounded at Vicksburg and at the Battle of Bull Run. General Beauregard used Henry House as his headquarters.[21]

After the war the family was dispossessed from their property, and Ebb's father took them down the Ohio River to a farm near Lake City, Minnesota. Life on the farm was far from the plantation lifestyle, and the family scratched out a living raising horses, cows, turkeys and chickens. Young Ebb enjoyed the life, learning to shoot a shotgun at an early age. It was a skill that would stand him in good stead in the future.

Young Ebb Johnson, considered a hated "reb" by some of his neighbours, learned to fight early. After one particularly brutal battle in the schoolyard when Ebb was 12 years old, he left home with a friend named Will Furlow. The pair made it to Camp Clark, Nebraska, a frontier town filled with miners, trappers and stockmen. Unfortunately, Will Furlow was shot and killed in a fight, and Ebb was left to make his way on his own.

It was the early 1870s, and longhorned cattle were just coming into

Nebraska from the great Texas plains. Johnson was befriended by one of the stockmen, just starting to be called "cowboys," and returned with him to Texas, acting as a wrangler for the returning horses. That trip gave him a chance to become adept with the six-gun and rope. The best ropes were made of rawhide braided with as many as eight strands and rubbed and oiled to make them pliable.

At the age of 14, Johnson headed back north to Minnesota with the intention of visiting his family but, on the way, encountered a Mexican who had escaped from the Texas Rangers and shot him as he rode away. The Texas Rangers were impressed with the marksmanship of the young man and offered him a job, but Johnson opted for a horse as a reward. Instead of returning to Minnesota, he got a job driving cattle over the Chisholm Trail. There were 12 to 20 cowboys, 100 horses and 2,000 Texas longhorns on that drive that ended up at Dodge City.

From Dodge City, Johnson headed back to Minnesota, where he discovered that his father had moved the family west to Rochester, where he ran a stagecoach line. Johnson took a job driving stagecoach and proved to be an excellent "whip," as the drivers were called. He found stagecoach driving boring but, when the stage line was sold to a man in the Black Hills of Dakota, he went with it and ended up driving a stage through the Dakota badlands to Deadwood. There, Johnson's fighting spirit got the better of him again, and in one fight he hit a man over the head with a neck yoke, leaving him senseless in the dust. Thinking that he had killed the man, Johnson fled Deadwood and worked for a time with a scout named William "Buffalo Bill" Cody, who was attached to the Fifth Cavalry under General Merritt. Cody had already begun to achieve fame through Ned Buntline's play, *The Scouts of the Plains*. In 1876, Cody was involved in an incident that he was to immortalize in his later Wild West Shows. As he later told it, he participated in a "duel" with the Cheyenne chief Yellow Hair, whom he supposedly first shot with a rifle, then stabbed in the heart and finally scalped "in about five seconds." Johnson's version of events was that Cody shot Yellow Hair at a great distance and then rode up and scalped him, "Buffalo Bill's first scalp for Custer," as Cody later told it. Although Johnson worked with Bill Cody and appreciated him as a fearless frontiersman, he was most appreciative that, through Cody, he met some of the great men of the American frontier. Johnson was particularly indebted to Cody for introducing him to John "Portugee" Phillips, whom Johnson considered to be a greater frontiersman. Following the massacre of 80 men of the 18th Infantry Regiment under William Fetterman in 1866, Phillips had ridden 190 miles in sub-freezing temperatures to report the massacre to Fort Laramie. When Johnson met him, Phillips was ranching at Chugwater Creek in Wyoming but was already regarded as

Ebb Johnson, age 22, when he worked for the Powder River Cattle Company in Wyoming. GLENBOW ARCHIVES NA-2924-12

a national symbol of courage and devotion to duty.

In 1878, Johnson drifted west to the Powder River country of Wyoming, where he found a place that he could call home. He later said that although the cowboy profession owed much to the Mexican, it was brought to perfection by the Texan. The cowboys in Wyoming were mostly Texans, and Johnson felt at home with them. In Cheyenne he met another Texas cowboy, Fred Hesse, an Englishman who had come north as a trail boss for "Texas" John Slaughter. The two became good friends and worked on ranches in the Powder River area along the Bozeman Trail. When Englishman Moreton Frewen set up a ranch on the trail, he asked Fred Hesse to be his foreman, and Hesse brought Johnson with him. In 1879, Hesse sent Johnson to Sweetwater, Montana, with a crew and wagon to bring back 3,000 head of cattle to stock the ranch. Because Johnson was only 19 years old at the time, Hesse told him to tell the men who worked for him that he was 21. At Sweetwater, Johnson branded the cattle with the 76 brand and then broke the herd into three to make herding easier. By 1881 the 76 had over 15,000 head of cattle; with the formation of the Powder River Cattle Company with English capital in 1882, the Draper and Van Tassel herds were purchased, bringing the total to close to 50,000 head of cattle.

Johnson was chosen as captain of the first Johnson County round-up while still 19 years old and kept this position as long as he was with the Powder River Ranch. There were two general round-ups in Wyoming, a spring one for collecting and branding calves and a fall one to gather mature cattle for market. The methods and equipment used in Wyoming were straight from Texas, just like the cowboys. Cattle were turned loose on the range and allowed to move with the weather. There was no such thing as winter feed, as cattle were expected to rustle for themselves. During winter storms, cattle were known to drift for 200 miles. Johnson rode a Texas saddle, double-rigged with an "A fork," and his saddle had a macheer (from the Spanish *mochilla*), a removable leather sheet that covers the entire underpart of the saddle. From this saddle, on a small Texas horse, Johnson could rope with the best Texas cowboys. Like them, he tied his rope to the horn so that whatever he roped, he held.

Johnson rose to be one of the most respected cowboys in Wyoming. He was considered a moral man who did not chase women and was considered honest, meaning he didn't rustle cattle. As Moreton Frewen was married to Clara Jerome, daughter of a wealthy New York financier, he had access not only to the money but also to the connections that came with his wife. His palatial ranch house saw a steady stream of easterners and titled Englishmen and Scotsmen who were fascinated with the ranching lifestyle. They were inevitably introduced to young Ebb Johnson, who seemed to represent everything that was wholesome and real about the cowboy.

Johnson also met Major Frank Walcott, owner of the VR Ranch on Deer Creek, a tributary of the North Platte River. In 1885 he was helping Walcott with some cattle when he met Owen Wister. Wister was fascinated by the quiet strength of the Virginia-born cowboy and made an effort to befriend him before immortalizing him in his 1902 novel. *The Virginian* is widely regarded as being the first cowboy novel and was wildly popular, being reprinted 14 times in eight months. Wister depicts the Virginian as a stern man with a soft side to his personality. Soon after the publication of the novel, Wister sent a copy to Johnson, now living in Canada, inscribed "To the hero from the author."

By the mid-1880s the cattle ranges of Wyoming were starting to show the effects of overgrazing, and Moreton Frewen considered moving at least part of his operation to Canada. He sent Johnson north to see if he could find a suitable location and, at Johnson's recommendation, leased seven townships of land in the Mosquito Creek area and had them recorded in the name of his foreman, E.W. Murphy.[22] But the directors of the Powder River Cattle Company in England vetoed the plan as being too costly. As a result of this, Frewen resigned in 1885, leaving the ranch in desperate financial condition. Belatedly, the directors in England decided that Frewen's plan had merit and agreed to move one fifth of the Powder River cattle to the lease.

In the spring of 1886, the Tongue River herds, consisting of 7,500 head of cattle in three bunches, were moved north with Ebb Johnson in charge of one of them. The herds comprised mostly "dry" (not bred) three- and four-year-old cows, but any calves born on the drive were killed at birth so as to not slow progress. A fourth herd, consisting of steers, followed the first three. The cattle arrived without incident or significant loss at the Mosquito Creek lease, and two of the crews, including Johnson and his cowboys, were immediately sent back to Wyoming.

The winter of 1886–87 was, as we have seen, a devastating one for ranches all across the Great Plains, from the north of Texas to Montana and the North-West. The losses for the Powder River Company at Mosquito Creek were relatively low, probably because the entire herd had comprised dry cows and steers. But it was quite a different story in Wyoming. Cattle losses were close to 70 percent, and the directors in England went into liquidation mode to try and cut their losses. In 1888 they were able to sell the entire Canadian branch of the company, including leases and cattle, to the Canadian Agricultural Coal and Colonization Company, headed by Sir Lester Kaye.

For Johnson, the situation in Wyoming was becoming untenable. The Powder River Ranch was deteriorating quickly, and the situation in Johnson County was becoming violent as the large ranches pitted themselves against the small farmers. The tensions escalated, culminating in the "Johnson County War" of 1892, in which Johnson's friend Frank Wolcott played a prominent part. By then Johnson had ridden north to Canada in search of work.

Upon his arrival in Calgary, Johnson met Charlie Berry and "Wild Horse" Johnson, who had just returned from British Columbia with a herd of horses. Johnson gave them a hand moving the horses to the Ghost River area west of Calgary and, for the rest of the year, worked for Major James Walker, a former Mounted Policeman who had homesteaded west of Calgary.

Johnson's credentials as a premier cattleman were not long in being recognized. In 1889, George Lane announced that he was stepping down as the foreman of the Bar U Ranch. His shoes would be tough to fill. D.H. Andrews, who had known Johnson in Wyoming and was working for the Canadian Land and Ranch Company, recommended Johnson as "a first rate cowman, in fact I think about the best all round cowman in this country and he is very good with young horses."[23] Johnson was offered the job and went to work right away.

While working at the Bar U, Johnson met Mary Eleanor Bigland from Windermere, England, who had come out to Canada with her uncle, William Laycock. She was a registered nurse and got a job looking after Mrs. Stimson at the Bar U. Eleanor was:

not exactly pretty but she was graceful, light on her feet and she could run like a gazelle. Raised in the Lake Country, she was adept at rowing a boat and at swimming. She was [a] good dancer, played the piano well and, as Johnson said, had a personality that one would never forget.[24]

The two fell in love and were married by the Reverend Herdman, minister of Knox Presbyterian Church in Calgary. The best man was Johnson's friend from Wyoming, Harry Longabough, who was in Canada hiding from the authorities for his outlaw activities as the Sundance Kid. For reasons that are unknown, Eleanor urged Johnson to leave his job at the Bar U. Somewhat reluctantly, Johnson agreed and left the Bar U in 1891.

Johnson found a job with the Military Colonization Company Ranch, which had a 92,000-acre lease managed by General Strange, east of Calgary in the Bow River Valley. Aside from running cattle and horses, the ranch was used as a centre for educating young British gentlemen who wanted to learn ranching. Johnson was an excellent instructor and mentor to those who really wanted to learn.

The years at the Military Colonization Company Ranch were happy ones for the new couple. Mary decorated their little house with cretonne, embroidered flour sacks for tea cloths and converted salt barrels for chairs. Their first son, Robert Everett Poindexter Johnson, was born in 1893 and, 15 months later, their second son, Lawrence Branch Johnson, was born on the last day of 1894. Johnson got along well with the neighbouring Blackfoot people, making an effort to learn their language and hiring them to work on the ranch. One Blackfoot chief, Old Brass, was a frequent visitor to the Johnson house, and his wife, referred to as Mrs. Brass, worked for Mary Johnson. Johnson displayed racial prejudice against Blacks, but not other races. His prejudice was most probably a result of his upbringing in the South, but he was fairly typical of his era. Interestingly, manifestations of racial prejudice in the North-West at the time were primarily against the Native people, and African Americans were generally accepted.

On a trip to Calgary during this time, Johnson was riding down Stephen Avenue, which was notorious for its mud. In addition to the usual saddle horses, buggies, wagons and pedestrians, on this day the street was the scene of a runaway buggy. As it careened down the muddy street, Johnson could see the potential for serious injury to bystanders or property. He spurred his horse, and it leapt over a large pile of lumber. As he alit on the other side, he threw a wide loop over the two runaway horses' heads and dallied up. When the horses hit the end of the rope they stopped, and Johnson was able to control them. Downtown Calgary has changed somewhat since those days.

Around 1896, Johnson was offered a well-paying job by the firm of Gordon, Ironside and Fares, Winnipeg cattle shippers who were looking to establish a ranch on which to raise their own cattle. Johnson located an excellent range in the Wintering Hills east of Calgary and laid out a home ranch for them similar to the Bar U. The family moved to the Two Bar Ranch, as it was called, and Johnson worked briefly for Gordon, Ironsides and Fares as a cattle buyer.

In 1895, Johnson took a few carloads of horses to Europe for them to see if there was a market for coach horses. It was quite an eye-opener for him to see the "Old Country," with its sprawling cities and easy way of life. Johnson was delighted with the fine dining available on his travel account and "packed in the grub" to the point where he gained weight that he would carry for the rest of his life. In Belgium, France and Germany, he drove a coach and four to demonstrate to potential buyers the capabilities of the teams and successfully negotiated good prices for the horses.

In 1897, Johnson and his friend Charlie Berry trailed a herd of 1,500 head of cattle through the Crowsnest Pass to Fort Steele. The trail was through thick timber and bush, and they were forced to follow the river or creek bed for miles. This was something the plainsman Johnson had never encountered before, and he declared it the most difficult cattle drive he had ever made. To add insult to injury, Johnson lost his favourite six-gun, a silver-mounted, ivory-handled beauty, in the bush.

When he got back from British Columbia, Johnson went into partnership with Captain d'Eyncourt, son of a prominent English family, and bought a ranch at Nose Hill, some 18 miles northwest of Calgary. Once again, Johnson was responsible for laying out the home site and overseeing the construction of the buildings and corrals. With Johnson in charge of operations, the ranch became known for its excellent horses. When the Boer War created a demand for remounts, the ranch was able to supply horses to the military. Johnson gloried in his own horses, which were known for their smooth performance. His favourite was a cutting horse named Sailor that was renowned in the area. One day a man in Bain's Livery stable in Calgary was boasting that his horse could jump 10 feet to head off a cow. Another man responded, "Ebb Johnson's Sailor would never let a cow get that far away." That shut the boaster up.

The ranch also ran cattle. Captain d'Eyncourt imported Sussex and Highland cattle. The Sussex were a beautiful cherry colour and were gentle and easily handled. But they were poor range cattle, as they could not fend for themselves and did not flourish. The Highland cattle, on the other hand, were quite adaptable to the North-West climate and took to the hills so that they became quite wild. But they were small and not very marketable. In all, Johnson felt that neither were "real cattle" and was not impressed with the captain's desire to see good British cattle introduced.

Throughout his time at Nose Hill, Johnson stayed involved in the Alberta cattle industry. He continued to work for Gordon, Ironside and Fares on a contract basis, on one occasion driving a herd of 500 head of five-year-old steers from Cochrane to the Two Bar Ranch. Around the same time, he was contracted by Gordon, Ironsides and Fare to round up John and Jim McKinnell's cattle, which had been left to range in the Little Red Deer River country all the way north to Fallen Timber River. The cattle had been allowed to range far and wide for some time and included steers up to seven years old. When the cattle were sold to Gordon, Ironsides and Fare, they asked Johnson to round them up. After an intensive search, Johnson and two cowboys managed to locate 200 head.

During his time at the d'Eyncourt ranch, Johnson was also contracted to move 500 head of cattle for the Jacques brothers, local jewellers, from their ranch near Calgary to Lane's Lake, 80 miles (130 kilometres) east of Lacombe. The crew included Johnson and five cowboys, one of whom acted as cook and drove the chuckwagon. Johnson was a stickler for moving cattle slowly so they would not lose weight and delivered the herd in good condition. His years in the dry Powder River country of Wyoming had taught him the need to keep weight on cattle while they were being moved.

One of the more pleasant encounters at the Nose Hill Ranch occurred when a man brought in a big black mare to have her cured of being a runaway. Johnson suggested that they put "draw lines" on her, and the mare was cured of her bad habit. The man thanked Johnson and introduced himself as W.D. Kerfoot, originally from Virginia. Kerfoot had been a cowboy in Montana and then the foreman of the Cochrane Ranch when it was located west of Calgary. He and Johnson became good friends and mutual admirers. Johnson maintained that he had never seen anyone mount a horse as beautifully as Kerfoot, who, as Johnson later recalled, "looked like a bird rising from the ground in one smooth motion."[25]

In 1901 the Duke and Duchess of Cornwall, later King George V and Queen Mary, visited Calgary and were given some "wild west" entertainment. As part of the show, Johnson, on his favourite horse, Sailor, roped, threw and tied two steers and was later introduced to the duke. Johnson was considered one of the best ropers in the country, along with Mike Herman and John Ware. Unfortunately, Johnson's prejudice never allowed him to compete with John Ware.

The d'Eyncourt Ranch was sold in 1904. Johnson had built a comfortable home in Calgary, from which he worked as a cattle buyer for Gordon, Ironsides and Fare. Later, he was appointed Mange Inspector for the Calgary District. But in 1909 he contracted typhoid fever and, after he recovered, sold the house in Calgary and moved to Cochrane to operate a meat market. During the Spanish flu epidemic of 1918 and 1919, Mary turned the Johnson home into a hospital to nurse the sick and dying. For a time the butcher shop was a success, but Johnson, realizing that his glory days were at an end, started drinking heavily. He retired to Calgary in 1923 and passed away in 1946.

Johnson was never really happy in Canada. Few people even got his name right, calling him "Ed" in their reminiscences. For a man who had lived through so much and met so many heroes of the American West, he was little known and unappreciated in Canada. Johnson's daughter-in-law noted that:

> Ebb was happy on the [d'Eyncourt] ranch; and yet he always seemed a sojourner in this new land, an exile from his own country. As he remained, in spirit, a son of Virginia throughout a boyhood and young manhood spent in the Western States, so he remained at heart an American although the greater part of his life was spent in Canada.[26]

His story is one that encompasses the history of the West like few others. He was "the Virginian."

Chapter Six

GREENHORNS

By 1891 the range cattle industry in Canada's North-West Territories had been around for about a decade. A number of large and small ranches were scattered from south of Fort Macleod into the foothills of the Rockies and north as far as the Bow River. An examination of the 1891 Canadian census for the southwestern corner of the North-West shows that almost 75 percent of the population was Canadian born, whereas only about 5 percent were born in the United States.[1] An additional 16 percent of the population originated from the British Isles. Many of these Canadians and British were likely involved in ranching in some way in this area, and many probably worked as cowboys. As there was no such profession as "ranch hand" where they came from, they must have learned the trade in the North-West. Most of the new arrivals to the North-West during the 1880s came there to earn a living, and many took jobs on ranches. While much has been made of the well-to-do "chinless wimps" who arrived from Britain or Canada with a monthly remittance to pretend to be cowboys, most of the newcomers showed a genuine desire to learn the skills of the cowboy quickly and thoroughly. These "greenhorns" would often be subject to a rough initiation into the ways of the cowboy but, where they showed persistence and good nature, they were readily accepted into the cowboy fraternity. Little did they know that only a small fraction of the American cowboys had been born into the life; most of them had started out just like the greenhorns.

Fred Ings, who was one of those Canadians who came to the West as a greenhorn, pointed out,

> Most of our best riders came from the States and they taught us all we knew of cattle lore. Over there cattle and roundups were an old story; to us they were a new game. We were young and learned quickly, we had to, as it was essential that we knew these things well.

Within a few years, newcomers were skilled enough to hold their own with their fellow cowboys, and a few went on to become expert cowboys. Many of them went on to own their own ranches and to contribute to the growing ranching industry well into the 20th century.

Bob Newbolt

I have heard talk about Canon Hollard's son being out here. He is close to this place but the account one hears of him here is very different to what you hear of him. He is one of the usual English sort who does nothing but play polo and drinks and plays the fool generally. His horse ranch is a myth. I believe he has some polo ponies and that is about all. The old Canon came out here to pay his debts and his son fed him about as roughly as he could, so the old man did not stop long. I think young Hollard is going back to England soon.[2]

This is how one Englishman described "the usual English sort" who came to the North-West to indulge themselves in playing "cowboy." One commentator described how they "dress themselves up in the garb of cowboys, spurs the size of small cart wheels, hat cut with a scissors [sic] and covered with mud to look old and tough."[3] They inevitably tried to copy the real cowboys in dress and mannerisms, but these "greenhorns" were scorned by the real men of the range. They ridiculed greenhorns of any sort but had the most fun with the Englishman who showed up on the range with the intention of becoming a working cowboy.

When William Robert Newbolt showed up in the Lemhi Valley near Deer Lodge, Idaho, Montana, with the cash to pay for 3,000 head of cattle destined for the Military Colonization Company in the North-West of Canada, the cowboys took one look at him and wrote him off as another ne'er-do-well Englishman. Certainly, he had all the credentials of a high-born wastrel. He was the son of a career Royal Horse Artillery officer and had been educated at the Uppingham Boys' School. After Robert Newbolt was turned down for the military due to his varicose veins, his father saw an advertisement in the *London Times* that had been inserted by a former member of the Royal Horse Artillery, Major-General Thomas Bland Strange, looking for young men of good means and character to work with him in a colonization scheme in Canada. At his father's urging, 18-year-old Newbolt left his family in 1884 to go to the North-West and become a part of the Military Colonization Company. This was not something to be entered into lightly. The "shareholder" was to pay $1,000 in cash and an additional $50 a month for the privilege of working for the company. In return, the shareholder could file for a homestead on land adjoining the company and start ranching for himself. The Military ·Colonization Company (MCC) had leased 92,000 acres and stocked a ranch east of Calgary on the Bow River.

Before leaving for Canada, Newbolt purchased a complete English riding outfit of the very latest style. Then he travelled on the steamship *Parisian* to Quebec City, full of anticipation for his new life. From there he took a train to Kingston, where he met with General Strange, who took one look at his riding outfit and forbade him to even consider wearing it

William Robert Newbolt in the riding outfit he brought to Canada. GLENBOW ARCHIVES NA-1046-5

in Western Canada. He persuaded Newbolt to "dispose of the bally lot to a riding academy for less than half of what it had cost in England."[4] Little did he know it at the time, but Strange had saved him a lot of grief in making him get rid of the "dude's outfit." But Newbolt insisted on keeping his bowler hat, something from which the cowboys would take particular pleasure in the future.

Newbolt was immediately dispatched to catch up with a group of shareholders from the MCC who were on their way to Idaho to take delivery of 3,000 head of cattle. He caught up with the others at Deer Lodge, Montana, and travelled to the Lemhi Valley where the cattle were being held. But, when they tried to pay for the cattle with a bank draft, the owner sent them back to Deer Lodge to arrange for a cash payment. Newbolt was sent on the mission and eventually returned with the necessary cash. When he arrived, he learned that the stagecoach before him had been held up by armed desperados. He knew then for sure he was in the wild west, a realization that provoked a mixture of excitement and worry in the newcomer.

Upon payment of the money, the herd was turned over to veteran cattleman Tom Lynch, who was to ensure that the herd arrived at the MCC in good shape. A better man for the job couldn't have been chosen; Lynch was the most experienced trail herder in the North-West and had picked a team of the best cowboys available. Newbolt was picked to join this trail-hardened group of westerners to look after the money needed for the trip back.

The rites of initiation for greenhorns varied but generally included giving them every dirty job available, and Newbolt was no exception. He later recounted:

> Because I was a greenhorn, of course they took all sorts of advantages of me. Along with driving the wagon all day, I was put on "night herding" and all night at that. I did not catch on for quite a while that the other riders were being relieved at midnight, because meeting them in the dark I would not know the difference.[5]

At the time, the sleep-deprived Newbolt was dressed in his English clothing of flannel trousers, puttees and bowler hat. But, as the ribbing grew more intense, Newbolt took an advance in pay and, when they reached Deer Lodge, purchased a complete western outfit, minus the six-shooter but including a cowboy hat. Satisfied with his new wardrobe, Newbolt returned to camp totally outfitted like one of the boys and carefully placed his old clothes and bowler hat in the bedroll wagon. But his fellow cowboys discovered his beloved bowler and found that, if you skimmed it through the air, it made a wonderful target. It was soon full of holes.

Newbolt had mercifully been given a quiet horse to ride on the trail, unlike some greenhorns who were immediately put on a mean horse that would test the skills of the best rider. He had ridden horses in England and had ridden to hounds a few times, so he began to train his horse to jump. This came in handy one day when some cattle got through the rail fence into a homesteader's property. Newbolt jumped his horse over the fence and herded the cattle along to the gate, much to the amazement of his companions. The trail boss saw his jumping skills and decided it was time Newbolt got a real horse to ride. He was assigned a half-broke horse from the herd with plenty of buck in it. Needless to say, Newbolt was sent flying, landing unceremoniously on his head. Undeterred, he got back on only to be quickly bucked off again. After his third landing in the dirt, a Mexican cowboy took him aside and showed him how to tie his stirrups together to keep his feet in the right place and how to pull on one rein to keep the horse bucking in a circle. Newbolt was a quick study; the next time he got on the horse, he survived the bucking and settled the horse down enough to ride off on it. The cowboys began to show a begrudging respect for the greenhorn, and Bob, as they began calling him, began to feel like he was being accepted by the rough men of the range. He remembered with pride:

> I was developing into a pretty fair cowhand and the boys were beginning to treat me with a good deal more respect than was the case at the start of the trip. I was enjoying the experience immensely and had developed a love for the great wide open spaces.[6]

Under the experienced hand of Tom Lynch, the cattle were moved at a leisurely pace, but the group reached the border in plenty of time to get the cattle delivered and settled down for the winter. Upon arriving at Fort Macleod, the Mounted Police carefully examined the herd for any signs of disease. As no one knew exactly where the MCC Ranch was located or how to get there, Newbolt, who now had the confidence of Lynch and the rest of the crew, went ahead to Calgary to get directions to the ranch. He then returned to join the herd and directed it along the old cattle trail that would later run to one of the major shipping points on the Canadian Pacific Railway at Strathmore.

The only major obstacle on their way was the Bow River, which was running high when the herd reached it. The cattle were crossed with little difficulty, but the wagons had to be dismantled and floated over a piece at a time. The cowboys crossed on their horses with the bedrolls and provisions held high over their heads. The herd finally arrived at the MCC Ranch in late summer, and Tom Lynch turned the herd over to General Strange. Newbolt bid his new friends goodbye and took stock of his surroundings. The MCC had taken out a lease on the short grass prairie between the Bow River to the south and the CPR line to the north, with Blackfoot Reserve to the east. The area was covered in grass that had not been grazed since the buffalo had disappeared and had numerous small lakes and sloughs that could provide water for the livestock. Newbolt effused, "This was an exciting adventure for a young greenhorn Englishman to be so suddenly transplanted from life in the Old Land to those great wide open spaces."[7]

Newbolt lost no time in staking himself a homestead with the intention of going into the ranching business. He purchased 10 head of cattle from the MCC and constructed a small log cabin and a horse stable before the winter set in. He chose DIO for his brand. He made an arrangement with the MCC to continue to work for them but without paying monthly wages to them. He worked for the MCC all through the winter, while at the same time caring for his own small herd and working on his property. The next spring, he went with the MCC wagon to the Chipman Ranch at Pincher Creek to pick up 500 head of cattle that the MCC had purchased. This time, Newbolt was the experienced hand and was well prepared for trail branding the cattle and driving them to the MCC along the same route he had taken the previous year. Upon arrival, he purchased 50 head of these cattle and drove them to his homestead. Somewhat concerned about the free range system that turned cattle loose on the range to fend for themselves, he proceeded to fence his land to keep his cattle within his property.

That summer, Newbolt received word that his father had passed away from old war wounds and that his mother and two sisters were coming to live with him. He scrambled to enlarge his log cabin to accommodate his family and continued to work on his homestead. They arrived in October, but it was Christmas before Newbolt had completed the addition and they could move into it. He was delighted to have his mother and sisters with him—and with

the stipend they received from the military because his father had died from wounds received in battle. This greatly assisted them in making a comfortable life for themselves in the North-West. Mrs. Newbolt was especially fond of the wooded area along the Bow River that formed part of the ranch. She referred to this wooded area by the English term "chase," meaning open parkland. And so the ranch was called Bowchase Ranch.

Newbolt, as a newcomer, was not bound by the antipathy that many ranchers felt toward grain farming. In 1886 he broke a few acres of prairie sod and planted it to oats. His method of planting without the aid of a seeder was unique: he had a hired hand drive a wagon over the area while he sat in the back and scattered the seeds on the ground. Then he cut a quantity of willow boughs and dragged them over the seed to cover it. Despite these somewhat primitive methods, the rain that summer was sufficient to produce an excellent crop. However, there remained the question of how to harvest the crop without a reaper or binder. Newbolt used his haying equipment

to mow and rake the crop into piles. Then the loose stalks were loaded on a hay wagon and hauled to a corral with hard-packed ground. There he spread the stalks on the ground and turned a bunch of horses loose to trample it down. Needless to say, the horses had to be bridled with their heads tied up so they would not eat the grain. Once the grain was sufficiently separated from the stalks, the mixture of oats and chaff was thrown up in the air on a windy day, and the grain effectively separated from the chaff. These methods produced a large quantity of oats to feed the horses as required.

Throughout the late 1880s, Newbolt continued to purchase and lease additional land and added cattle to his herd. He preferred the Hereford breed and purchased good "white faced" bulls to keep his bloodlines healthy. He also began to raise Hackney-blooded horses that were in demand by the Mounted Police and the military. With his increased land base, he put up

Bob Newbolt, the cowboy, in his western gear. Note the *tapaderos* over the stirrups, an indication of the Mexican *vaquero* influence in Alberta. GLENBOW ARCHIVES NA-1046-18 large quantities of hay to bring his livestock through the occasional killing winter. His growing pride in his operations and his own abilities as a rancher was justified:

> My ranching operations were proving to be very successful and I had developed into a top notch rancher. I could ride and rope with any of them, could hold my own in a poker game, and had acquired a special liking for good whisky.[8]

Newbolt's mother left to return to England in 1891, and he returned to a bachelor life, adding friends and neighbours to his social life. He was close enough to the booming town of Calgary to regularly visit to play polo and rugby, and he also became a charter member of the Ranchmen's Club. His sisters remained in the area, one of them marrying Oswald Chritchley. The Chritchleys hired a governess, Mabel Frazer, to look after their children. In the North-West, where men outnumbered women enormously, single women were inevitably the focus of attention from the myriad eligible young men. Bob Newbolt successfully wooed Mabel, and the two were married in 1899.

The Newbolts lived at the Bowchase Ranch for many years. Bob remained committed to mixed farming and grew larger crops with more sophisticated equipment than he had used for his first crop. He also remained enthusiastic about raising Hackney horses and purchased a world-class stallion named Romance, whose offspring won many prizes. The Newbolts spent much of their time in the winter exhibiting Hackney horses. Bob had a particularly good roping horse, Slippery, on which he earned a deserved reputation as a "heeler" when it came to roping for the branding fire.

As more and more settlers arrived in the area, Newbolt found his leased land diminished and even his regular roads to town fenced off. This made him extremely antagonistic toward new settlers. He was eventually forced to move his horses and cattle many miles every spring to available pasture. The livestock placed on an unfamiliar range made every effort to return to the home site, resulting in many of them going astray or disappearing. Despite his unhappiness with the changes taking place in the new Province of Alberta, formed in 1905, Newbolt continued ranching. He was always successful in turning a good profit on his cattle and horse sales and was able to build a brand-new ranch house. But the open prairies were rapidly being taken over by grain farmers, and the writing was on the wall. Newbolt eventually disposed of his land and livestock. He kept only his original homestead and specialized in hog raising. In later life, he mused:

As I look back over the 66 years which I have spent at Bowchase, they have been full of interesting experiences and I have made my mistakes like everyone else. One of my happiest memories is to think back into the past of these great, beautiful, open spaces as they were before being marred and scarred by the forward march of civilization. I suppose if I had broken up the sod on my beloved sections of prairie I would, perhaps, be a wealthy farmer today. Nevertheless, after I have been called to the "Last Great Roundup" and this land becomes worn out and useless, it will not be recorded that "Bob Newbolt was the one who turned it upside down."[9]

Hugh Bayliff

Clement Fitzalan Cornwall eyed the gawky 18-year-old before him. He noted the soft voice and even softer hands, and the aristocratic face with its penetrating intense eyes. The lad was soft, a definite "greenhorn" in the parlance of the frontier: in other words, a novice. He handed Cornwall a letter of introduction giving his family credentials, most important to an Englishman. The letter went on to state that he had been sent out by his family to learn the ranching business and they were willing to pay for it if Cornwall could find a suitable position. Quite an interesting idea: pay a rancher in the distant colonies to teach a younger son the rudiments of ranching in hopes that he might amount to something. Cornwall had seen it before. In most cases the young man turned out to be a wastrel, and the rancher lost time and patience in trying to fit him in with the hardened cowboys who did a real day's work. The locals called such a one a "mud pup." He was unsure of the origin of the term, but it seemed to express the harmless puppy-like innocence of the young men and the mess they could create.

Clement Cornwall was from Gloucester, England, and his lineage could be traced as far back as Richard I in the 12th century. Clement and his brother Charles had pre-empted land on the Thompson River in 1862 and established a successful ranch and stopping house, which they called Ashcroft after the family home in Gloucester. The lad in front of him was none other than Hugh Peel Lane Bayliff, who boasted a family heritage at least as prestigious as Cornwall's. The Lanes had been mayors of Hereford for generations and traced their origins back to Adam de la Lone, who arrived with William the Conqueror in 1066. His mother was a Peel, related to Sir Robert Peel, who had twice been prime minister of Britain.[10]

Being a magistrate, Cornwall knew all the possible places where young Bayliff could learn whether he liked the ranching life or not. The fact that Bayliff brought with him a stipend to be paid to the rancher who took him in made him particularly attractive. He decided that William James Roper, who had a ranch at Cherry Creek, would be an excellent choice. Roper was from Dorset in England and came from a good family. He had arrived in the Colony of British Columbia in 1862 and, for a time, tried his hand at mining in the Cariboo. Like most of the great horde that had rushed to the Cariboo, he made a living but never remotely approached "striking it rich." In 1865 he had joined the miners who rushed to Wild Horse Creek in the Kootenays and achieved the same measure of success. He then went to work as a "bullpuncher" on the Cariboo Road, driving a freight wagon for the Hudson's Bay Company. He came to Kamloops in 1871 to take charge of the Hudson's Bay Company horses, and the next year he pre-empted land at Cherry Creek just west of Kamloops and also bought property from Nicholas Hare (whose son Alex was to gain fame as the accomplice to the infamous McLean brothers—the McLean boys—who terrorized the Interior in 1881). Roper used the land to operate a very successful cattle ranch eventually comprising some 15,000 acres. He had been the first rancher to work at improving the bloodlines of his cattle, importing the first Hereford cattle and Clydesdale horses in the area.

Roper had trained mud pups before. In 1873 he had agreed to take in his nephews, William and John Roper Hull. Under their uncle's guidance, the brothers had grown from greenhorn cowboys to become excellent ranchers. They were now organizing a scheme to drive horses to the North-West Territories. William Roper was a man who would brook no nonsense, but he also knew when to look the other way, so Cornwall sat down and wrote a letter to Roper, offering Bayliff and his healthy stipend to cover his "apprenticeship." In the meantime, he offered Bayliff a place to stay until they heard back. The answer was not long in coming: Bayliff would be welcome, and the money should be paid up front.

At the beginning of December 1882, Hugh Bayliff rode to Cherry Creek Ranch, just a half-day's journey, and introduced himself to William Roper. His new boss and mentor was quick to inform him, "I don't care who your family is. If you don't work, you won't be here for long." This was, of course, mostly bluff. Roper was glad to get the money and had seen as Bayliff rode in that he was a natural in the saddle. The somewhat awkward boy nodded agreement and took his gear to the bunkhouse. When he entered, he met two cowboys who were at the home ranch, Hugh Armstrong, an Irishman, and Joseph Bernard, a Frenchman. Knowing that neither of these nationalities was particularly fond of the English, Bayliff kept his mouth shut and did what he was told. He set to work right away. As the Kamloops *Inland Sentinel* noted in an 1886 article, most cattle were left to fend for themselves through the winter unless the snow became too deep, when they would be fed hay:

WINTERING STOCK: Persons coming from the east are sometimes astonished at the way stock is kept in this country in winter when snow, as at present, is from four inches to two feet deep where drifted. Notwithstanding the recent cold spell by far the greater part of horses and cattle picked up their daily supply. Horses paw the snow to get at the grass for food and eat snow for drink; there are a large number of horses in the mountains back and to the southeast of Kamloops. Bands of cattle roam over the ranges and find sufficient, especially where the hills are bare, to retain their fat gained in the fall; numbers may be seen at times going to water holes in the ice along the river; others, we are informed, satisfy thirst with snow. Certain it is that the stock look [sic] in remarkably good condition at present. Even spring calves are running with the cattle. It is true a number of ranchers have to look after the younger portion of their bands and sometimes drive them into places prepared.[11]

Heifers that were due to calf were usually kept close to the home ranch, where they could be watched and helped in calving. William Roper was a "progressive" rancher who always put up a lot of hay as insurance against the severe winters. Bayliff was responsible for helping feed hay to the cattle and keeping the watering holes open so the cattle were able to drink. He also rode among the cattle looking to see if they needed help in calving. Since the cattle did not take a day off, neither did Bayliff. It was only when spring began to arrive, on March 9, that he was given a Sunday afternoon off. In working seven days a week, Bayliff never got a chance to go to town and purchase necessities. His clothing began to grow old and, in a letter home, he lamented his situation:

We are all much too big. I am so tall, in cold weather, the ends of one are so far away from the centre of warmth . . . I am getting so horribly mean and miserly . . . I hope mother will send me some socks. I try to hide the fact that mine are worn out.[12]

Roper also supplied beef to the Canadian Pacific Railway construction crews on a subcontract with JB Greaves of the Douglas Lake Cattle Company. Bayliff would have been involved in driving cattle to the holding areas, from where the Douglas Lake cowboys would supply them to the construction camps. Always a superb rider, he soon became adept at roping and handling cattle in a herd. After his first year of working for his board, he was put on the payroll by William Roper, who was genuinely pleased with the progress Bayliff was making. His prowess as a cowboy prompted Roper to choose him as cow boss on the cattle drives to the CPR construction sites.

Bayliff was given more and more responsibility. It was clear that he loved the rugged demanding outdoor life that ranching involved. Once he had served his apprenticeship, he began to consider his options. He wanted to have a ranch of his own, but the Thompson, Nicola and Okanagan Valleys were already in the hands of competent ranchers. Bayliff knew that the only way to make a profit in ranching was to own or lease enough land to hold a large volume of cattle. The possibilities of purchasing a large enough acreage to ranch successfully were limited in the southern Interior and, besides, he was concerned that the bunchgrass ranges of the region were being overgrazed and not able to recover in the hot dry climate. He had heard good things about the Chilcotin, where there were still large tracts of land available for pre-emption and purchase. So, in the summer of 1886, as the southern Interior baked in a stifling heat wave, Bayliff took a "leave of absence" from the Roper ranch and set out to find a place of his own. He rode through Clinton and crossed the Fraser River near the mouth of the Chilcotin River.

About 45 miles up the Chilcotin River, he came across the trading post operated by Tom Hance and Benjamin Franklin "Doc" English in the Chilcotin Valley. They encouraged Bayliff to settle in the area but warned him that the Chilcotin Natives were suspicious and unfriendly toward Whites. Hance suggested that Bayliff travel with a pack train that Hance was sending to Ulkacho, far to the northwest. Bayliff agreed and spent a good part of the summer travelling through the Chilcotin. When winter set in, he decided to stay and constructed a little log cabin overlooking the Chilcotin River and spent the winter alone there.

In the spring, Bayliff returned to an area he had been particularly impressed with, where Alexis Creek ran into the Chilcotin. When he got there, the Chilcotin River was in flood and overflowing its banks, creating a natural irrigation for the bottomlands on either side. After his years in the dry Kamloops country, Bayliff was impressed. He also saw the survey stakes that passed along the north bank of the Chilcotin, indicating that the Canadian Pacific Railway survey passed right through the area. Convinced that this location was the place for him to settle, Bayliff rode back to Cherry Creek Ranch to have a talk with William Roper.

He told Roper of his discovery of the ideal place to set up a cattle ranch and asked if Roper could help him get started. Roper had done very well by Hugh Bayliff; he had had free labour out of him for a year and, after that, he had had an excellent cowboy who was not only capable but also intelligent enough to be put in charge of things. While Roper was reluctant to see a good man go, he was smart enough to know that it was inevitable that Bayliff would want a place of his own. He made Bayliff a business proposition: he would provide Bayliff with 100 yearling heifers with the understanding that, in five years, Bayliff would return the original herd plus 50 percent of the increase. Bayliff thought about it. In five years, the chances were that the 100 heifers would produce over 400 calves and some of these calves would have produced their own offspring. That would still leave about 500 head for Bayliff after he had repaid Roper. It was not a bad deal and showed Roper's confidence that, under Bayliff's care, the original investment of 100 heifers would triple over the five-year term. The two men shook hands, and Bayliff had himself a herd.

He hired Shuswap Native cowboys to help drive his cattle to the Chilcotin. They were happy to drive the heifers to the Fraser River but, because Shuswaps were not welcome in Chilcotin Native territory, they refused to cross the river. They roped and branded all the cattle with Bayliff's Bar 11 brand and then left Bayliff alone to drive them to his property. Bayliff managed to get them to Alexis Creek, where he laid out his original pre-emption of 320 acres of the Chilanko Ranch.

The following year Bayliff met Norman Lee, who was also from England, and the two agreed to go into partnership. They pooled their money and purchased a team and wagon that they loaded with a few provisions to start a store to trade with the Chilcotin Natives. Lee pre-empted adjoining land to Bayliff and the two held their cattle in common. But by 1891 they had decided to part ways and broke up their partnership. To choose who would keep the land and cattle, they opted to flip a coin. Norman Lee won the toss and made a hurried trip back to England to try to secure enough money to buy out Bayliff. When he failed to do so, it was Bayliff's turn to try. He went back to Hereford and obtained the money to buy Lee's share of the ranch. Not only was he successful in finding the financing, he also found a bride, Gertrude Tyndle, a daughter of the editor of the *London Times*. The couple travelled together to the Chilcotin.

Despite their comfortable upbringing, the Bayliffs took to frontier life with enthusiasm. Gertrude was a skilled horsewoman and rode sidesaddle to help round up the cattle. She eventually purchased two racehorses that she entered in the yearly races at Becher's Prairie, near Riske Creek, often bringing home trophies. Since both Bayliffs were excellent riders, it was only natural that they would organize polo games among the local settlers.

Gertrude also had a basic knowledge of medicine, which she used to assist any neighbours in need, whether Native or white. While she was undisturbed by the roughest surroundings, she always insisted on dressing for dinner, which was served on a table set with the finest silver and china. The Bayliffs' son, Gabriel Thomas Lane Bayliff, known as Gay, was born in 1898 and was

Hugh (left) and Gertrude Bayliff in their parlour with their friend Tommy Young.

sent to Charterhouse School in England. At the outset of the First World War, Gay enlisted in the British Army and served in the Tank Corps. He was captured and served as a prisoner of war, only returning to Canada in 1919.

After the war, Hugh Bayliff purchased the original Tom Hance lumber mill and sawed boards to construct a big house on the ranch. He hired two young men whom Gay had met in England in the British Army, Stuart and Gordon MacKay, to hand plane the boards into a smooth finish. Their new home became the scene of Gabriel's wedding to Dorothy Dyson, from Kent, England, in 1923. The new couple left on their honeymoon in a 1917 Dodge, one of the few cars in the Chilcotin at the time.

When Hugh died in 1934, he left the 3,000-acre Chilanko Ranch to Gay, who continued raising Hereford cattle. The beautiful ranch and its fine herd of cattle were a legacy of one "mud pup" who worked out.

Lachlin McKinnon

Lachlin McKinnon's first job as a cowboy seemed like a breeze. All he had to do was take a herd of mares out to pasture and keep an eye on them all day long. His horse, named Sneezer, seemed content enough to stay close at hand and graze, so McKinnon found he could dismount, take the bridle off and tie his 40-foot lariat to the hackamore. Then, with the rope attached to his wrist to let him know if the horse had gone too far, he lay down in the prairie grass. All went well until Sneezer stepped over the rope and it came up between his legs. Like a shot, Sneezer was off through the herd with McKinnon bouncing along behind him over rocks and buffalo bones, up and down the undulating prairie. Eventually, Sneezer decided he wanted to return to the herd and slowed to turn around. This gave the dazed McKinnon enough slack to untie the rope from his wrist and limp back to the ranch buildings about two miles away. He was a sorry sight: his clothes in tatters; his hands, elbows and hips scratched and bleeding; but, other than that, intact. Arriving at the bunkhouse, he found a cowboy named Frank Smith, who used scissors and a razor to trim the loose skin off the torn and tattered parts of his body, all the time muttering, "Stupid greenhorn!" under his breath.

Lachlin McKinnon was born on a small farm near Durham in Grey County, Upper Canada, in 1865. His parents came from Scotland and carved a small farm out of the bush. To help supplement the meagre farm income, young McKinnon worked in lumber camps in northern Michigan. In 1886 he travelled on the Canadian Pacific Railway to Calgary in hopes of becoming a rancher in the new country that was opening up. Arriving in Calgary in the middle of March with $7.50, he immediately made the rounds of the nearby ranches looking for work. He could ride a horse and knew one end of a cow from the other, but he had absolutely no experience in handling cattle. Not surprisingly, none of the ranchers in the area were interested in hiring a greenhorn like him, so he spent his first two months in the North-West looking for any job that he could find. He managed to get a job working on the railway near Calgary but found he hated the work. He never returned for his second day and never picked up his one-dollar wages for the first. At that point, he considered walking back to Ontario along the train tracks, but a quick calculation of the time it would take discouraged him from that idea.[13]

In the middle of May he heard that General Strange of the Military Colonization Company (MCC) was looking for a flunky to help with the chores around the ranch and assist him in his daily activities. General Strange had recently broken his leg and needed help getting around. One of McKinnon's daily chores was to help Strange navigate from his opulent ranch house, called Strangemuir, to the Bow River and pour buckets of cold water over his injured leg. McKinnon also cut firewood, carried water and helped with general household chores—not exactly the general duties of a cowboy, but he performed them with diligence and quietly resigned himself to a life of drudgery.

It only took General Strange 17 days to see that McKinnon was no stranger to hard work. After that short apprenticeship, McKinnon was promoted to the rank of ranch hand at forty dollars a month and began to learn the cowboy way of life. His first job was to look after a herd of about 250 mares during the day and ensure that they all made it back to the corral in the evening. The mares had been brought into the home ranch for breeding purposes, and McKinnon worked with the stallion groom, Neil Neilson, in the evenings to bring the mares to the stallions.

McKinnon's incident with Sneezer happened about two weeks into his "career" as a cowboy and taught him the first of many valuable lessons: leave a horse's bridle on if you tether him. Riding back to the herd on a borrowed horse, McKinnon attempted to catch Sneezer, but the newfound freedom was too much for the experienced horse, and he refused to be caught. McKinnon cut off the small bunch of mares around Sneezer and drove them back to the corral, where he caught his recalcitrant horse, turned the borrowed one back and proceeded back to the mares. His lunch was still securely tied to the saddle, and everything was back to normal. McKinnon looked at his pocket watch and found it was just eight o'clock in the morning.

Once the mares were bred, McKinnon was given a job riding line at one of the MCC cow camps. But, in a few days, the regular cowboys returned from round-up and, by the law of the range, a more experienced cowboy was given the job. McKinnon, as a green hand, was assigned the job of helping MCC shareholder Arthur Goldfinch for the winter on his homestead, five miles up the Bow River. The winter of 1886–87 was a hard one, and the winter storms scattered the Goldfinch cattle far to the south. McKinnon was sent to the Little Bow to join the round-up and look out for the strayed cattle. When he rode up to the round-up camp, the round-up boss informed him that, according to the practice on round-ups, he needed two more horses if he was to take part and he had to pay a fee in order to be a "rep" (representative of a given ranch). McKinnon turned around and headed back to the Goldfinch ranch before returning and joining in the round-up.

McKinnon was rapidly learning the skills and techniques of the cowboy and beginning to gain confidence in his abilities. But he was still regarded as a greenhorn and, as such, available for any job around the ranch. His next job was back at the MCC, where General Strange had left as manager and a new foreman, Charlie Brown, was in charge of the work. Brown's first decision was to move the ranch headquarters to the extreme west side of the lease so that they would be closer to Calgary. McKinnon was put to work helping construct the new buildings and, by fall, they had finished a shack to live in, some corrals and a stable for horses. Brown had decided to expand the horse-raising operations in anticipation of an influx of homesteaders who would need good horses. He was also responsible for keeping expenses to a minimum and so laid off most of the cowboys, including McKinnon, for the winter.

McKinnon returned to Calgary and, as he put it, "put in time with 'Street and Walker.'" After putting in a few days digging a domestic well, he got a job in a logging camp for the winter. In the spring, he found employment with the CPR between Canmore and Banff, where he was able to spend Sundays at the hot springs. After a few more months with the CPR, he returned home to Ontario for a visit and didn't arrive back in Calgary until July.

Upon his return, he reluctantly agreed to go back to work for the MCC. He was used as a line rider, travelling across the huge lease of 70,000 acres from the new headquarters to the old ones. The original ranch house, Strangemuir, was on the far eastern side of the lease, now called the Lower Camp, and McKinnon rode to the extreme western side of the lease, keeping an eye on the range. He spent that winter alone at the Lower Camp "batching" for himself and living in the old bunkhouse, the frame ranch house being too hard to heat. It was a lonely time and, on occasion, McKinnon would stand on the steps of the house and shout as loudly as he could just to hear his echo. As spring approached, he would ride the surrounding range and keep an eye on cattle that were calving or that might be in trouble. On one particularly sunny day, he became completely snow-blinded. He let his horse find its way back to camp, then stayed indoors for a few days to allow his eyes to recover.

In the middle of April, McKinnon drew his winter wages of $280 and decided to head to Calgary for a few days off. But, on his way, he noticed smoke on the southern part of the MCC range and, concerned that it was prairie fire, he returned to headquarters. Charlie Brown told him to hurry to the Lower Camp and burn fire guards around the buildings and pasture. As the prairie fire raged toward him, he threw off his chaps and coat and, clutching a handful of matches, hastened off to burn his fire guards. Just as he finished, a few riders from headquarters arrived to see the huge fire hit the fire guards. The fire was diverted and continued on toward the Blackfoot reservation. The buildings and a few hundred acres of grass were saved but, in the process, McKinnon lost his winter's wages out of his pocket. The next morning, he headed back to headquarters:

> The range was a sorry looking sight; nothing but black ground; what little grass there was around the sloughs was all that was left for the stock to feed on till the new grass started to grow.
>
> I arrived back at headquarters from where I had started out a little more than twenty-four hours before, in such high spirits, and with my money all in my pocket. Now there was no use going to Calgary because I was flat broke so I started back at my old job of line riding.[14]

While riding line that summer, he was pushing some horses back to their home range when his horse, none other than old Sneezer, stepped in a badger hole and fell. McKinnon was thrown and broke his collarbone. Once again, Sneezer refused to be caught and McKinnon had to walk all the way back to the homestead of Alex Strange, the general's son. Thoroughly disgusted by the intrusion, Strange refused to go catch Sneezer but, instead, rode all the way to headquarters. A buckboard was dispatched and McKinnon was taken back to headquarters, where a doctor was sent for. The only one that could be found was Dr. Bannister, a horse doctor, who confirmed that the collarbone was broken. McKinnon was thrown back on the buckboard and taken to Calgary where, after some delay, his collarbone was set some 30 hours after it had been broken.

After a few days' convalescing in Calgary, McKinnon was taken back to the MCC headquarters. In the absence of Charlie Brown, who was away at round-up, McKinnon was asked to act as boss around the headquarters. Things had changed for the young greenhorn who had arrived at the MCC as a chore boy. He was recognized as a reliable hand and good cowboy.

Undeterred by his broken collarbone, he oversaw the branding of calves at the Lower Camp and helped drive them back to headquarters. In driving them into a corral, his horse slipped and, as McKinnon tried to protect his damaged collarbone, his left leg got caught under the horse and was broken in two places. The other cowboys rolled him onto a door and carried him to the bunkhouse. One of the cowboys headed for Calgary to fetch the doctor. On the way back in the dark, they got lost and didn't arrive until the next morning. McKinnon, however, was glad that this accident had only taken the doctor 12 hours to deal with. Frontier medicine was rough and ready at the best of times, and treatment for the broken leg was no exception. Because McKinnon's broken bones had pierced the skin, the doctor decided that the leg should not be put in a cast; instead, he built a box that the leg could be placed in and covered with sandbags to keep it stable. The contraption was effective in setting the leg bone, but the pressure on his heel caused secondary damage and slowed down the healing process.

McKinnon was laid up all season and only went back to work in December, returning to the Lower Camp for another lonely winter. Nonetheless, he was happy to be back at the work he loved and happy to be working at all. Most of the cowboys at the MCC and other ranches had been laid off for the winter. The winter of 1889–90 was a bitter one, and McKinnon watched in despair as the MCC cattle struggled through the snow. Many of them did not make it to spring.

In the spring, McKinnon was given the good news that he would be paid forty dollars a month for the time he had been laid up, and his medical fees would be covered. His good luck was compounded in April. He was riding near the fence where his fire break had been set when he spotted the remains of his wallet. Bills were scattered about and a few had been eaten by gophers, but he was able to recover about $260 of his lost $280.

Following this lucky find, McKinnon was sent to be the rep for the MCC in the High River round-up as part of the Bar U wagon under the leadership of Ebb Johnson, one of the best cowboys in the West. The round-up took seven weeks, and McKinnon arrived back at the MCC with 30 head of cattle. He spent the rest of the summer working on haying crews and breaking horses that were sold as remounts to the Mounted Police and as workhorses for homesteaders. The following winter he was back at the Lower Camp, looking after the cattle on that range.

By the spring of 1891 the MCC was in decline. The "shareholders" were taking up more and more of the land leased by the company, and those who had controlling interest in the ranch were located in Kingston, Ontario. McKinnon decided to quit while he could and, on May 15, 1891, went to

Lachlin and Sarah McKinnon in 1893. GLENBOW ARCHIVES NA-2198-1

work for the Canadian Agricultural Coal and Colonization Company, known as the CCC. The CCC had taken possession of the Powder River Cattle Company's lease and cattle in the Little Bow River area. McKinnon was sent out with top cowboy Bob Thornton to go through the round-up with the Oxley wagon and gather CCC cattle for slaughter in Calgary. They returned with 300 head of steers. McKinnon spent the rest of the summer with Thornton and continued to learn under the guidance of this top hand. In the fall, the two went to Willow Creek to rep on that round-up, spending the month of September gathering CCC cattle and driving them back to the home range. These round-ups put McKinnon in contact with the best cowboys of his day, and he realized that he could hold his own among them. His apprenticeship as a greenhorn was complete. In 1894, McKinnon was appointed the foreman of the CCC. He had risen to the top ranks of the working cowboy hierarchy and had proven his worth as a cattleman.

In 1893, McKinnon had married Sarah Whitney and the two had moved into the large farmhouse called Strangmuir, where McKinnon's cowboy life had started. In 1895 he took out a homestead about five miles from Strangmuir and built a house of his own. His initial purchase of a small herd of cattle with his very own LK brand continued to grow, as did his land holdings. McKinnon went on to be a successful rancher, horse breeder and grain farmer. He passed away in 1948.

Greenhorns to Cowboys

The "greenhorns" who arrived on the western Canadian ranching frontier did not stay green for long. They either adapted to the way of life and made the best of it, or went home. Those who stayed usually showed an enthusiasm for the cowboy way of life that was only matched by their love of the country. They responded to the challenges of survival and of learning a new business. Most often, they learned from the experienced cowboys—the "top hands"—who ended up as their informal teachers. These top hands were the products of years on the ranching frontier and tended to prefer, and to stay loyal to, the techniques and equipment that they had learned with. Bob Newbolt learned how to stick with a bucking horse from a Mexican cowboy who probably got his training west of the Rockies. Another young Englishman, Ted Hills, wrote from a round-up camp near Fort Macleod in 1885 that a man named John Ware had taught him how to drive a herd of horses across a river.[15] Ware had learned his trade on the cattle drives north from Texas. Mike Herman, who became one of the best ropers in the North-West, was called the Emerson Kid because he learned his skills from George Emerson.

By the time the ranching industry had become established in southern Alberta, there were so many techniques and varieties of equipment to choose from that a young cowboy would most likely pick what his peers were using or what was readily available. Early photographs show that the greenhorns probably looked the part of the cowboy long before they acted the part. Whatever they wore and how they roped a calf made little difference to their employers as long as they accomplished the job. And, in most cases, the newcomers soon developed into seasoned cowhands. Most went on to own their own ranches and to make a contribution to the ranching industry and way of life.

Chapter Seven

THE FORGOTTEN COWBOYS

Shortly after his arrival in Canada, the Virginian cowboy Ebb Johnson stopped at the Quorn Ranch on the south side of Sheep Creek, where a horse-breeding program was producing some fine mounts. After admiring the famous stallion Eagle's Plume, Johnson went up to the house for dinner. The first man to sit down for dinner was John Ware, the well-known black cowboy. Johnson's Virginian upbringing overcame him, and he left the table in disgust, revealing a strong streak of racism that had not been extinguished by his time in the racially and culturally mixed society of the American West.

There is something basic to human nature that makes us look down on those who look different from ourselves, particularly when it comes to race. When Northern Europeans set forth to colonize the world, Caucasians looked down on the darker-skinned races of Africa, Asia and the Americas. As the Europeans exerted their cultural dominance through force of arms and advanced technology, their attitude was one of superiority. Discrimination against African Americans, Mexicans, Chinese and Native peoples in western North America—a society where equality of opportunity was considered to be the norm—was widespread. Where different language speakers from Europe were begrudgingly accepted into the melting pot, probably because they looked no different from the dominant English speakers, the same could not be said for those who "looked" different. And, since the politically dominant Whites were most often the writers of early history, the story of the significant role that the Native people—and, to a lesser extent, African Americans and Mexicans—played in the development of the American and Canadian West has only recently begun to emerge.

While the Canadian experience was not unlike that of the United States, there were differences. Some racial minorities were more accepted than others and the situation in frontier British Columbia was different from that in the North-West. Discrimination was strongest against those "minorities" that were present in greater numbers, indicating that prejudice was driven to some extent by a jealousy or resentment that these "others" were taking too large a share of the available resources. In British Columbia, there were thousands of Chinese in the mining areas, and they were therefore considered to be the greatest threat. Only a limited number of Blacks were in the colony, and there was a greater tolerance toward them, except by Whites from the American South. The same applied to the small number of Mexicans, who dominated the occupation of packing much-needed supplies into the isolated mining areas. The Native people also found a niche for themselves as cattle drovers on the frontier, something that contributed to their being accepted in the cattle trade. However, their acceptance by the ranching industry did not mean that they were accepted by society in general.

Across the Rocky Mountains, in the North-West, the Chinese were few in number and never considered a threat. The Native people, however, were feared and distrusted and, while some ranchers maintained good relations with their Native neighbours, most preferred to keep them at a distance.

On the Alberta ranching frontier, the Native people were marginalized and took years to be accepted as working cowboys. Blacks, however, were accepted, even though the term "nigger" was invariably applied to them. Later writers would insist that the term "was a purely descriptive nickname such as Shorty or Red,"[1] but it nonetheless indicated in no uncertain manner a person who was "different" from the European establishment.

For individuals of Native, African or Mexican background to make it in the largely White-dominated frontier took an extremely strong character and an ability to ignore much of what was directed their way. That some succeeded in rising to the top of the cowboy profession despite the discrimination is a testament to their strong personalities and physical abilities.

Natives

As we have previously seen, fully one-half of the labour force driving cattle into the Colony of British Columbia during the gold rush days was Native, primarily Yakima, Palouse, Cayuse and Umatilla. Once these Native drovers were finished driving the cattle north, they inevitably returned to their homes. But, during the years from 1858 to 1868, Native drovers firmly established themselves as a significant part of the labour force in British Columbia.

Perhaps the most significant contributing factor in the relatively easy assimilation of the Native people into the ranching community was that language was not a handicap, as it was east of the Rockies. Almost all the Natives and Whites spoke the trade language, Chinook, which had developed during fur-trade times in the Pacific Northwest. This made basic communication possible. So, if a trail boss were to say "Mamook kishkish moosmoos kah cole chako," everyone in his party, whether Native, European or, for that matter, Chinese, would know he meant, "Drive the cattle north." Chinook was the common language of the different races in British Columbia right up until the early 1900s. In fact, it was said that "Early British Columbia cowboys were masters of three languages, English, Chinook and profane."

This bridging of the language barrier was the most important factor in the acceptance of the Natives as drovers. The ability to communicate can break down many of the prejudices that so often divide races. The acceptance that came from easy communication, combined with the sometimes grudging admission that the Natives were superb horsemen, led to the tension between the Native people and the white intruders being much less than it would be on the east side of the Rockies when that area came to be settled.

In the earliest days of ranching in the Colony of British Columbia, Natives formed a majority of the labour force. John Fall Allison used Similkameen Native cowboys to help him drive cattle from Princeton to Hope from the early 1860s, and most of the ranchers in the Okanagan and Nicola valleys employed Natives for various aspects of ranch work, from handling cattle to assisting in haying. In almost all these cases, the Natives were already living on reserves close to the rancher. It made sense for the white ranchers to put aside their racial prejudices and look to the nearby reserves for their source of labour.

Also in the Similkameen Valley, Barrington Price used Okanagan and Similkameen Natives on his ranch near present-day Keremeos. One of the Native cowboys he hired in 1872 was named Susap, also known as Yankin or Silitoe. Susap was an Okanagan, one of three brothers who became well known for their honesty and ability to handle livestock. He soon showed himself particularly talented at handling horses, which attracted the attention of John Carmichael Haynes, who had a large ranch near Osoyoos Lake. Susap took over the care and training of Haynes's large herd of horses and proved he could break and handle even the most difficult. His skill with horses made Susap an excellent packer, and he was entrusted to take pack trains over the Dewdney Trail to Hope to purchase supplies for the isolated Okanagan Valley. In 1880 he became the guide and packer for Bishop and Mrs. A.W. Silitoe over the Dewdney Trail. He was given the name Silitoe in commemoration of that trip. While many would consider being named after a "more important" White a slight, Susap accepted the name as an honour for the care he had shown to the well-loved bishop. Susap worked for ranches all over the South Okanagan and lived to be 106 years old.

The acceptance of Natives took another form in the predominantly male frontier. Many of the earliest ranchers in British Columbia married Native women, and the children of these mixed-race marriages worked on the ranches of the Interior. The young men of mixed blood proved to be among the best working cowboys in British Columbia as the ranching industry grew and prospered among the bunchgrass ranges of the Interior. One of the best of these children was Antoine Allen. He was born in 1855 in the Willamette River Valley in Oregon Territory, the son of a white miner and his Native wife. In 1864 he travelled with Jerome and Thaddeus Harper on one of their cattle drives to British Columbia and remained with them for many years afterward. They taught him the cattle trade, and he worked for them on their ranches west of Kamloops and in the Cariboo.

Allen was one of the cowboys on the famous drive that Newman Squires conducted for Thaddeus Harper in 1876. Allen and a number of well-known BC cowboys started the drive in May in the Dog Creek and Alkali Lake areas and worked their way to Kamloops and through the Okanagan to the United States. The cattle were forced to swim the Columbia River at the mouth of the Okanagan, and from there the drive proceeded south through the Grande Coulee and crossed the Snake River near Fort Walla Walla. By then the drive had been going for almost seven months, and Newman Squires decided to winter the cattle. Only a few men remained to winter-herd the cattle, and Allen returned to British Columbia with many of the other cowboys. He remained in the Kamloops area: in 1881 he was working for James Todd on the South Thompson River east of Kamloops, and some years later appears to have worked for Thaddeus Harper on the Gang Ranch.

In 1910 the 55-year-old Allen took part in another major cattle drive. Ulysses Campbell, son of Kamloops area rancher Lewis Campbell, recruited him in Kamloops to be one of the head cowboys in a drive to supply beef to the construction camps of the Grand Trunk Pacific and Pacific Great Eastern railways (now the BC Rail). Pat Burns had secured the contract and, after an experimental drive from the Chilcotin to Hazelton led by Joe Paine had proven successful, Burns had contracted Ulysses Campbell to take a series of drives north. Allen and the other cowboys took the train to Ashcroft to collect the saddle and pack horses that Burns had sent from Alberta. The cowboys spent a couple of weeks gathering cattle from all over the Chilcotin and assembled a herd of 800 steers at Riske Creek. The steers were carefully inspected and 300 of them culled from the herd. On May 10, the drive of 500 select steers left the Chilcotin. It took eight days to reach Quesnel. They then battled through another 500 miles (about 800 kilometres) of brush and mudholes to reach Hazelton, where Burns and Company had a slaughterhouse. That year, Allen accompanied another three drives of cattle, taking a total of 2,000 head to Hazelton. He remained involved in the drives until 1913, by which time a total of 12,000 head of Chilcotin cattle had been driven to market.

Allen was 57 years old when he married Catherine Frise in Kamloops. After he completed his work for Burns and Company, he and his wife settled down and lived in the Kamloops area near their three daughters. Allen died

Native cowboys branding at the Alkali Lake Ranch, BC. Note the traditional braids worn by two of the Native cowboys. MUSEUM OF THE CARIBOO CHILCOTIN, WILLIAMS LAKE

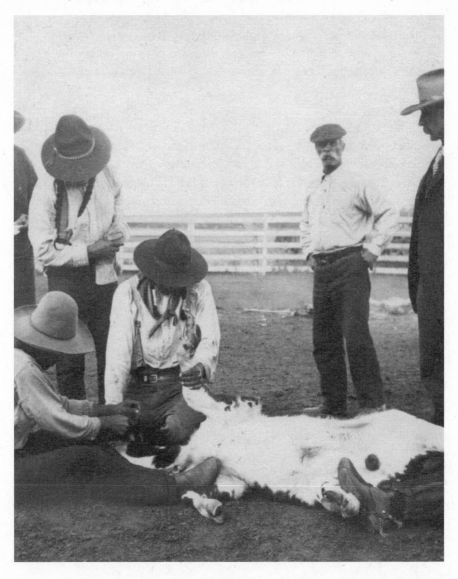

in 1935 and was recognized as one of the true pioneer cowboys who saw the cattle industry grow and change in the Interior of British Columbia.

Native cowboys' contribution to the development of ranching in British Columbia was significant, and they continue to be an important component of ranching in the Interior, despite the discrimination to the Native people in other areas of employment. A look at the ranches in the Interior reveals that Native cowboys still play a major role in the ranching industry of the province.

Things unfolded rather differently in Alberta. Across the Rocky Mountains on the plains, the Blackfoot were the People of the Horse. Their stories tell of the origin of the horse:

> The Blackfoot tell of an orphan boy from their community who made a long and difficult journey. At its culmination he dove into a lake. There a spirit chief helped him to retrieve an elk-dog which he brought back to his people.[2]

By the middle of the 1800s, the Blackfoot Confederacy was regarded as the most powerful military force on the northwestern plains. With the use of the horse, their territory was greatly expanded. There is no question that the horse played a special role in the life of the Plains peoples but, when the buffalo began to be hunted out, the Canadian government saw the potential for cattle raising among the tribes of the plains. In 1877, Treaty Number Seven stipulated:

> And further, Her Majesty agrees that the said Indians shall be supplied as soon as convenient, after any Band shall make due application therefor [sic], with the following cattle for raising stock, that is to say: for every family of five persons, and under, two cows; for every family of more than five persons, and less than ten persons, three cows, for every family of over ten persons, four cows; and every Head and Minor Chief, and every Stony Chief, for the use of bands, one bull.[3]

David Laird, who was Lieutenant Governor and Special Indian Commissioner, reported on the treaty negotiations:

> The number of cattle promised may appear large; but when it is considered that cows can be readily purchased at Fort McLeod [sic] for twenty or twenty-five dollars per head, and their delivery to the Indians will cost an inconsiderable sum, the total expense of supplying the articles promised by this treaty will, I am convinced, cost less than those under either Treaty Number Four or Number Six.[4]

Unfortunately, the government assumed that there was plenty of time for these obligations to be met and did not supply the cattle as promised. As the buffalo disappeared in the late 1870s, the starving Natives had little recourse but to steal the cattle belonging to the few white ranchers in the North-West. This brought about an animosity on the part of the ranchers that effectively eliminated the possibility of their hiring Natives for ranching activities, even though the Natives were incredible horsemen and would have taken little time to adapt to the ranching way of life. And so the acceptance of the Natives as ranch hands evolved slowly on the prairies. Another factor was the language barrier that could not be bridged with a jargon like Chinook, as well as American prejudice against the Natives that came north with the cattle from Montana. This prejudice was fuelled by the continuing battles on the northern plains between the Native people and United States Cavalry, which the media had made much of. While the treaty with the Sioux and Cheyenne in 1876 placed the Natives on reserves and opened the vast region north of the Platte River and east of the Bozeman Trail, Montana cattlemen regarded the Natives with fear and suspicion.

As the ranching frontier advanced into southern Alberta, Native or mixed-blood riders were occasionally hired by ranchers for round-up or branding activities. But language difficulties and prejudice continued to be a barrier to their wholesale entrance into the workforce. Nonetheless, as the years went on, Native cowboys could be seen on many of the ranches, particularly for seasonal work or specialized activities. Typical was a Blackfoot named Cupa-nis-ti, nicknamed "Cupi," who was regularly hired to help guide cattle across the Bow River. Another early Native cowboy was Joe Red Blanket, also a Blackfoot, who worked in the 1890s as a night herder and later as a cook's helper. Red Blanket eventually owned the largest herd of cattle on the Blackfoot Reserve and established the Teepee Ranch.

In the early 1880s the government established herds of cattle on the reserves in fulfillment of treaty obligations and hired Natives to take care of the stock. Soon, many of them began to dress in cowboy attire while retaining many elements of their traditional culture, particularly their long braids. By the turn of the century, ranching was flourishing on the reserves, especially the Blood Reserve, home of men like Bobtail Chief, Heavy Head and Bottle, who were experienced cowboys and successful ranchers. The Blood Reserve had an estimated 15,000 head of cattle before the turn of the century. Later, residential school graduates like Cecil Tallow and Chris Shade started as cowboys and became successful ranchers.

By the time of the First World War, Native cowboys were working on ranches throughout southern Alberta and, most visibly, Natives were excelling in the rodeo events being held in the ranching community. The earliest "hero" was Tom Three Persons, born on the Blood Reserve, who became the bucking horse champion at the first Calgary Stampede in 1912. Three Persons was the only Canadian to win a top award, and he became an instant celebrity. His success paved the way for Native cowboys in the rodeo world and, to a lesser extent, on the ranches of the Canadian prairies.

Blacks

In 1858, Governor James Douglas of British Columbia accepted nearly 800 free Blacks who were looking to escape the oppressive racial conditions of San Francisco for a new life on Vancouver Island. Governor Douglas invited them to settle in British Columbia, and these pioneers enriched the political, religious and economic life of the colony. While many of these newcomers became involved in mining activities in the Cariboo and other goldfields, there is no record of any of them working on ranches or as ranchers. While there was a strong contingent of US Southerners in British Columbia at the time, few incidents of racial prejudice against the Blacks are recorded. Unfortunately, as time passed, racial antagonism grew and, after the American Civil War, many Blacks returned to the United States, and the Black population in British Columbia fell to less than 300.[5]

In 1884 the remarkable John Fremont Smith pre-empted land on Louis Creek, which runs into the North Thompson River. Fremont Smith was born on the island of St. Croix (then the Danish West Indies). As a young man he earned scholarships to a school in Copenhagen and then to the Jesuit College in Liverpool, England, where he also learned the boot-making trade. After travelling in Europe, Peru and the United States, he arrived in Victoria, British Columbia, in 1872 and set up a shoe store. He spent one season in the Cariboo goldfields and then returned to Victoria, where he married a black woman named Mary Miller in 1877.

In 1881 the couple moved to New Westminster and later to Lytton, where Fremont Smith was active in the community and served as a juror before Judge Matthew Baillie Begbie. This indicates that Blacks were not barred from holding public office or from public institutions and enjoyed legal and political equality with other citizens. In Lytton, Freemont Smith met James B. Leighton, who recommended he move to Kamloops, which was destined to become a Canadian Pacific Railway centre. Fremont Smith bought land from fellow Black Jesse Lee Smith and built a small house and shoe store in Kamloops. He also pre-empted land up the North Thompson River and started a ranch, but his commitment to ranching was limited. He used the ranch as a base from which he did a lot of prospecting. He opened a store at Louis Creek and then, leaving his wife to run the store, he cut a trail through to Adams Lake, collecting mineral samples along the way.

Fremont Smith was appointed the first postmaster at Louis Creek and, during his time there, became a freelance journalist, contributing to the *Cincinnati Tribune*, the *Plain Dealer* and the *Detroit Times*. He made an expedition to the upper reaches of the North Thompson, where he prospected and established a mine that he later sold to an American company. After that, he stayed close to his cattle ranch, where he also experimented with a variety of crops and promoted the valley to newcomers. After his house at Louis Creek burned down in 1898, he and his family moved to Kamloops, where he was variously a businessman, alderman, city assessor and Indian agent. He also helped organize the Agricultural Association, the Conservative Association and the Board of Trade in Kamloops. However, he did not forget his ranching career and was one of the promoters of the first Kamloops Bull Sale. He died in October 1934, having on the same day written an article on early settlement for the *Kamloops Sentinel*. John Fremont Smith was a pioneer in the true sense, leaving his mark on ranching, business and mining in his adopted country.

If there is little evidence of black cowboys in British Columbia, there is ample in the North-West. Because the cattle and many of the cowboys in the early North-West came up from the United States in the years following the Civil War, thousands of emancipated Blacks went to work on ranches in south and west Texas and subsequently rode the cattle trails northward. Many black cowboys were involved in the beginnings of ranching on the northern plains, but far and away the most famous was John Ware. While only in Canada from 1882 until his death in 1905, more has been written about him and his 23-year career than about any other cowboy of the time.

John Ware was born a slave somewhere near Fort Worth, Texas, in about 1840 and learned the cattle trade from an early age. Legend has it that he worked on a ranch with 15,000 head of cattle and 5,000 horses.[6] After the Civil War, when the cattle industry spread northward with hundreds of thousands of longhorn cattle, Ware travelled north with it along the Chisholm Trail. He also seems to have driven cattle along the Oregon Trail and spent some time in eastern Oregon, where he came in contact with cowboys from California.[7]

In the spring of 1882, Ware was in Lost River, Idaho, with his friend Bill Moodie when Moodie was approached by Tom Lynch, who was contracted to drive a herd of 3,000 head of cattle north for the North-West Cattle Company. Moodie suggested that he hire his friend Ware, and Lynch, unaware of Ware's abilities, agreed that he could join the drive. And here the legend begins. According to the story later told, Ware was given an old plug of a horse and a dilapidated saddle and put on night herding, prompting him to request "a little better saddle and a little worse horse." The trail boss, Abe Cotterell, convinced he had a greenhorn on his hands, provided Ware with a better saddle and a horse known for meanness and grit, one that had bucked off the best riders on the cattle drive. Of course, Ware rode the outlaw horse "from ears to tail." From then on, Ware was given more and more respect and responsibility on the drive.[8]

The cattle drive, which started in May, did not reach the Canadian border until September. From there, the cattle were driven to the North-West Cattle Company home site, from then on known as the Bar U Ranch. Abe Cotterell and Tom Lynch told manager Fred Stimson about Ware's ability to ride horses and herd cattle, and Stimson offered him a job on the Bar U. Ware, impressed with the beautiful country around the Highwood River, agreed to stay. Stimson also offered Moodie a job, but it involved cutting timber for the ranch buildings that were being constructed at the home site. Moodie replied, "If I can't do the job on a horse, I won't do it" and rode back to the United States.

While working for the Bar U, Ware was widely admired, not just for his ability to sit a horse but also for his genial nature and courage. His simple, open nature prompted many of the cowboys to pull pranks on him, but Ware gave as good as he got. During the 1883 round-up, 17-year-old Ed McArthur was night rider and pulled a joke on Ware. The next day Ware quietly stole into the tent where McArthur was sleeping and tied his foot to a tent stake. Then he made a racket and banged on the side of the tent shouting "Whoa!" McArthur, thinking he was about to be trampled by a bronc, jumped out of his bedroll, got about 10 feet from the tent and was yanked flat on his face.

While riding with the Bar U on round-up, Ware's strength and horsemanship were demonstrated when he came to the rescue of newcomer Frank Bedingfeld. Bedingfield was wearing a pair of loose leather chaps while they were gathering cattle for branding. His bronc began to buck and threw him out of the saddle, hooking his chap leg on the horn of the saddle and leaving him hanging upside down within inches of the horse's hooves. Ware, who was some distance away supervising the wagons, turned his horse and ran it right into the bronc. Loosening his feet from the stirrups, he threw himself on the bronc's neck, letting his own horse run out from under him. He then grabbed the bronc's bridle with one hand and lifted Bedingfield back onto the bronc with the other hand.[9]

Ware had been working for the Bar U for two years when he was approached by John Barter, foreman of the Quorn Ranch on Sheep Creek, which had been established by the Quorn Hunt Club of Leicestershire, England. Although the Quorn ran a large herd of cattle, the primary purpose of the ranch was to raise hunting horses for the sport in England. To achieve this, they imported 210 Irish hunter-type mares and 20 fine thoroughbred and Cleveland Bay stallions. John readily accepted the job of caring for the horse herd and breaking the young horses. During the round-up of 1885, the *Macleod Gazette* described Ware:

> John is not only one of the best natured and most obliging fellows in the country, but he is one of the shrewdest cow men, and the man is considered pretty lucky who has him to look after his interest. The horse is not running on the prairie which John cannot ride.[10]

Ware was a bear of a man, standing six foot three inches in his stockings and weighing well over 200 pounds. He was also agile and quick as a cat. He could hang by his arms from the corral gate crossbar and drop onto a horse as it passed through the gate. He broke every one of the big hunting horses that came his way and earned a reputation as the best bronc rider in the North-West. The English members of the Quorn Hunt Club who came to visit the ranch were delighted to meet Ware and encouraged him to ride with them on their "hunts" after coyotes or jackrabbits across the countryside with their pack of hounds.

The cowboys at the Quorn Ranch were very proud of Ware's incredible strength and often presented him with tests to see just how strong he was. On one occasion, they arranged a challenge between Ware and another hefty cowboy. The first lift using hay hooks on a weigh scale was a draw, so the beam was set at 200 pounds. Ware lifted with all his might and straightened out the hay hooks. The opponent did not bother to proceed.

A.E. Cross wrote about Ware's participation in the 1887 round-up, describing him as "A splendid cow hand and the greatest broncho rider in the West. It was like a snubbing post when a broncho [*sic*] came up against the end of John's lariat, a beautiful roper and a perfect horseman." Later in the round-up, Cross was having a particularly hard time staying on a grey horse in his string:

> I never shall forget when riding this grey one, one day having a bad time to keep in the saddle, the same old . . . John rode up saying, "let me ride dat hoss." You bet I changed on to his gentle one in record time saying,

"you can ride him or kill him if you like." You never saw anything more astonished than that horse was. He was spun round like a top, made to stop, lope, trot, walk and was mighty glad to do anything that old John could think of doing.[11]

Like many working cowboys, Ware dreamt of having his own ranch, and by 1888 he had saved enough to locate on land on the north fork of Sheep Creek, where he turned out a small herd of cattle. Ware had previously registered his 9999 ("four nines") brand and happily applied it to his little herd on his own property. When he was established on his ranch and had constructed the necessary cabin and outbuildings, Ware met and courted an attractive black woman, Mildred Lewis, whose father, Daniel Lewis, had come west from Whitby, Ontario, and taken out a homestead in the Shepherd district. Although Mildred was deathly afraid of cattle and horses, the two were married in 1892 in Calgary's First Baptist Church. The *Calgary Tribune* reported on the wedding and commented that "probably no man in the district has a greater number of warm-personal friends, than the groom."[12]

Mildred settled into ranch life as best she could. Although she never rode a horse, she did eventually learn to milk a cow. But she loved her home and always welcomed visitors. As her husband was illiterate, she wrote all the correspondence and kept the books for the ranch. By 1902 the Wares had five children, and John was beginning to be concerned about the encroachment of settlers on grazing land in the area. Like many other ranchers, he decided to move out onto the open prairie to carry on his ranching endeavours as there was more unoccupied government land available for grazing leases. The family sold the Sheep Creek property and moved to the short-grass range country along the Red Deer River east of Calgary. To drive his herd of cattle to the new ranch, Ware had to take them through Calgary and was informed that he could not use the east Calgary bridge to cross his cattle as there was a City ordinance forbidding the use of the bridge by cattle. Ware, never one to let regulations get in the way, was up at dawn and had his cattle across the bridge before the City authorities were out of bed.

Ware constructed a log cabin on the river flat along the Red Deer River but, after waking up to knee-deep water in the house one spring morning, he rebuilt up the bank overlooking the river. The family was not to enjoy their new home for long. Mildred Ware died of typhoid and pneumonia in April 1905, and most of the children were sent to live with relatives in Blairmore, Alberta.

Opposite: John and Mildred Ware with their children Robert and Nettie. GLENBOW ARCHIVES NA-263-1

That fall, John Ware was attempting to cut out a steer from the herd when his horse stumbled in a badger hole and fell on him. Before his 11-year-old son, Bob, could get help, Ware was dead. His funeral in Calgary was attended by all the old-timers from the ranching country of southern Alberta.

Green Walters was another black man who had a significant impact on the ranching country. Like John Ware, he came north with one of Tom Lynch's trail herds in 1883. While not a proficient cowboy, he was valued as a cook and worked for the Oxley, the Bar U and the CC Ranch at various times. While on the CC Ranch, he was allowed to accumulate a small herd of his own, on which he used the Yoke brand.

In 1886, when J.L. Douglas visited the CC Ranch, he took a trip to visit George Emerson, but unfortunately Emerson was out on a round-up. Green Walters was staying at Emerson's place at the time, and Douglas described him as:

> a sort of general servant, who is about the most original specimen I have ever come across; he is a very little fellow and built in the most extraordinary way imaginable; he sang plantation and other minstrel songs all the time and kept us in roars of laughter and the more we laughed the funnier he became; he would be worth a fortune to anyone who could transplant him home as a music hall artiste.[13]

Fred Ings tells the story of Walters, while he was cook at the High River Horse Ranch, stopping by one cold winter evening on his way to a distant ranch. Walters seemed to be well bundled-up against the cold, and Ings invited him to stay for the night as his bunkhouse was vacant. Over supper, Walters told how he was working for a bunch of Englishmen who kept getting parcels of clothing from home. These contained, among other things, clothing of all sorts, none of which the Englishmen would wear, preferring to look the part of cowboys. When Walters headed to the bunkhouse for the night, Ings followed at a distance, intrigued by Walter's appearance. He seemed to have on so many clothes that his usually round shape was even rounder. When Ings burst into the bunkhouse, he saw in an instant that Walters was layered in brightly coloured silk pyjamas that he had appropriated from the Englishmen.[14]

Walters was a great round-up cook and ran a tight wagon. One day the night herder complained to Tom Lynch that the cook was not getting up early enough for him. Lynch replied, " For G—'s sake do not tell the old man this. He will not allow us any sleep." Sure enough, from then on, Green roused the cowboys at 4:00 AM.[15] A.E. Cross, who recounted this story, went on to tell of Walters:

Old Green was a very emotional religious old [Black] in his own particular way. Some of the boys would start him up with his camp meeting songs, the favourite one being "Climbin' up de Golden Stairs." He would start with a low note, gradually getting higher and higher until his emotional feeling would overcome him. With tears streaming down his cheeks he wound up exhausted. The old man was not what you would call a methodical or clean cook. One minute his hands were covered with dough, mixing up the baking powder biscuits, the next cutting beef or washing dried apples or prunes, but the prairie was clean and pure and it was all right anyway, the grub tasted good after a long ride.[16]

Around 1890 Walters settled along the North Fork of the Highwood River, where he had previously cut logs and rails for the Bar U Ranch. He brought his few head of cattle with him and was getting a good start on a herd when he badly froze his feet and had to have most of his toes amputated. This made it impossible to walk and put an end to his ranching career. Discouraged, he sold out and returned south to Kansas, where he spent the rest of his days.

There were other black cowboys on the Canadian ranges, of course. Tom Rengald was a cowboy for the Chipman Ranch near Pincher Creek, where he was considered a top hand. Felix Luttrell, who was nicknamed "Big Enough" because of his huge size, rode for the Little Bow River round-up. In 1908, Jim Whitford, a black cowboy who worked for the Hyssop Ranch, was struck by lightning and killed. He was described as "a hard-working fellow and consistently steady in his habits" who had ridden for several outfits in the Lethbridge area.[17] No doubt there are many more black cowboys whose lives and exploits are not recorded in the historical records. Unfortunately, in an industry where cowboys tended to be a transient lot, there were many who came and went without leaving any traces.

Mexicans

Although the influence of the Mexican *vaquero* was felt as far north as British Columbia and Alberta, very few cowboys of Mexican origin found their way to the northern ranges.

One notable exception to this was in the area of horse or mule packing. The Spanish and Portuguese had brought this form of transporting goods to the New World and, in mountainous areas where water or wagon transport was impossible, packing supplies by horse or mule was widespread. Packing was the most important form of transport in Mexico, Peru, Bolivia and southern Brazil and, when the United States conquered the Spanish-speaking southwest, packing remained the most effective form of transport. In the early years of the gold rush in British Columbia, most of the packers were Mexicans, with some Chileans and other Spanish Americans.[18] In June 1859 the secretary of the British Boundary Commission commented in his diary, "You must first of all understand that all of our muleteers & packers are Mexicans."[19] A year later, in June 1860, the Anglican Bishop of Victoria, the Reverend George Hills, travelling from Yale to Lillooet, recorded talking "to Mexicans who are the muleteers of the country."[20] In the frontier, where non-Europeans were marginalized, the other minority groups were soon to take advantage of packing as a way to make a living. The Native people of British Columbia soon learned the art of packing, as did the Chinese. David Wiggins, an African American who had learned the art of packing in California, worked on the frontier. But perhaps the most long-lived and best-known packer was a European named Jean Caux, a native of the French Pyrenees who began his life in British Columbia as a gold miner.

The make-up of the workforce is in no way surprising. The Mexicans had dominated packing in both California and the Oregon Territory during the gold rush, and many men simply moved north when the British Columbia boom began. The size of the new finds in the Pacific Northwest attracted packers directly from Spanish America. Pancho Gutierrez and his two brothers arrived at Victoria by steamer from Mexico.[21] Some of the men did not stay long or did not survive, but others contracted a union with Native women and stayed in British Columbia. The descendants of Manuel Alvarez, Jesús García, Pancho Gutierrez and José Maria Tresierra—to name but four of these early packers—can be found across the province to this day.

Jesús García was born and raised in Mexico and, in the first years of the gold rush, worked for packer Raphael Carranza. After two years in British Columbia, he approached his boss to let him know he was thinking of buying a few mules and starting business for himself. Carranza, in a generous gesture, offered to sell him half of his mule train. The two shook hands and the deal was completed. Through hard work and careful management of his resources, García made an excellent living. Like many of the Mexican packers in the early 1860s, García would winter his mules and horses at the forks of the Nicola River, the first inhabitants of what was to become the town of Merritt. García spent his summers packing to the Cariboo gold mines, but he also began to accumulate a few head of cattle and keep them on the excellent bunchgrass ranges of the Nicola Valley. In the early 1870s he established a ranch, which he operated successfully.

Emanuel Barcelo took the same route in establishing his ranch in the Similkameen Valley. He was born in Guaymas, Mexico, and worked for a time as a farmer and woodcutter before finding work as a packer in the California goldfields. His work eventually brought him to British Columbia, where he ran his own pack train to the Cariboo and over the Dewdney Trail from Hope to Osoyoos, and Wild Horse Creek in the Kootenays. By 1879 he had saved enough to establish himself as a cattle rancher and squatted on land in the Similkameen Valley. That year he also married Lucy Hunter, the daughter of Englishman Henry Hunter, a gold miner whom Barcelo had met in his packing business. Then he returned to Mexico, where he bought cattle, which he then proceeded to drive overland all the way to the Similkameen, trading with miners along the way. He arrived back in British Columbia, and his land acquisition was accepted by the government in 1885 as it did not interfere with the Similkameen Native Band reserve. Aside from raising large herds of cattle that he drove to market over the Dewdney Trail to Hope, Barcelo specialized in raising light horses for riding and stagecoach purposes.[22]

One notable, if short-lived, Mexican cowboy who found his way to the North-West was Jesús Lavarro. He was born in Mexico, but his family moved to Idaho when Jesús was a boy. He had grown up on horseback and had learned the cattle business in Idaho. After two severe winters had devastated the Cochrane Ranch herd west of Calgary, leaving about 4,000 out of the 12,000 head that had been purchased over the course of the previous two years, the owners decided to move their lease farther south to the Waterton Lakes area. The cattle drives of 1881 and 1882 had pushed the cattle from Idaho and Montana at a much too rapid rate for them to maintain their health and weight and, when winter came, they could not survive. The Cochrane Ranch Company, determined not to repeat this mistake, hired the best cattleman they could find, Jesús Lavarro, to take the remaining cattle to the new ranch site in good condition. However, the Company had not bargained on frontier prejudices being a problem.

Lavarro was referred to as "Ca Sous" or "Qusoose" because the English-speaking cowboys could not wrap their tongues around the Spanish pronunciation of Jesús (hay-soose). Even though his credentials as a cowboy were impeccable, the western frontier prejudice against darker-skinned races made it difficult for him from the start to maintain authority. The fact that he was travelling with his Peigan Native wife, Almost an Owl Woman, and their nine-year-old son, Joe, didn't help matters. But Lavarro did what he was paid to do: get the cattle to their destination in good condition. Despite the undisguised attitude of the cowboys, he maintained order and kept the drive moving at a slow, steady pace.

Frank Lawrence, who was on that cattle drive, reminisced:

The Cochrane foreman Qusoose, a half-breed Mexican and in many respects a remarkable ranch hand as a working stockman probably had few equals in the country. He took charge of the final round up and went south with the cattle. The men did not appreciate working under a Mexican but nevertheless what Qusoose said went, and he made good stockmen out of them . . . All had come in from the nor'western ranges but Raikes, Smith and myself. They drifted in from across the border with the various herds and remained for the bigger wages that were paid in the new country.[23]

The drive was accompanied by a chuckwagon that travelled ahead with the extra saddle horses to set up camp before the crew arrived. Lavarro's handling of the drive south was a textbook example of the most effective way to handle cattle on a long drive.

On the drive south we moved slowly, not averaging ten miles a day. We divided into two parties, the first rode out of camp to herd from sundown to midnight, slowly bunching up the herd as they settled for the night. At midnight one rode into the camp and roused the relief; they in their turn now held the cattle until dawn when they would be relieved by those who had breakfasted and the herd was again set drifting and grazing.[24]

Despite Lavarro's excellent handling of the cattle drive and the men, he was replaced as foreman for the Cochrane Ranch by Jim Dunlap, an experienced American cowboy. Lavarro, not impressed with his treatment at the hands of the Canadian directors, returned to Montana, where he lived for a while on the Blackfoot Reservation with his wife's family.[25]

Chapter Eight

Ranching Women

Elizabeth Coughlin came to British Columbia in the late 1870s to visit her uncle Cornelius O'Keefe at his ranch in the North Okanagan. She and O'Keefe's partner, Thomas Greenhow, soon fell in love and were married in 1879. Elizabeth proved to be an excellent wife and mother, and the Greenhows prospered in the burgeoning cattle industry of the 1880s, when the Canadian Pacific Railway was being built. Unfortunately, Tom Greenhow died in 1889, leaving his wife and two children. O'Keefe, no doubt concerned about his niece's survival in the rough-and-tumble cattle industry, offered to manage her ranch for her. She looked him in the eye and stated, "Thank you, Uncle, but I'll run my ranch by myself." Such a thing was unheard of. Women at that time did not become involved in business of any sort, and the very idea of Elizabeth dealing with cowboys and cattle buyers seemed ludicrous. Nonetheless, Elizabeth Greenhow went on to manage her ranch most successfully and eventually sold it for $304,000 in 1907.

The story of Elizabeth Greenhow is remarkable because it was so unusual. In the Victorian era, middle-class women were expected to stay at home and raise the children, not become involved in the world. But the ranching frontier was different from the normal Victorian setting. Strong women took their place alongside their husbands and did what they could to make the ranch a success. There were no boundaries. Not only did they cook the food and care for the children, they could rope and ride if they had to. They were, after all, ranching women.

Lucy Richter

Francis Xavier Richter was born in Friedland, Austria, in 1837. At the age of 16 he sailed for America in search of fame and fortune. He landed in

Galveston, Texas, and travelled to San Antonio, where he landed a job in a wholesale grocery establishment. But the grocery business was too tame for a young man who yearned for adventure, and he headed to the Arizona silver mines. In 1862 he made his way to San Francisco and mined for placer gold in Florence, California. Then he heard of gold being discovered in Idaho, so he travelled to Lewiston to try his hand there. Finding no success, he proceeded to Fort Colville and on to Rich Bar on the Columbia River, near the mouth of the Okanogan River, where he opened a store and ran a freight boat on the Columbia. While there, a former Hudson's Bay Company employee named King told him of the excellent pasturage and potential for raising stock across the 49th Parallel in British territory. The two men decided to pool their resources and start cattle ranching in British Columbia. They travelled to Butter Creek near Pendleton, Oregon, and purchased 42 head of cattle. Frank Richter had become a drover.

The partners drove the cattle north and paid the customs duty at Osoyoos. Then they crossed over what is now called Richter Pass to the lower Similkameen Valley, where there was plenty of bunchgrass for their cattle. Frank was totally without assets, aside from his share of the cattle, and went to work for the Hudson's Bay Company, which was constructing a new post a few miles up the valley from its earlier post, constructed in 1860. In the spring of 1865, Richter went to Fort Colville for supplies, and then he and King helped to move the trade goods from the old Hudson's Bay Company post to the new one.

Richter and King dissolved their partnership in March, but Richter continued to work for the Hudson's Bay Company at their new post. His duties included looking after the Company's small farm and livestock and helping with the trade for furs with the Similkameen Natives. On one of these trips, he met Lucy, a Similkameen, and married her "in the fashion of the country." This phrase, a translation of the Canadian French *à la façon du pays*, had been used to describe the marriage of white men to Native women since the beginning of the fur trade. In the absence of clergymen, it was common for the ceremony of exchange to be enacted between the man and the family of the proposed bride. Native customs varied, but once the parents consented to the marriage, tradition often called for the payment of a bride price, gifts given by the groom to the bride's parents, probably to compensate for their loss of her labour. Once the bride price had been agreed upon, the pipe was smoked to seal the agreement, and sometimes the bride was lectured by her parents about her new life and responsibilities. The new couple then went to the husband's home, where the Native woman often adopted new European-style clothing. According to Native tradition, the couple was free to separate at any time, at least until the first child was born, but the bride price would not be returned. There is no question that the ceremony was recognized as a binding obligation by the Native people.

This was in strong contrast to customs in Europe at the time, in which legal marriages were made for life by the clergy. Many non-Native men regarded the formal ceremony between the white man and Native woman as representing a lifelong commitment equivalent to a legal marriage, while others viewed it as a common-law union that could be dissolved by either partner at any time. Still others saw their new mates as women they were just "sleeping with," and treated them like goods that could be acquired or discarded as desired. The practice of taking Native wives was widespread in British Columbia on the ranching frontier, where the ratio of white men to women was disproportionate. Fully half of the early ranchers in British Columbia had Native wives.[1]

Lucy proved to be an excellent wife and mother. She supplemented her existing knowledge of Native ways with knowledge about her husband's culture. Her son Joseph described his mother's ability to provide necessities for her family:

> When I was little, coal oil was brought 70 miles from Hope on the backs of horses. It was used sparingly. My mother made candles in a special mould and after the cotton wick was threaded, it was filled with our own tallow. She made soap from waste fat and lye. Some of our clothing was made from buckskin traded from the Indians. Mother fashioned it into coats, shirts and pants. Take it from me, buckskin garments are warm, soft and comfortable.[2]

Lucy also milked the dairy cows that had been brought in by her husband and churned butter from the cream. This butter was salted and packed into wooden tubs made on the ranch and provided a much appreciated income to the family. It sold for one dollar a pound to the various Hudson's Bay posts in the area.

Lucy and Frank Richter had five sons: Karl (Charlie) in 1869, William in 1872, Joseph in 1874, Edward in 1876 and Hans (John) in 1878. All were born at the R Ranch, and they all attended the school at Okanagan Mission (Kelowna); they boarded with Frederick Brent and his Native Okanagan wife and were taught by William Smithson, who also had a Native wife. The great Canadian geologist George Mercer Dawson commented in 1877 that "there is a school with about 20 scholars (all half-breeds) some of whom we met on our way to the mines, with lunches & books, neatly dressed."[3] The greatest difficulty in schooling the mixed-race children was language. The teacher in 1883 reported:

> With one exception the pupils are half-breeds, & speak better Chinook & Indian than English, & those who have a French father speak French, Indian and Chinook at home, & English only when at school, consequently their written English is very inferior.[4]

The boys returned home for summer holidays to help with the ranch work and, when they completed their seven years of schooling, became full-time workers on the ranch. All five sons were enthusiastic cowboys, working with their father's cattle and driving them to market when necessary. They helped to cut hay with scythes and put it up with a pitchfork; they built fences for pastures and whipsawed lumber for new buildings.

The family spoke mostly Chinook, the trade jargon developed during fur-trade days, at home, as that was the common language spoken between Natives and Whites at the time. According to Joseph:

> At first our only neighbours were Similkameen Indians. We often hired them to help in the fields or on the range. Fluency in Chinook jargon was necessary and I learned to understand but not to speak the Okanagan tongue. . . . I suppose that today most people would think that our early days were rough. We worked hard, we had everything we needed. We were a closely knit, affectionate family, self-sufficient, yet depending on one another, each respecting the other's worth under the guidance of wise parents. Our dealings with the Natives were those of mutual respect. They regarded our father as their trusted friend and counsellor.[5]

Frank and Lucy Richter cared deeply for each other and demonstrated that love to the children on many occasions. But, as is the case with most married couples, their relationship could be stormy at times. A friend of the Richters, Richard Louden, who lived in Loomis, Washington, just across the border, told a story that illustrates the mix of mutual affection and occasional frustration. "That Lucy respected him as well as loved him was clearly demonstrated one time in a near tragedy that had a humorous ending." One time, while crossing the Similkameen River in full flood, Frank was crossing and lost his footing and struggled in deep water to make it to shore. Lucy ran and grabbed a fence rail that she extended to him so he could hold on and let her pull him to shore. "She pulled him to safety then beat him soundly with the fence rail for risking his life unnecessarily."[6]

As the Interior of British Columbia opened up to more and more settlers, couples in mixed-race relationships like the Richters began to find themselves in the minority and subject to discrimination. White men who had arrived early in the Interior, and who were owners of extensive

The Richter family ranch house in the 1890s.
BC ARCHIVES A-03621

lands and regarded as "pillars of the community," were pressured to discard their Native concubines. The ugly discrimination that newcomers showed against the men with Native wives (referred to sneeringly as "klootch," from the Chinook word for "woman") is encapsulated in the reminiscences of Sydney Russell Almond, recorded sometime after white settlers had become a majority in the area, which reveal a disappointingly common attitude. He says of early Similkameen rancher Barrington Price:

> He came of a good family in England and evidently had rich connections . . .
> He married a klootch and wrote home to his friends that he had married
> an Indian princess. I don't know what idea his friends had of an Indian
> princess as they come in British Columbia, but it is safe to say that they had
> no such picture of her as the actual Indian klootch as we know here, even
> when married to a self-respecting white man.[7]

While other white ranchers began to dispose of their Native wives, Frank Richter remained steadfastly loyal to his wife and partner. But the pressures were starting to build. He confessed to a friend that he was becoming increasingly concerned that, while he was away, Lucy was inviting her family and friends to entertain them and shirking her housewifely duties. Richter confided that he had arrived at a way of controlling the situation. He invited another Similkameen woman to live with them, a woman who was very fond of Richter and would tell him everything that went on while he was away. This succeeded in keeping Lucy's entertaining to a minimum, but the unconventional arrangement strained their otherwise healthy relationship. Richter had to admit that the "third party" interference was a bad idea and asked the other woman to leave. But perhaps the damage had been done.

In 1894, Richter, then 56 years old, agreed to escort the Loudens' 17-year-old daughter, Elizabeth, to school in Victoria. The two returned to the Similkameen married. Richter, on his return, had a cabin built for Lucy and she quietly agreed to leave the home they had occupied for over 25 years.

Lucy's main legacy was her five sons, who went on to be prominent members of the Okanagan Similkameen community. When Joseph was married in 1900, his father gave him the Ingram Ranch near Midway, complete with a large log house, stable and other buildings, machines and herds of cattle and horses. Frank Richter bought Charlie butcher shops in Princeton and Hedley. William inherited the Kruger Ranch at Osoyoos, and Edward inherited the large Nicholson Ranch at Rock Creek. Hans used his inheritance to purchase bucking horses to supply the growing rodeo circuit in British Columbia and Washington State.

The history of the British Columbia Interior is replete with stories of ranchers taking Native wives who helped them develop their ranches and who bore their children and cared for their homes. But the sad truth of these stories is that they almost all ended with the Native woman being pushed aside by the rancher so he could marry a white woman and gain respectability for himself in the eyes of his peers. One notable exception was North Okanagan rancher, Edward Tronson, who remained faithful to his Okanagan wife, Nancy, despite the sneers of his neighbours.

Some may have sneered at the Native women, but the early development of the ranching industry in British Columbia could not have taken place without them, and their legacy lives on in the names of so many excellent cowboys of mixed blood in the BC Interior.

Susan Allison

Susan Moir was already quite an experienced traveller when she arrived in Victoria in the new Colony of British Columbia in August 1860. Born in Ceylon to Louisa and Stratton Moir, she travelled to England at the age of four after the death of her father. She spent most of the year in London, but her summers were spent in Aberdeen, Scotland. In 1860 her mother married Thomas Glennie who, by then, had already inherited and squandered several fortunes. Attracted by the prospect of free land in the new colony, he packed the family up and took them via the isthmus of Panama to British Columbia.

The family did not stay long in Victoria, but headed by steamship to the ramshackle stockaded fort and collection of huts that comprised Fort Hope. What the frontier town lacked in elegance, it made up for in bustle. It was located at the head of navigation on the Fraser River and in the heart of the gold excitement that had bred the creation of the Crown Colony of British Columbia two years earlier.

Glennie lost no time in pre-empting 160 acres on a location two miles from the fort on the Coquihalla River. He then contracted the construction of a substantial log house, designed somewhat like a hunting lodge in Scotland, which he dubbed Hopelands. The family settled in, getting to know the neighbours, who consisted of a large number of "upper-class" British, many of whom would rise to fill significant positions in the government of the new colony. While her parents were making the acquaintance of the ruling members of the community, Susan was exploring the town with a curiosity that was to remain one of her lifelong traits. She enjoyed meeting representatives of the mixture of races and classes that constituted a frontier community.

In March 1864, Susan's sister Jane married Edgar Dewdney, who would hold many government positions in the years to come, including Lieutenant Governor of the North-West Territories. That same year, Thomas Glennie's propensity for spending more than he could afford caught up with him again. Without a word to anyone—not even his wife—he sold Hopelands and disappeared, leaving Mrs. Glennie homeless and without funds, even though she still owned property in Ceylon. She and Susan moved to New Westminster to be with Jane while her husband worked on the construction of the Dewdney Trail west from Hope to Princeton and beyond. Susan, never one to sit around and feel sorry for herself, found employment as a governess in Victoria for a time and then returned to New Westminster to be with her mother. By 1867 the Dewdneys were preparing to move to Soda Creek in the Cariboo, so Mrs. Glennie and Susan moved back to Hope, where they shared teaching duties in the little school there.

Although Hope was now a backwater, with New Westminster having been chosen as the colony's capital, there were still fascinating people to meet. Two or three times a year, John Fall Allison would pass through Hope, driving cattle from his ranch in the Similkameen to markets at New Westminster and Yale. On one of these drives, Susan was introduced to him. Susan's curiosity about the Similkameen helped her establish a friendship with Allison, some 20 years her senior. When he discovered that she was fond of riding, Allison bought her a cream-coloured mare and sometimes she would ride out with him partway on his return trip to the Similkameen. In September 1868 the two were married, and Mr. and Mrs. Allison headed out to the Similkameen. They had urged Mrs. Glennie to come, but she preferred to remain in Hope and run the school rather than brave the wilderness.

John Fall Allison had been born in Leeds in West Yorkshire, England, in 1825 and had come to the Lower Fraser River in 1858. Two years later he was prospecting around Vermillion Forks (Princeton), where he staked gold, copper and coal claims and, on his way back, he liked what he saw of the valley and pre-empted 160 acres. He returned in the fall with a partner named Hays, and the two set up a ranch, purchasing 80 head of Durham Shorthorns from a rancher in Washington State.[8] In 1862 he married a Native Similkameen woman named Nora Yacumtekum, with whom he had four children. The details of John Allison's Native wife seem to have escaped him when he first entertained Susan with tales of his adventures. In addition, Susan Allison's account of her fascinating life as a rancher's wife in the Similkameen, *A Pioneer Gentlewoman in British Columbia* (1931) contains no mention of her husband's first wife, but she must have known of her and, given Susan's soft heart for all people, no doubt made sure she was well looked after.

The Allisons set off, with Susan riding sidesaddle on her cream mare. Only one white woman had crossed the Hope Mountains previously, but Susan was unperturbed. They were being led by Cockshist, the Similkameen Native guide who had led Dewdney when he planned the trail from Hope. With them were Johnny Suzanne, the Native packer, and Yacumtecum, another Similkameen Native who was related to Allison's Native wife. Yacumtecum was the bell boy, who cooked for the party and who led the pack horse, which wore a bell. Yacumtecum also led Susan's horse up the steep switchbacks. Although she must have felt some trepidation at the thought of settling in the wilderness with Similkameen Natives as her only neighbours, she wrote about this phase of her life as being the beginning of "my camping days and the wild, free life I enjoyed till age and infirmity put an end to it."[9]

The couple arrived at the new log house Allison had just finished constructing, and Susan took in her surroundings. John Allison's partner, whose name Susan always spells as Hayes, was probably Silas Hays, who is mentioned as a "stock raiser" in Osoyoos in the 1881 census. Obviously a little put out at the termination of his bachelor existence, he protested Susan's dressing for dinner, "a habit I was drilled in as a child," but seemed somewhat placated when he learned that she could milk a cow and was not afraid to go into a corral full of cattle.

The couple had little time to enjoy the snug log cabin to which Susan had already begun adding feminine touches. Allison had to make another pack trip to Hope and then, at the beginning of November, had to drive his cattle and horses to the Okanagan Valley to winter. By then the partners had 500 head of cattle, which they wintered across the lake from the Okanagan Mission at a location they called Sunnyside (later Westbank). It took three or four days to gather the cattle and horses, and then they headed down the river. In those days, the partners drove the cattle down the Similkameen River to Penticton and then up the west side of Okanagan Lake to the winter range.

The winter passed with relative ease as the couple settled in to married life in their cozy cabin. With the coming of spring, life became a good deal more hectic. As a rancher's wife, Susan was expected to perform all the household chores, run the trading post, where gold dust was the medium of exchange, operate the post office and keep the account books for the ranching and trading post operations. To this was added the burden of bearing and rearing children. The first child, Edgar, was born the following July, with the help of a Native midwife, Suzanne. Over the next 23 years, she would give birth to 13 more children, all without medical assistance and all of whom lived to maturity. Despite its regularity, childbirth was never easy for Susan. In her memoirs, she wrote that "Suzanne was very good to me in her way—though I thought rather unfeeling at the time. She thought that I ought to be as strong as an Indian woman but I was not."[10]

Susan was left alone and began to meet the Native Similkameens who would be her neighbours for many years. She began to learn Chinook, the trade language that had been developed by fur traders and Native people in the Pacific Northwest, and was able to get help by hiring Similkameen boys and girls to look after certain chores. This contact with the young Natives allowed her to master the Chinook language, which in turn allowed her to entertain the adult Similkameens in her home. Susan's natural curiosity made her want to learn more of their customs and stories and, over the years of living in close proximity to the Similkameen and Okanagan people, she learned much about their ways and made close friendships with many. In fact, she notes in her recollections that "they told me more than they told most white people." She carefully recorded their stories and myths and entertained her children by retelling the stories to them. In addition to her recollections, Susan's later writing included a long narrative poem titled *In-Cow-Mas-Ket* (published under the pseudonym Stratton Moir in 1900), scholarly articles on the Similkameen people published in British journals, a collection of 10 stories based on Aboriginal myth, other pieces published by the *Okanagan Historical Society*, numerous letters, and a number of private papers with accounts of people and events. Years later, she was able to write with authority about the Native people of the Interior in a number of articles, some of which were published during her lifetime and some of which are available in archives and from descendants.[11]

During the early 1870s the ranchers in the British Columbia Interior were optimistic that the railway promised by the Government of Canada to BC when it entered Confederation would soon link the province to eastern Canadian markets. Allison shared this optimism and continued to acquire land for ranching, going into debt to purchase an additional 300 acres. He also decided that he needed to upgrade his cattle by acquiring a purebred bull and, in the spring of 1872, when Hays left to visit his family in Maine, it was agreed that he would return via California and purchase a purebred shorthorn bull from Colonel Younger in Greenwood, Missouri. Hays bought an excellent bull and had it shipped to Hope. He started driving the bull back from Hope during an extremely hot summer and after he had driven it nine miles, it appeared to give out with the heat. Hays left the bull and continued on his way, only to learn a few days later that the very expensive bull had succumbed to the heat and died. Allison went to his wife and had her count out all the money she had, some $1,400. He took it, telling her he was going to Missouri for another bull. Some weeks later he was back with Red Oak, one of the finest shorthorn bulls in the country and one that would leave its mark on the cattle from Princeton to Chilliwack in the years to come. Allison's concentration on upgrading his cattle paid off. His beef began to be highly valued at the coastal markets, where it was referred to as "Similkameen beef."

For some time, Allison had been driving his cattle to winter in the Okanagan at Sunnyside, where he owned property and there were excellent hay meadows. In October of 1873, when he was preparing to move his cattle there, he asked Susan if she would like to relocate to the Okanagan. By then he had cut a trail from Sunnyside to Princeton that very much shortened the trip, enabling him to drive his cattle to Hope without too much difficulty. Allison promised to build a house and to make his wife and children comfortable. As Susan wrote, "I loved adventure, so in spite of my growing family, I agreed to this plan and never have I repented of the decision."[12]

For some time John McDougall of Okanagan Mission had been cutting hay for Allison, and he was contracted to build a house for the family. In November the entire family, in a caravan described by Susan, were on their way:

> In November we started out on the journey. First went the cattle, Mr. Hayes and his packs and outfit. Then the pack train with winter stores and belongings, then myself and Marie who carried one of the children. I carried two—one in front, and the other at my back. My husband rode first with one outfit then the other and relieved me when he could of one of the little ones. We had a jolly time in spite of the bad roads and went rather a roundabout way by Dog Lake . . . It was round a cliff—such a narrow ledge the horses with the packs could barely make it. My husband told me to trust my horse and not to try to guide him, and this I did. In one place where the cattle had broken down the trail one could see down a dreadful abyss into the lake. I was afraid, but the Indians did not seem to be and the horses took it in their stride. I had learned that even if you are terrified it is best not to show it, then you get credit for being fearless—I certainly was not.[13]

The Allisons arrived to find that their cabin was not yet finished and so they spent their first month in the Okanagan in tents. As they began to meet their new neighbours, they found that, for the first time, they were in a community of Natives, Whites and mixed-blood people living together harmoniously. Across Okanagan Lake from Sunnyside was the Okanagan Mission, founded in 1859 and run by Fathers Pandosy and Richard. Next to the Mission was Eli Lequime's trading post and ranch. Mrs. Lequime was the first white woman whom Susan could call a "neighbour" since she had married. Other ranchers on the Okanagan Mission side of the lake included

Cyprian Laurence and his wife, Therese; Fred Brent, who also ran a primitive flour mill; and the Christian brothers. Isadore Boucherie had established his ranch on their side of the lake, not far from the Allisons.

The Allisons moved into their new house on Christmas Eve of 1873. The only drawback was the lack of close water, which John Allison eventually remedied by diverting a stream running down from the mountains into their yard. The hardships of frontier life were continuous. In the spring of 1874 the Okanagan Natives nearby suffered from an epidemic of grippe, and several died; the following year there were rumblings of a general uprising by the Okanagan people; John Allison suffered a head injury from a fall from which he never really recovered; and the family had several anxious weeks when the outlaw McLean brothers were on the loose. Even though things were far from tranquil, Susan thoroughly enjoyed her time at Sunnyside. She made fine clothes and moccasins for her children, baked bread in a primitive oven, smoked fish and dried venison. She plowed and planted a small garden and also became quite adept at braiding rawhide lariats, for which there was a ready market among the cowboys. Her children were able to enjoy a carefree life, they tamed some deer as pets and, in the summer, they could fish in the streams and lake and wander the hills. Susan's sister Jane and her husband, Edgar Dewdney, came to visit in 1876 and were soon put to work cleaning kokanee fish for drying and helping in the ranch chores.

But during the winters of 1869–70, 1873–74 and 1877–78, the Okanagan suffered through intensely cold weather and Allison lost stock each winter. The winter of 1879–80 was the last straw; severe weather killed off fully half of Allison's livestock. This came at a time when he had just dissolved his partnership with Silas Hays and had to pay $3,000 to buy him out. Down but not out, Allison was forced to sell off his Okanagan property to John Phillips and moved the family back to Princeton in 1880.

Susan begged her husband not to sell, but Allison had little choice. Susan wrote:

> It was with a sad heart I went around our old haunts, said goodbye to my little mountain garden . . . [and] the little mountain spring which my husband had led down to the house in an underground ditch. It was a sad cavalcade that left our dear little home where we had been so peaceful and happy. It had been a busy life too; no day was spent in idleness.[14]

After seven years in the Okanagan, the family moved back to Princeton with the remaining "small band of about 120 head of cattle—but they were every one thoroughbred Shorthorn Durhams . . . Then 75 horses, pack and saddle animals." The time at Sunnyside had been a happy one for Susan Allison. Four more children had been born during that time, and her relationship with the Okanagan Natives had been friendly and mutually cooperative. The Okanagans had shared their stories with her, including the one about the great Okanagan Lake monster later dubbed Ogopogo. Susan appreciated their culture and wrote, "My husband always laughed at Indian yarns but I did not, for I thought there must be some foundation for what they said."

The return to Princeton did not bring about a change in fortune for the Allisons. There they found that the snowfall the previous winter had been so heavy, its weight had crushed the roof of their house. The family moved into the milk house and made the best of the situation until the roof was repaired. Once the family was finally settled into their home, Susan took over her previous duties of operating the trading post and dealing with the common ailments of her children and the Similkameen Natives, who always consulted her for remedies.

The next calamity struck the family a year after their return. While John Allison was away, their home and everything in it was destroyed in a fire. Susan managed to escape with a small photo of her brother, Stratton Moir, her dressing case (containing $100 in gold), a small piece of bacon and 15 pounds of flour. Susan and the children, with only the clothes on their backs, set up house in a small, mouse-infected cabin. They found a few horse blankets for bedding and, rummaging in the cabin, located a coffee can full of rice and an old Bible. The rice and flour would be their main food, and the Bible would be their literature. Susan started a fire in the fireplace at one end of the cabin, and the children nestled into their horse blankets. One of her daughters found a flat rock to use as a bread board, and an empty whisky bottle served as a rolling pin. For the next few days, the family struggled with the meagre rations and with mice chewing their hair at night as they slept. Susan tired of cooking over an open fire and built herself a bake oven with the half-melted door from their old stove. After five days, a pack horse loaded with flour, beans and bacon arrived from their Keremeos neighbour, Barrington Price. Another neighbour, Richard Cawston, rounded up a lot of old clothes from his aunt, Ella Lowe, who also sent calico, needles, thread and scissors. Susan later wrote:

> That month I learned two lessons that have lasted me through life. First, that money in itself is valueless, and second, that contentment is invaluable . . . the gold did not feed us when we were hungry or clothe us when we were cold. I also found that when the children's minds were active they

did not notice the hunger so much. The old Bible was hunted for stories and when it was exhausted I told them stories I could remember . . . and so was able to interest the children sufficiently to make them forget their troubles.[15]

John Allison, on his return, immediately began the construction of a new home and, once again, the family returned to a somewhat normal life.

Located as she was on the Dewdney Trail and with her husband often away, Susan Allison entertained many travellers on the trail and offered her warm hospitality to one and all, regardless of race or station. While her new house was under construction, she was visited by the French artist Jules Tavernier and his companion. Without hesitation, she fed them the three ducks and huge custard that she had prepared for her family and had cooked in her outdoor oven. They ate the entire meal and washed it down with "coffee" made from roasted peas. The very next day, Sir Thomas Hesketh, Seventh Baronet of Rufford, and his valet passed through and did some duck

hunting in the area. Later, she was visited by the Anglican Canon Cooper and, not long after, the famous Father Pat (Reverend Henry Irwin) of the Catholic Church. But perhaps her most famous visitor came in 1883, when General William Tecumseh Sherman, the great American military man, visited the Allisons. Susan, having no sitting room to receive him, placed chairs outside the door and the great general asked her to "parade" all her children. She was impressed with the man and recorded the visit:

> General Sherman was a healthy, intelligent man with shrewd piercing eyes that seemed to take in everything and look into your mind . . . [He] was delighted to see my boy, Jack, just seven, perched on his big horse, riding back and forth with his messages and little Jack was proud to ride the General's horse. They did not stay for long for some of the men deserted, so they passed through the country as quickly as they could. Before leaving he presented Jack with a sword.[16]

One of General Sherman's aides also recorded the visit:

Allison's place was a comfortable dwelling with a few outbuildings. In one of the latter was a small store. Allison was at Victoria but his courteous wife received us with hospitality. She was a rosy cheeked woman of about 25 [*sic*], born in Ceylon, and she had 10 children, healthy, handsome urchins, which goes to show that the more distant and difficult of access the place, the more prolific are the human inhabitants. Residing here she appeared cheerfully happy and contented in her isolated home.[17]

Susan Allison and eight of her children in front of her home at Princeton in 1880.
BC ARCHIVES D-08228

Life continued on an even keel for the Allisons as they built up their ranch and regularly drove cattle to the coastal markets. The gold rush to Granite Creek, just a short distance from the ranch, brought an even closer market, and Susan regularly drove pack trains of supplies to the camps. However, before long, large stores were constructed at Granite Creek. They brought in their own supplies, and the Douglas Lake Cattle Ranch provided all the beef that was needed at a lower price than the Allisons could provide.

One more calamity was to strike the Allisons. In 1894 both the Similkameen and Tulameen Rivers rose and overflowed their banks, washing away all 14 buildings, including the Allisons' house. Just when John Allison thought he was getting ahead, he was forced to start over again. He began to reconstruct the ranch buildings but had to mortgage his lands. The ranching industry was changing, and greater competition from ranches closer to railways made it difficult to continue. He became more interested in mining ventures and convinced his brother-in-law, Edgar Dewdney, to invest as well. Dewdney was appointed Lieutenant Governor of British Columbia in 1892, bringing Susan's sister and mother closer to home. Susan went to visit them often at their new home, Cary Castle, and Edgar reciprocated, visiting the Allison Ranch often.

John Fall Allison died in October 1897 and was laid to rest on his own property at the foot of Castle Rock. Susan stayed on the ranch and ran it as best she could under the circumstances. Little by little the land had to be sold off to keep up with payments. Unlike many of the early ranchers in the southern Interior who had founded ranches and eventually sold them off to syndicates for land development, Susan was hampered from doing so because of the remoteness of Princeton. Eventually, a subdivision was marked out on Allison's Flat and Susan moved out of her log house and built a small house on the lot. There, Susan continued to write down her experiences and to advocate for her friends, the Native Similkameen and Okanagan people. After her 80th birthday in 1925, she began to spend the winters with one of her daughters in Vancouver, and in 1928 she moved to Vancouver. She died at the age of 92 in 1937. In her later years she was lovingly referred to as the "Mother of the Similkameen."

Pioneer Women of the North-West

Fred Ings, in his book *Before the Fences*, pays tribute to the pioneer women of the North-West for their incredible contribution to the opening of the country to settlement:

> Whether they were in a cabin or more pretentious dwelling, they were quite
> as isolated and as far from their former friends. There were no means of

quick communication. Later, when the farmers came, they rigged up wire telephones, but in the range days there were no fences on which to rig them.

He goes on to tell the story of a pioneer wife who described the hardest day she had to face in her daily challenge of survival. She said, "the worst day I ever spent" was when her newborn baby was sick and she thought she may have given him the wrong medicine. There was no one to ask for advice, as her nearest neighbour was 20 miles away. She could do nothing but pray that help would come and, before nightfall, her neighbour drove by for a visit:

> When I look back at these brave women in their first little cabins and think of the hardships, privations and anxieties that must have been their lot, I wonder if these later comers realize how greatly they have contributed to the upbuilding of this country . . . in those days of struggle in bare little log houses, far from neighbours, doctors, and for many, across the world from friends. Whether they came from humble homes or those of luxury, from cities, or from quiet countrysides, whether they had training in home-making or not, when they threw in their lot with the pioneer men they took up cheerfully their part of the burden; the heavy monotonous work that is a woman's share in empire building. Wheresoever a woman lived there was generally a bright plant in bloom on the narrow sill, if only in a tomato can, a little fence about the shack, and an attempt at a garden in the door yard.[18]

Perhaps the first rancher's wife to appear in the North-West came in 1875. That year, John and Annie Armstrong drove a herd of mostly dairy cattle north from Montana and settled with their two adopted Native American daughters, Julia and Ellen, an arrangement that was quite uncommon at the time. They were accompanied by Annie's 21-year-old son, James, from another marriage and their hired man, Oscar Morgan. They settled on the Oldman River just upstream from Fort Macleod, having brought with them some beef cattle and a herd of dairy cows, always referred to as Annie Armstrong's. She made a decent income selling dairy products to the Mounted Police. John Armstrong does not seem to have been home very much, as most reminiscences from the era mention only Annie Armstrong. When the first round-up in what was to become southern Alberta took place in 1879, it was Oscar Morgan who represented Annie Armstrong and, along with the other small ranchers in the area, found a significant number of cattle missing and blamed it on the Blackfoot in the area. About this time, Annie Armstrong complained to the Mounted Police that she had lost one of her cattle to the Natives. Governor Edgar Dewdney mentioned this in his report:

I had heard that even the night before a Mrs. Armstrong, who kept a dairy, had one of her cows shot through the head and it was in her corral at the time. The chiefs assured me that they knew nothing of it.[19]

When neither Governor Dewdney nor the Mounted Police could assure the ranchers that they would take responsibility for the missing cattle, as the country was not yet ready for settlement, Annie Armstrong and a few others rounded up their cattle and headed south to Montana. The Armstrongs settled on the Teton River in Chouteau County to await the opening up of the country.

In June 1881, while John and James Armstrong were away, a man named Brackett E. Stewart stopped by their ranch and said he was looking for some lost cattle. With typical western hospitality, he was invited to stay. On the second night at the ranch, he brutally murdered Annie Armstrong and Oscar Morgan. He didn't realize that the two girls were outside checking their horses and, when they heard the shots, they hid. Stewart looted the house and then set it on fire, assuming that the girls were inside. When it was safe, the girls rode to their nearest neighbour and were taken to the nearby town of Old Agency, where the local storekeeper, Alfred Hamilton, was sheriff. His store was crowded with cowboys in from the nearest round-up, and Julia recognized and pointed out the murderer. The cowboys grabbed Stewart and searched him, finding a large amount of money and a gold watch that was recognized as belonging to Morgan. Sheriff Hamilton locked Stewart up in one of the storerooms until he could be tried for murder. But the local cowboys, outraged by the crime, took the matter into their own hands. The Fort Benton newspaper, *The River Press*, reported that:

> a party of masked men rode up to Mr. AB Hamilton . . . levelled their guns at him, and demanded his prisoner. These men were immediately joined by about twenty more, and they took the prisoner by force from Mr. Hamilton, and hung him to a tree.[20]

Another notable pioneer woman was Katherine "Kate" Quirk who, with her husband, John, left Ireland in the early 1850s and travelled to the United States, eventually ending up in Detroit. There they joined an overland party going to the California goldfields. After making a bare living in California, John decided to head to the new goldfields at Virginia City, Montana, and left Kate behind until he got established. A few years later, Kate tired of waiting and joined John in Montana, where the couple established a ranch near Missoula. At this time, there was great unrest among the Native people, who frequently raided and burned settlers' cabins. The Quirks would make their bed out on the open prairie, where they could hear anyone approaching and where they would be safe if the cabin was lit on fire.

After ranching for five years in Montana, the Quirks heard that the North-West was being opened for settlement and headed north with 450 head of cattle. The neighbour boys had given them a hand for a few miles but turned back as soon as they reached Blackfoot country. John drove the cattle with the help of a talented cow dog that was as good as three men, and Kate drove a covered wagon. The journey took them over prairies, mountains and five rivers. When they reached Mosquito Creek in the summer of 1882, they asked two men, Jim Meinsinger and Herb Millar, where the best available range could be found. The men suggested the Crossing, but the Quirks found that Mosquito Creek was well named. John would later joke, "The mosquitos were so bad that Mrs. Quirk scraped them off the tent and made soup."[21]

The next night, after leaving Mosquito Creek, the herd was bedded down near the Highwood River, where a grove of cottonwoods stood. Kate looked at her husband and said, "John, that is as far as I am going." They settled on the south side of the river. The Quirk home became a favourite place to stop for the community, proving even more popular than the local hotel, thanks to the couple's true Irish hospitality. Quirk, who loved an argument, would always find a way to disagree with something that a guest had said, and the fun would begin. One evening he was getting very hot under the collar and his language a little ripe, even though two of his visitors were Roman Catholic priests. When Kate gently remonstrated with her husband, pointing out that there were Fathers present, John hotly replied, "Oh, to hell with the Fathers!" and continued his tirade.

In 1887 the Quirks moved west onto the north fork of Sheep Creek, where there was better range for their cattle. Eventually, the little town of Kew, named after the Quirks' Q brand, was established there. Both the John Ware and Sam Howe families were neighbours and became good friends. Kate decorated her home in typical pioneer fashion, lining the walls with brightly coloured cretonne. The Quirks' Sheep Creek Ranch became prosperous under their diligent stewardship, their herd eventually numbering 2,000 head on 6,000 acres of deeded land and an equal amount of leased acres. In 1912 the Quirks sold their herd and property to Pat Burns and returned to Detroit, where they had started out 60 years earlier.

Building a good relationship with the Native people was a key contribution of women in the North-West. While their husbands were out on the range, they kept their small cabins and dealt with Native visitors regularly.

John Quirk, Henry Sinnot (with horse), Kate Quirk and W.H. King in front of the Quirks' home.
GLENBOW ARCHIVES PD-374-2-44

In the early days, the Blackfoot people were often hungry, and they saw the newcomers as owing them something for their intrusion in what was once all Blackfoot territory. A pioneer woman who lived on one of the many ranches in the North-West was once asked what had been her worst experience. She laughed and answered, "My most desperate day was one when my husband was off on the range, and three big Indians pushed their way into the kitchen." Asked how she responded, she laughed and said, "I fed them 'heap plenty,' and they became my best friends, often bringing me presents of really lovely skins and bead work and also all their relatives to sample my fare."

Another pioneer woman, Susan Brown, who had arrived from Scotland and settled on a ranch southwest of Calgary, was noted for her hospitality to Natives and Whites alike. A nearby lake was given the name Slick-Up Lake because that is where the cowboys would "slick-up" themselves before visiting. Not long after she had settled in the area, she heard that a daughter of a Blackfoot chief was ill and, gathering all her home remedies, she drove her horse and wagon to the reserve and asked if she could help. The parents gladly accepted her assistance, and she applied various treatments to the sick girl. The girl quickly recovered, and Brown was, from that point on, revered by the Blackfoot people, who called her "White Angel" in Blackfoot in recognition of her powers as a healer.

Unfortunately, not all ranching women displayed the same compassion toward the Native people. Mary Ella Lees, for example, left her home in Perth, Ontario, in September 1883 and travelled on the new Canadian Pacific

Railway to the end of the rail, where she was met by her brother, who was working at a lumber mill near Pincher Creek. The following year, she met and married James Inderwick, who, along with others, had formed the North Fork Ranch and leased 100,000 acres between the two forks of the Oldman River. Mary Inderwick loved the ranching way of life and, as an expert rider, was accepted and esteemed by the cowboys, but she did not extend a similar acceptance toward the Native people from the nearby Peigan Reserve:

> I think the Indians should have been isolated in the mountains and left with their own lives and ways of living and never allowed to eat of the fruit of knowledge as revealed by the white men who came to live among them. They could teach civilization a great deal too, but our inconsistencies are too subtle for his direct mind and when he tries to follow he is lost, and under the circumstances the sooner he becomes extinct the better for himself and the country.[22]

Granted, Inderwick's attitude was shaped after only limited contact with the Native people and an observation of the devastating effect the coming of the Whites had had on the Natives, but her attitude was far from unique. Many in the North-West adhered to her view that assimilation was the only way the Native people would adapt to "civilization."

Inderwick represents a segment of the North-West ranching community who were of British or Canadian "upper-class" backgrounds. With widespread investment from the eastern Canadian and British establishments, many ranches were operated by people who arrived with substantial financial backing. This allowed them to build themselves comfortable homes and hire servants to care for them. Inderwick insisted that the cowboys "dress for dinner" and, to that end, the cowboys all kept a black alpaca coat that they could pull on over their flannel shirts to give themselves the required appearance. She also described her attempt to "make use of a squaw who is nominal wife of a white man near to us to do the washing but had to give it up" because she did not understand how to do it. Inderwick:

> gave up the task of training her ... and I now send my washing to a dignified coloured lady in Pincher Creek ... Time is nothing to her and if I were an ordinary woman, and not a bride with a good trousseau, I shiver to think what might happen to me when weeks go by and no laundry can be cajoled from our aristocratic Auntie's stately dwelling.[23]

Many of the upper-class newcomers were much more open to the intrinsic equality of everyone in the North-West and became respected and

Mary Inderwick.
GLENBOW ARCHIVES NA-1365-2

valuable members of the community. In 1895, Walter Skrine of Somerset, England, who had been ranching near Mosquito Creek since 1884, returned to Britain and married Agnes "Nesta" Higgonson. Nesta had been writing poetry for some time under the pen name of Moira O'Neill and found in the North-West an environment not unlike that of her native Ireland. But in many ways the prairies were very different from her home. Her impression of the classless society of the North-West is quite different from Mary Inderwick's:

> No one is rich here. On the other hand, hardly anyone is distressingly poor, of those at least who live on their ranches like ourselves, and make their money by horses and cattle. As to whether they make or lose most, and how they make or why they lose it, I know just enough to be silent on the subject for fear of making some "bad break" . . . This, however, I know, that it is a very novel and pleasant experience to belong to a community of which all members are more or less equal in fortune . . . As to the want of congenial society, that complaint may be preferred from many a corner of the British Isles with as much reason as from North-Western Canada. But one observes that those who are always complaining of the society round them are not, as a rule, its most useful or brilliant members.[24]

Nesta Skrine had brought a maid out with her from Britain but "in course of time the mistake rectified itself, and she went the way of all womankind in the west [marriage]." Nesta took up a broom and duster and did the housework herself, taking pleasure and pride in having a well-ordered household, even when she learned her best salad bowl had been used as a water dish in the henhouse. Still, she had a Chinese cook to look after the meals, except for the time when he had taken a knife to one of the cowboys and been tied to a chair in the kitchen.

Like most well-to-do ranching wives, Nesta gloried in the outdoors. After doing a couple of hours of housework, she was able to ride for hours, exploring the countryside. She was delighted to be able to hunt coyotes with hounds and was fearless in their pursuit. Her husband, Walter, would watch in horror as she leapt her horse over a creek that he and others would search out a place to cross. In the fall, the men would hunt for grouse, and Nesta would ride alongside to help in locating the fallen birds. One neighbour, Ruth Hanson, remembered her as a "fearless, splendid rider."

While Nesta Skrine was enjoying ranch life in the foothills, she was gaining a literary reputation as Moira O'Neill in Britain, publishing *Songs of the Glens of Antrim* in 1900, from which composer Charles Villiers Stanford selected six poems for his song-cycle "An Irish Idyll," published the following year. Many more of her poems, both of Ireland and the North-West, were published individually. She was torn between these two of her favourite places on earth and, whenever she returned to Ireland, she found "now 'tis wanting back I am to that lone land; 'tis the other house I'm seein' on the green hills' breast, an' a trail across the prairie goin' south an' west."

In her memoir, *A Lady's Life On a Ranche*, published in 1898, she recorded her love for the North-West:

I like the simplicity, the informality of the life, the long hours in the open air. I like the endless riding over the endless prairie, the winds sweeping the grass, the great silent sunshine, the vast skies, and the splendid line of the Rockies, guarding the west. I like the herds of cattle feeding among the foothills, moving slowly from water to water; and the bands of horses travelling their own way, free of the prairie. I like the clear rivers that come pouring out of the mountains with their great rocky pools and the shining reaches of swift water where we fish in the summer-time; and the little lakes among the hills where the wild duck drop down to rest on their flight to the north in the spring . . . I like the work and the play here, the time out of doors and the time for coming home. I like the summer and winter, the monotony and the change. Besides, I like a flannel shirt and liberty.[25]

Chapter Nine

THE LEGACY OF THE *VAQUERO* AND TEXAS COWBOY

The ranching industry in British Columbia developed during the years of the gold rush, from 1858 to 1868. At that time, there was nothing but buffalo on the prairies, which were still the traditional territory of the Blackfoot. So the cattle and cattlemen that came to the Colony during the gold rush were almost entirely from the south. When the rush to British Columbia began, there was already a thriving cattle industry in California, Oregon and Washington. This industry had originated in California when it was Spanish territory, and many of the Mexican/California practices and almost all the equipment used in raising cattle remained. Even the Spanish term for the ranch labourers, *vaqueros*, was retained, albeit with an Anglicised pronunciation, "buckaroos." The practices and equipment of the *vaqueros* were accepted almost entirely by the English-speaking labourers. They adopted *chaparreras*, or chaps, as leg coverings, the California stock saddle, the hackamore, the braided rawhide *reata*, and many more of the equipment refinements and practices of the *vaquero*.

Much of the traditional Mexican way of handling cattle was adapted and adopted by the cattle herders who travelled north into Oregon and Washington. There, cattlemen were further influenced by the thousands of new settlers who had come over the Oregon Trail from the Midwestern states. Large herds of Durham and Devon cattle added to the already predominantly shorthorn bloodlines, so the cattle in the Pacific Northwest were large and heavy. This meant that the horses used to handle these cattle had to be larger and heavier as well, and the addition of French Norman and Breton horses during the fur trade days had to a great extent addressed this need. The bloodlines of the horses were further enhanced with the importation of Morgan horses along the Oregon Trail.

The cattle that were driven into British Columbia during the gold rush years were all fine beef cattle of the shorthorn variety. When driven at a leisurely pace and allowed to graze on the ample bunchgrass along the way, they arrived in British Columbia in prime condition. The foundation stock for the British Columbia ranching industry were these excellent beef cattle and, because of their size, the horses that were used to drive them were also large but not as agile as the Native "cayuses" that had been bred from wild stock. It was generally accepted in British Columbia that a certain amount of cayuse blood was needed to keep the horses agile and more capable of cutting out and roping cattle. The result was the "British Columbia horse" that was so prized in the early ranching days on the prairies.

As might be expected, the drovers who brought cattle into British Columbia were mostly from Oregon and Washington, with a significant minority from California. They brought with them the California practices and equipment that had travelled north into Oregon and Washington and had been modified along the way by the cattlemen who had brought in herds along the Oregon Trail. Nonetheless, the influence of the California *vaquero* was still present. Photographs taken during the gold rush days show a distinctly "California" saddle on horses, *tapaderos* over the stirrups and romals (reins woven together to form a whip at the end). References to the braided rawhide *reata* are common, suggesting that the technique of roping from the single-cinched saddles was the *vaquero*'s dally (from the Spanish *dar la vuelta*, or take a wrap). In the mid-1870s, Susan Allison was braiding rawhide ropes to sell to the mostly Okanagan Native cowboys who had become the expert ropers of their day.

Some of the most accomplished cowboys to travel to British Columbia in the early days came from California. The Harper brothers, who effectively controlled the cattle trade in the Colony, had spent years in California and their earliest drives were from California, using personnel selected from the *ranchos* of the central valley. Their most talented and best-known cowboy was Newman Squires, who became recognized as the premier British Columbia cowboy. He influenced a generation of young cowboys with his distinctly Californian way of handling cattle. His skills as a roper had been learned from Spanish-speaking *vaqueros* on the California ranges and brought to British Columbia, where his prowess as a roper was acknowledged and influential, as was his manner of breaking and handling horses.

The horses that were brought into British Columbia in the gold rush days were invariably the large, tough horses of the Pacific Northwest, with Norman, Breton and Morgan blood. They proved to be the ideal mounts for cowboys working the heavier cattle that had predominantly shorthorn breeding. The techniques for breaking these horses were derived from California, where the hackamore was preferred to the bit and where a snubbing post was usually situated in the middle of the breaking pen to secure the horse prior to breaking. The cowboys who broke horses using this equipment were referred to as "buckaroos" until as late as 1880.

There were, however, many aspects of handling cattle that had been brought to California and the Pacific Northwest by the English-speaking drovers who had come west. They brought with them the equipment and techniques that had been transplanted to the eastern US from Britain. Stock whips were common, and herder dogs were used to control cattle. Fencing of pastureland was not uncommon, and the careful attention to cattle breeding also derived from the highlands of Britain. In general, the open range system of raising cattle was impractical in British Columbia, where the mountainous terrain necessitated a closer herding of cattle and a seasonal movement of the herds to the high country in the summer months. Although these practices were carried on at a time when there was not a fence to be seen on the rangelands and cattle were known to wander long distances in the winter storms, the emphasis was on more diligent herding of cattle.

Well into the 1880s, the ranching industry in British Columbia was similar to its counterparts in California, Oregon and Washington. The buckaroo influence, even though it had been significantly modified as it spread north from California, was present in British Columbia. The cattle and the horses that herded them were distinctly different in size from those on the east side of the Rockies. It is safe to say that the cowboy of British Columbia remained a northern version of the California "buckaroo" well into the 1880s, when the cross-mountain traffic began to meld both British Columbia and Alberta ranching into similar systems.

The ranching frontier in what was to become southern Alberta opened much later than in British Columbia. During the intervening time, major importations of cattle from Oregon and Washington had taken place in the mining camps of western Montana. These cattle were primarily of shorthorn blood and were much larger than the Texas longhorns that were being driven into eastern Montana at the same time. Both of these types of cattle were available to the early cattle importers to the North-West. Tom Lynch and George Emerson, who were the earliest large cattle importers, purchased their cattle in the Sun River and Choteau areas of western Montana and eventually in Idaho, where the cattle were mostly shorthorn crosses. The suggestion that the earliest cattle in the North-West were Texas longhorns is unfounded.

Not only did the cattle breeds originate from west of the Rocky Mountains, so too did the horses. The first large herds of horses in the North-West were from British Columbia, and these large tough horses were enthusiastically accepted by the pioneer cattlemen. They proved to be the best horses to handle the larger cattle that were being brought into the Canadian prairies. With the horses came a lot of the California methods of horse breaking and some of the equipment. The hackamore was very popular in the North-West, but the single-cinched California saddle was not widely accepted. It was deemed too light and too easily shifted when a large steer hit the end of a rope tied to the saddle horn. So the heavier double-cinched Texas saddle was generally used, especially by the Texas via Wyoming ranch hands who tied their ropes to the saddle horn and questioned the effectiveness of dallying their ropes around the horn.

The braided rawhide lariat was used by some cowboys in the North-West, but the hemp rope, mass-produced and more easily available, was by far the most popular. The experienced cowboys who drove the cattle into the Canadian prairies were mostly from the Midwestern states but had learned their trade from the Texas cowboys who had driven cattle north to Wyoming and Montana. Although there had already been enough cross-mountain intermixing that some aspects of the California *vaquero*'s dress were being adopted east of the Rockies, the Montana cowboy and his counterpart north of the border were distinctly "Texan" in their clothing, their saddle and their rope.

The open range system of ranching, where cattle were left untended on the range for extended periods of time, travelled north from Texas and was widely accepted on the northern ranges. When the huge leases were granted by the Canadian government to eastern and British investors, the attraction of the prairies was the extremely low cost of caring for the cattle. Unfortunately, the open range system was not really suited to the northern climate. As early as 1886, when an extremely severe winter had decimated the cattle herds east of the Rockies from Texas to the North-West, a writer had asked, "Where are the million or more head of largely longhorn breeding stock that had been driven north from Texas during the previous 10 years?" He went on to answer his question:

> In a suitable climate these cattle would have been alive today. Where are they? The bones of thousands . . . lie bleaching on the wind-swept flanks of the foothills. They pave the bottoms of miry pools; they lie in disjointed, wolf-gnawed fragments on the arid, bunchgrass ranges, they are scattered over the short buffalo-grass. They have died of hunger, they have perished of thirst, when the icy breath of winter closed the streams; they have died of starvation by the tens of thousands during the season when the cold storms sweep out of the North and course over the plains, burying the grass under snow . . . [they were] frozen into solid blocks during blood-chilling blizzards.[1]

The reality was that the northern plains were not ideally suited for the open range system of raising beef cattle, but it took ranchers many years to realize this. The buffalo had been much hardier and had possessed a much thicker coat to protect them from the cold. Although the ranchers put up more and more hay in anticipation of the occasional hard winter, they simply were not ready for the worst.

The winter of 1908–09 marked a turning point in the cattle industry in Alberta. The winter was the worst on record and, by spring, hundreds of thousands of cattle had perished. Coming at a time when the prairies were rapidly filling up with settlers who were more interested in growing grain, the days of the open range could be considered to have passed away. In isolated pockets of the open prairies, cattle were still turned loose to wander on the ranges. But the more sheltered foothills became the preferred terrain for raising cattle. Even here, where there was ample water and good shelter, the ranchers saw the continuing need to put up large quantities of hay for winter feed. The great round-ups of the last two decades of the 19th century became a thing of the past, and smaller, local round-ups took their place. Most ranches were small holdings with some government land leased for grazing. The great days of the open range had passed into history.

Looking back at the stories and the reminiscences of the earliest cattlemen in British Columbia, it is safe to say that, in those early days, the cowboys of the province were direct descendants of the *vaqueros* of California. The ranch hands of the 1860s and 1870s were the northernmost extension of the buckaroos who came out of California and were the working class of ranching in Oregon, then Washington and, finally, British Columbia.

In Alberta the story was more complicated. As we have seen, from the beginnings of ranching in what is now southern Alberta, cattle, horses and ranch hands from British Columbia had crossed the "Great Divide" of the Rocky Mountains and had an impact on that area. Even in the early days of ranching in the North-West, the Texas cowboy practices and equipment were meeting and blending with the California way of raising and handling cattle. For a time, however, the distinction between cowboys in British Columbia and those in the North-West Territories was clear. One could spot a buckaroo from a distance by his dress and his saddle—and by even the horse that he rode. The same would apply to the cowboy from east of the Rockies. His double-rigged saddle and his plain undecorated tack and clothing spoke of the Texas tradition that had travelled north and found a home on the northern prairies.

By the turn of the 1900s, the distinction between the cowboys on either side of the Great Divide had blurred. Although subtle differences lingered, the cowboys of BC and Alberta began to look alike in their clothing and gear. But even though the open range era had come to an end, the legacy of the Texas cowboy endured in Alberta, and his descendants can be seen on the ranches of the province. In British Columbia as well, the young cowboys of today prefer the flat-brimmed hats and tapaderos that came north from California 150 years ago. The cowboy is alive and well on either side of the Great Divide.

ENDNOTES

Introduction
1. Badger Clark. "The Passing of the Trail," *Sun and Saddle Leather*.
2. Charles M. Russell. *Trails Plowed Under*, pp. 2–3.
3. David Dary. *Cowboy Culture: A Saga of Five Centuries*, p. 4.
4. Much of this section is derived from what is acknowledged as the most comprehensive study of the origins of North American ranching: Terry G. Jordan, *North American Cattle-Ranching Frontiers: Origins, Diffusion, and Differentiation*.
5. Ibid., quoting "Stock-Raising," *Texas Almanac for 1861*. Galveston, Texas, 1860, pp. 217–18.
6. Ibid., p. 167.
7. Hazel A. Pulling. "A History of California's Range Cattle Industry, 1770-1912," p. 342.
8. Jordan. *North American Cattle Ranching Frontiers*, p. 280.

Chapter One: Drovers
1. James Watt. *Journal of Mule Train Packing in Eastern Washington in the 1860's* (Fairfield, Washington, 1978), p. 34.
2. E.B. Bronson. *Reminiscences of a Ranchman*, p. 298.
3. *Oregon Farmer*. May 1859.
4. Lieutenant R.C. Mayne. *Four Years in British Columbia and Vancouver Island*, pp. 99, 104.
5. A. J. Splawn. *Ka-mi-akin: Last Hero of the Yakimas*, p. 51.
6. Splawn. *Ka-mi-akin*.
7. Daniel M. Drumheller. *"Uncle Dan" Drumheller Tells Thrills of Western Trails in 1854*, pp. 65-66.
8. Ibid., p. 123.
9. Ibid., p. 128.
10. Splawn. *Ka-mi-akin*, p. 288.
11. Myron R. Brown diaries, 1867, 1868.
12. Splawn. *Ka-mi-akin*, pp. 288–89.
13. R.C. Lundin-Brown. *British Columbia: An Essay*, p. 39.
14. Myron R. Brown diaries, 1867, 1868.
15. Branwen C. Patenaude. *Trails to Gold, Volume Two*, p. 87.
16. *British Colonist*, April 15, 1862.
17. *Pacific Christian Advocate*, January 12, 1921, p. 19.

Chapter Two: Frontiersmen

1. Viscount Milton & W.B. Cheadle. *The North-West Passage by Land*, p. 287.
2. Alfred Selwyn. *Journal and Report of Preliminary Explorations of British Columbia* (the Canadian Naturalist and Quarterly Journal of Science, Montreal, 1875), p. 18.
3. Andrew Birrell. *Benjamin Baltzly: Photographs & Journal of an Expedition through British Columbia: 1871.*
4. Sanford Fleming. *Report of the Progress on the Explorations and Surveys up to January 1874*, p. 123.
5. *Cariboo Sentinel*, Barkerville, November 7, 1874, p. 1.
6. L.V. Kelly. *The Range Men: Early Ranching in Alberta*, p. 115.
7. Edward Brado. *Cattle Kingdom: Early Ranching in Alberta*, pp. 138-39.
8. Kelly. *The Range Men*, p. 166.
9. *Journal of the Royal Agricultural Society of England*. London, 1885, p. 295.
10. BC Provincial Archives, Victoria. Letter from Joseph Ashley to Colonial Government claiming discoverer's rights on Wild Horse Creek, signed by John S. Fisher, J.N. Stephens, J.P. Brien, T.P. Myrer, J. Larese and J. Shaw. Cited in Fred J. Smyth, *Tales of the Kootenays*, p. 53.
11. Smyth, *Tales of the Kootenays*, p. 56.
12. Orin J. Oliphant. *On the Cattle Ranges of the Oregon Country*, p. 67
13. *The Mountaineer*. August 17, 1872. Cited in Oliphant, *On the Cattle Ranges*, p. 67.
14. Penticton Archives, Esther White Papers, "Account of Minnie Ashton of Enderby."
15. John McDougall. *Opening the Great West*, p. 12.
16. Glenbow Archives. M-477-586. Richard Hardisty Fonds, Series 14. John Bunn to Richard Hardisty, August 14, 1875.
17. Ibid., M-477-587.
18. McDougall. *Opening the Great West*, p. 26.
19. Hugh Dempsey. *Calgary: Spirit of the West*, p. 24.
20. McDougall. *Opening the Great West*, pp. 37–38.
21. Kelly. *The Range Men*, p. 117.
22. High River Pioneers and Old Timers' Association. *Leaves from the Medicine Tree*, p. 21.
23. Kelly. *The Range Men*, p. 116.
24. *Leaves from the Medicine Tree*, p. 21.
25. A.E. "Bovis" Cross. "Reminiscences of Round-Up of 1887," *Farm and Ranch Review*, August 5, 1919, p. 854.
26. *Leaves from the Medicine Tree*, p. 22.
27. Homestead Records. File 535112, statement made by George Emerson, June 15, 1900. Cited in Simon Evans, Sarah Carter and Bill Yeo (Eds.), *Cowboys, Ranchers and the Cattle Business*.
28. *Leaves from the Medicine Tree*, p. 22.
29. Mark H. Brown and W.R. Felton. *Before Barbed Wire: L.G. Huffman, Photographer on Horseback*, p. 96.

Chapter Three: Mounties

1. Hugh A. Dempsey. *The Golden Age of the Canadian Cowboy*, pp. 85-86.
2. Canada, House of Commons Debates, April 28, 1880, p. 1814.
3. Kelly. *The Range Men*, p. 131.
4. William Naftel. *The Cochrane Ranch*, p. 88.
5. Brado. *Cattle Kingdom*, p. 131.
6. Kelly. *The Range Men*, p. 187.
7. Edward Maunsell. "Maunsell's Story" in William Kelly (Ed.), *The Mounties as They Saw Themselves*, p. 12.
8. Ibid., p. 13.
9. Ibid., p. 14.
10. Ibid., p. 16.
11. Hugh Dempsey. "The West of Edward Maunsell—Part One" *Alberta History*, Volume 34, No. 4 (Autumn 1986), p. 1.
12. Ibid., p. 3.
13. Ibid., p. 4.
14. Ibid., p. 16.
15. Kelly. *The Range Men*. p. 160.
16. Hugh Dempsey. "The West of Edward Maunsell—Part Two." *Alberta History*, Volume 35, No. 1 (Winter 1987), p. 25.
17. Ibid.
18. Kelly. *The Range Men*, p. 263.
19. "Maunsell, Edward Herbert" in the *Dictionary of Canadian Biography Online*. Vol. XV.
20. Colonel S.B. Steele. *Forty Years in Canada*, p. 157.
21. Lee M. Rice and Glenn R. Vernam. *They Saddled the West*, p. 123.
22. Donald Klancher and Roger Phillips. *Arms and Accoutrements of the Mounted Police, 1873-1973*, pp. 166-67.

Chapter Four: Horsemen

1. Mark S. Wade. *The Thompson Country*, p. 69.
2. John R. Craig. *Ranching with Lords and Commons or Twenty Years on the Range*, p. 37.
3. *Leaves from the Medicine Tree*, p. 355.
4. Art Downs. *Wagon Road North*, p. 51.
5. Frederick W. Ings. *Before the Fences: Tales from the Midway Ranch*, p. 15.
6. *Inland Sentinel*. Kamloops, November 27, 1884.
7. Naftel. *The Cochrane Ranch*, p. 129.
8. *Inland Sentinel*, Yale. April 7, 1881.
9. *Leaves from the Medicine Tree*, p. 71.
10. Ibid., p. 23.
11. Ings. *Before the Fences*, p. 78.
12. Kelly. *The Range Men*, pp. 434-35.

13. Ibid., p. 10.
14. Dary. *Cowboy Culture*, p. 48.
15. Ings. *Before the Fences*, p. 96.
16. Ibid., p. 70.
17. *Leaves from the Medicine Tree*, p. 72.
18. Ibid., pp. 135, 95.
19. Ibid., p. 367.

Chapter Five: Top Hands

1. David H. Johnson. *Sonora Pass Pioneers: California Bound Emigrants and Explorers 1841-1864*, p. 69.
2. "Sonora Pass Emigrants" and "1853 Sonora Pass Emigrants." Available at www. sonorapasspioneers.com.
3. *Inland Sentinel*. Kamloops, May 1927.
4. *Cariboo Sentinel*. October 5, 1872.
5. *Cariboo Sentinel*. December 15, 1874.
6. *British Colonist*. February 14, 1875; September 14, 1876.
7. *British Colonist*. August 19, 1876.
8. *British Colonist*, Victoria. April 20, 1876.
9. T. Alex Bulman. *Kamloops Cattlemen: One Hundred Years of Trail Dust*, p. 16.
10. *British Colonist*, Victoria. May 21, 1876.
11. *British Colonist*, Victoria. February 5, 1878.
12. *Inland Sentinel*. May 26, 1881.
13. *Inland Sentinel*, Kamloops. November 27, 1884.
14. A.W. McMorran, Western Canada Ranching Company Manager, in the *Ashcroft Journal*, February 9, 1939.
15. F.W. Laing. "Some Pioneers of the Cattle Industry." *British Columbia Historical Quarterly*, Vol. 6, #4 (October 1942), p. 275.
16. *Leaves from the Medicine Tree*, p. 374.
17. C.J. Christianson. *My Life on the Range*, p. 88
18. *Macleod Gazette*. September 4, 1882.
19. *Leaves from the Medicine Tree*, p. 373.
20. Christianson. *My Life on the Range*, p. 89.
21. Information for this section is primarily from a typescript by Jean Lamont Johnson, *A Virginian Cowboy: His Life and Friends*. Glenbow Alberta Archives, M-4018.
22. *Leaves from the Medicine Tree*, p. 454.
23. Glenbow Archives, M2388, "Stair Ranch Letterbox," p. 350.
24. Johnson. *A Virginian Cowboy*.
25. Ibid.
26. Ibid.

Chapter Six: Greenhorns

1. Simon M. Evans. "Some Observations on the Labour Force of the Canadian Ranching Frontier During its Golden Age, 1882-1901." *Great Plains Quarterly*, Winter 1995, p. 6.
2. Claude Gardiner. *Letters from an English Rancher.* Glenbow Alberta Institute, Calgary, 1988, pp. 40-41.
3. *Alberta Tribune*, Calgary. July 2, 1895.
4. W.R. Newbolt. "Memories of Bowchase Ranch." *Alberta History*, Vol. 32, #4, Autumn 1984, p. 2.
5. Ibid., p. 3.
6. Ibid., p. 4.
7. Ibid.
8. Ibid., p. 7.
9. Ibid., p. 10.
10. Douglas E. Harker. "The Bayliff Story." Provincial Archives of BC. MS-2528.
11. *Inland Sentinel*, Kamloops. January 28, 1886.
12. Harker. "The Bayliff Story."
13. Lachlin McKinnon. *Lauchlin McKinnon, Pioneer*, pp. 1-2.
14. Ibid., p. 17.
15. Glenbow Archives M-7988, "Edward J. Hills Letters", Number 43, May 25, 1885.

Chapter Seven: The Forgotten Cowboys

1. *Leaves from the Medicine Tree*, p. 444.
2. Peter Iverson and Linda MacCannell. *Riders of the West: Portraits from Indian Rodeo.*
3. Alexander Morris. *The Treaties of Canada with the Indians of Manitoba and the North-West Territories*, p. 371.
4. Ibid., p. 262.
5. Daniel Francis. *The Encyclopedia of British Columbia*, p. 78.
6. *Leaves from the Medicine Tree*, p. 369.
7. Glenbow Archives. MS-1281-2. Typescript: "John Ware, Famous Cowboy, of the Bar U." Slim Marsden, Vulcan, Alberta, nd.
8. Kelly. *The Range Men*, p. 154
9. Ings. *Before the Fences*, p. 16.
10. *Macleod Gazette*, Fort Macleod, Alberta. June 23, 1885.
11. Cross. "Reminiscences of Round-Up of 1887."
12. *Calgary Tribune*, Calgary, Alberta. March 2, 1892.
13. Glenbow Archives, MA337. J.L. Douglas. "Journal of Four Months Holiday to Canada and the USA, August to September 1886." p. 35
14. Ings. *Before the Fences*. p. 18.
15. Cross. "Reminiscences of Round-Up of 1887."
16. Ibid.

17. *Lethbridge News*. June 5, 1908.
18. Roderick J. Barman. "Packing in British Columbia: Transport on a Resource Frontier." *Journal of Transport History, 21*(2), p. 147.
19. Diary entry of 19 June 1859, transcribed in George F.G. Stanley (Ed.), *Mapping the Frontier: Charles Wilson's diary of the survey of the 49th parallel, 1858–62*, p. 52.
20. R.L. Bagshaw (Ed.). *No Better Land: The 1860 Diaries of the Anglican Colonial Bishop George Hills*, pp. 150, 184
21. Barman. "Packing in British Columbia," p. 147.
22. Doug Cox and Elizabeth Pryce. "The Barcelos of Cawston." *Fifty-fifth Report of the Okanagan Historical Society* 1991), pp. 99–105.
23. H. Frank Lawrence. "Early days in the Chinook belt." *Alberta Historical Review, 13*(1), Winter 1965, p. 11.
24. Ibid.
25. Dempsey. *Golden Age of the Canadian Cowboy*, p. 16.

Chapter Eight: Ranching Women

1. Duane Thompson, "A History of the Okanagan: Indians and Whites in the Settlement era, 1860-1920."
2. Eric D. Sismey. "Joseph Richter." *Thirty-Fourth Report of the Okanagan Historical Society* (Vernon, BC, 1970), pp. 13-14.
3. Douglas Cole and Bradley Lockner (Eds.). *The Journals of George M Dawson: British Columbia 1875-1878.*
4. Provincial Archives of BC, GR1468.
5. Sismey. "Joseph Richter," p. 15
6. From an original manuscript by Richard Louden entitled "An Odyssey: The Louden Family in Retrospect." In Jean Barman, "Lost Okanagan: In Search of the First Settler Families." *Okanagan History, 60th Report* (1996), p. 12.
7. Sydney Russell Almond. "History of the Kettle Valley District." *Tenth Report of the Boundary Historical Society* (Grand Forks, BC, 1985).
8. Margaret Ormsby, ed. *A Pioneer Gentlewoman in British Columbia: The Recollections of Susan Allison*, p. 21.
9. Ibid., p. 24.
10. Ibid., p. 28.
11. Ibid., pp.xliii, appendices.
12. Ibid., p. 40.
13. Ibid.
14. Ibid., p. 55.
15. Ibid., p. XXXV.
16. Ibid., p. 67.
17. Ibid., p. xxxvi.
18. Ings. *Before the Fences*, p. 82.
19. Kelly. *The Range Men*, p. 129.

20. *The River Press*, Fort Benton, Montana. July 6, 1881.
21. *Leaves from the Medicine Tree*, p. 39.
22. "A Lady and Her Ranch." *Alberta Historical Review,* 15(2), Autumn 1967, p. 4.
23. Ibid.
24. Moira O'Neill. "A Lady's Life On A Ranche." In *Leaves from the Medicine Tree,* p. 502.
25. Ibid., p. 505.
26. Frank Wilkeson. "Cattle Raising on the Plains." *Harpers New Monthly Magazine.* 72 (April 1886), p. 789.

Chapter Nine: The Legacy of the *Vaquero* and Texas Cowboy

1. Frank Wilkeson. "Cattle Raising on the Plains." *Harpers New Monthly Magazine.* 72 (April 1886) p. 789.

REFERENCES

Published Sources

Bagshaw, R.L., ed. *No Better Land: The 1860 Diaries of the Anglican Colonial Bishop George Hills*. Vancouver BC: Sono Nis Press, 1996.

Birrell, Andrew. *Benjamin Baltzly: Photographs & Journal of an Expedition through British Columbia: 1871*. (n.p., n.d.)

Brado, Edward. *Cattle Kingdom: Early Ranching in Alberta*. Victoria, BC: Heritage House, 2004.

Bronson, E.B. *Reminiscences of a Ranchman*. Nebraska: University of Nebraska Press, 1962 (reprint of 1908 McClure Co., New York edition).

Brown, Mark H. and W.R. Felton. *Before Barbed Wire: L.A. Huffman, Photographer on Horseback*. New York: Henry Holt & Co., 1956.

Bulman, T. Alex. *Kamloops Cattlemen: One Hundred Years of Trail Dust*. Winlaw, BC: Sono Nis Press, 1972.

Christianson, C.J. *My Life on the Range*. Lethbridge: Southern Publishing, 1968.

Clark, Badger. "The Passing of the Trail," *Sun and Saddle Leather*. Boston, MA: The Gotham Press, 1922.

Cole, Douglas and Bradley Lockner, eds. *The Journals of George M Dawson, Vol. 1.1: British Columbia 1875-1876*. Vancouver, BC: UBC Press, 1989.

Craig, John R. *Ranching with Lords & Commons, or Twenty Years on the Range*. Victoria, BC: Heritage House, 2006.

Cross A.E. "Bovis." "Reminiscences of Round-Up of 1887." *Farm and Ranch Review*. August 5, 1919, p. 854.

Dary, David. *Cowboy Culture: A Saga of Five Centuries*. New York: Avon Books, 1981.

Dempsey, Hugh A. *The Golden Age of the Canadian Cowboy*. Calgary, AB: Fifth House Ltd., 1995.

———. *Calgary: Spirit of the West*. Calgary, AB: Fifth House Publishing, 1993.

Downs, Art. *Wagon Road North*. Quesnel, BC: Northwest Digest Ltd, 1960.

Drumheller, Daniel M. *"Uncle Dan" Drumheller Tells Thrills of Western Trails in 1854*. Spokane, WA: Inland American Printing Company, 1925.

Evans, Simon, Sarah Carter and Bill Yeo, eds. *Cowboys, Ranchers and the Cattle Business*. Calgary, AB: University of Calgary Press, 2000.

Fleming, Sanford. *Report of the Progress on the Explorations and Surveys up to January 1874.* Ottawa, ON: MacLean, Rogers & Company, 1874.

Francis, Daniel. *The Encyclopedia of British Columbia.* Madeira Park, BC: Harbour Publishing, 2000.

Gardiner, Claude. *Letters from an English Rancher.* Calgary, AB: Glenbow Alberta Institute, 1988.

High River Pioneers' and Old Timers' Association. *Leaves from the Medicine Tree.* Lethbridge, AB: High River Pioneers' and Old Timers' Association, 1960.

Ings, Frederick W. *Before the Fences: Tales from the Midway Ranch.* Calgary, AB: McAra Printing, 1980.

Iverson, Peter and Linda MacCannell. *Riders of the West: Portraits from Indian Rodeo.* Vancouver, BC: Greystone Books, 1999.

Johnson, David H. *Sonora Pass Pioneers: California Bound Emigrants and Explorers 1841-1864.* Tuolumne County, CA: Tuolumne County Historical Society, 2006.

Jordan, Terry G. *North American Cattle-Ranching Frontiers: Origins, Diffusion, and Differentiation.* Albuquerque, NM: University of New Mexico Press, 1993.

Kelly, L.V. *The Range Men: Pioneer Ranchers of Alberta.* Toronto, ON: Coles, 1980.

Kelly, William H. *The Mounties as They Saw Themselves.* Ottawa, ON: Golden Dog Press, 1996.

Klancher, Donald and Roger Phillips. *Arms and Accoutrements of the Mounted Police, 1873-1973.* Bloomfield, ON: Museum Restoration Service, 1982, pp. 166-167.

Laing, F.W. "Some Pioneers of the Cattle Industry." *The British Columbian Historical Quarterly,* 6(4), October 1942.

Lundin-Brown, R.C. *British Columbia: An Essay.* New Westminster, BC: Royal Engineer Press, 1863.

Mayne, Lieutenant R.C. *Four Years in British Columbia and Vancouver Island.* London, UK: John Murray, 1862.

McDougall, John. *Opening the Great West.* Calgary, AB: Glenbow-Alberta Institute, 1970.

McKinnon, Lachlin. *Lachlin McKinnon, Pioneer.* Calgary, AB: John D. McAra, 1956.

Milton, Viscount and W.B. Cheadle. *The North-West Passage by Land.* London, UK: Cassell, Petter & Galpin, 1865.

Morris, Alexander. *The Treaties of Canada with the Indians of Manitoba and the North-West Territories.* Reprint of 1880 edn., Belfords, Clarke & Co. by Prospero Books, 2000.

Naftel, William. *The Cochrane Ranch.* Canadian Historic Sites, No. 16. Ottawa, ON: Government of Canada, 1974.

Oliphant, Orin J. *On the Cattle Ranges of the Oregon Country.* Seattle, WA: University of Washington Press, 1968.

Ormsby, Margaret A., ed. *A Pioneer Gentlewoman in British Columbia: The Recollections of Susan Allison.* Vancouver, BC: UBC Press, 1976.

Patenaude, Branwen C. *Trails to Gold, Volume Two*. Victoria, BC: Heritage House, 1996.

Rice, Lee M. and Glenn R Vernam. *They Saddled the West*. Centreville, MD: Cornell Maritime Press, 1975.

Russell, Charles M. *Trails Plowed Under*. New York: Doubleday & Company, 1927.

Selwyn, Alfred R.C. *Journal and Report of Preliminary Explorations of British Columbia*. (Geological survey report to Parliament, 1872.)

Smyth, Fred J. *Tales of the Kootenays*. Vancouver, BC: Douglas & McIntyre, 1977.

Splawn, A.J. *Ka-mi-akin: Last Hero of the Yakimas*. Oregon: Oregon Historical Society, 1941.

Stanley, George F. G., ed., *Mapping the Frontier: Charles Wilson's diary of the survey of the 49th parallel, 1858–62*. Toronto, ON: Macmillan, 1970, p. 52.

Steele, Colonel S.B. *Forty Years in Canada*. (n.p.): Dodd, Mead & Co., 1915; re-issued by Prospero Books, 2000.

Wade, Mark S. *The Thompson Country*. Kamloops, BC: Inland Sentinel Print, 1907.

Watt, James. *Journal of Mule Train Packing in Eastern Washington in the 1860's*. Fairfield, WA: Ye Galleon Pr., 1978.

Unpublished Sources

Johnson, Jean Lamont. *A Virginian Cowboy: His Life and Friends*. Glenbow Alberta Archives, M-4018.

Pulling, Hazel A. "A History of California's Range Cattle Industry, 1770-1912." Ph.D thesis, University of Southern California (Los Angeles, CA, 1944).

Thompson, Duane. "A History of the Okanagan: Indians and Whites in the Settlement Era, 1860-1920." Ph.D Thesis, Department of History, UBC, 1985.

Archival Sources

BC Provincial Archives, Victoria.

Glenbow Archives, Calgary.

Myron R. Brown diaries, 1867, 1868. Washington State Library, Olympia, Washington.

Penticton Archives, Esther White Papers.

Newspapers and Periodicals

Alberta Historical Review, Alberta History.
Ashcroft Journal, Ashcroft.
British Colonist.
Cariboo Sentinel.
Farm and Ranch Review.
Great Plains Quarterly.
Harpers New Monthly Magazine.
Inland Sentinel. Kamloops.
Journal of the Royal Agricultural Society of England. London.
Journal of Transport History.
Lethbridge News.
Macleod Gazette, Fort Macleod, Alberta.
Oregon Farmer.
Pacific Christian Advocate.
Report of the Boundary Historical Society, Grand Forks, BC,
Report of the Okanagan Historical Society.
The River Press. Fort Benton, Montana.